Understanding Other Persons

Understanding Other Persons

Edited by

THEODORE MISCHEL

BASIL BLACKWELL · OXFORD

ISBN 0 631 15100 1

Printed in Great Britain by
Western Printing Services Ltd, Bristol
and bound at Kemp Hall Bindery, Oxford

Notes on Contributors

JOHN H. FLAVELL Professor of Psychology, Institute of Child Development, University of Minnesota (Minneapolis, Minn.), is known for his experimental studies of cognitive development. His books include *The Developmental Psychology of J. Piaget* (1963) and *The Development of Role-Taking and Communication Skills in Children* (1968).

DAVID W. HAMLYN Professor of Philosophy, Birkbeck College, University of London, has written extensively on epistemology and the philosophy of psychology. His books include *The Psychology of Perception* (1957), *Sensation and Perception* (1961) and *The Theory of Knowledge* (1971).

ROM HARRÉ University Lecturer in Philosophy of Science and Fellow of Linacre College, Oxford University, is known for his contributions to the history and philosophy of the sciences. His books include *The Logic of the Sciences* (1963), *The Anticipation of Nature* (1965), *Principles of Scientific Thinking* (1970) and *The Explanation of Social Behaviour* (1972, with P. Secord).

THEODORE MISCHEL, Professor of Philosophy, State University of New York (Binghamton, N.Y.), has written on the history and methodology of the psychological sciences in both psychological and philosophical journals. He edited and contributed to *Human Action* (1969) and *Cognitive Development and Epistemology* (1971).

RICHARD S. PETERS Professor of the Philosophy of Education, Institute of Education, University of London, has made many contributions to the analysis of psychological concepts and to analytic philosophy of education. His books include *The Concept of Motivation* (1958), *Ethics and Education* (1966) and *The Logic of Education* (1971, with P. H. Hirst).

PAUL F. SECORD Professor of Social Psychology, Department of Urban Studies, Queens College, City University of New York, is known for his contributions to the empirical study of personality and the self-concept. His books include *Social Psychology* (1964, with C. Backman) and *The Explanation of Social Behaviour* (1972, with R. Harré). BARBARA H. PEEVERS, Lecturer in the Department of Psychology, University of Nevada (Reno), has co-authored a number of papers on the development of person-concepts with Paul Secord.

STEPHEN E. TOULMIN Professor of Philosophy and Provost of Crown College, University of California (Santa Cruz) has contributed extensively to the history and philosophy of the sciences and epistemology. His books include *The Philosophy of Science* (1953), *The Uses of Argument* (1958), *Foresight and Understanding* (1961) and *Human Understanding* (Vol. I, 1972).

Contents

Introduction

This volume is part of a continuing attempt by a group of philosophers and psychologists to explore issues at the intersect of cognitive psychology and epistemology. Over the last ten years or so, some psychologists have grown increasingly disenchanted with positivistic prescriptions for developing psychology as a hypothetico-deductive science based on the 'hard' data of laboratory experiments with animals. The ways in which the epistemological tenets of empiricism and logical positivism had constrained the theoretical and methodological assumptions of the behaviorisms that had dominated psychology became apparent and psychology became self-critical; partly as a result of developments in such fields as linguistics and anthropology, a far more open and liberated conception of the nature and task of psychology was emerging. Many psychologists began to abandon attempts to deal with complex human behavior as if thinking and the use of concepts made no difference; as they turned to the investigation of 'conceptual behavior', 'cognitive processes' and the like, their inquiries began to relate less to biology and more to the study of language and investigation of various rule-following social behaviors.

Philosophers, on the other hand, beginning with the work of Ryle and Wittgenstein, were developing an extensive body of 'philosophical psychology' and their analyses of the way our ordinary psychological concepts work seemed to have some relevance for the conceptual structure and methods of a psychology concerned with human cognitive and social behavior. Moreover, some philosophers came to appreciate the significance for their own work of what was now being done in cognitive psychology and related areas; indeed, some even found it increasingly difficult to draw a very sharp line between their epistemological investigations and cognitive psychology. The time thus seemed propitious for an attempt by a small group of philosophers and psychologists to map out areas in which their interests seemed to overlap and to co-operate, if not in the investigation of the same questions, then at least in the sorting out and clarifying of questions that were arising for them in their different, yet related, areas of special competence.

We began with an attempt to explore rather broad issues relating to the conceptual framework needed for the explanation of human actions (see T. Mischel, ed., *Human Action*, 1969). Since we found that many of these issues were connected with questions about the way in which language, thought, and purposive, rational behavior develop jointly in the child, we decided to focus next on Piaget's theory of cognitive development. That theory provided a point of departure for an exploration of interrelations between empirical studies of cognitive development and conceptual analyses of human knowledge and cognition. In particular, we tried to get clearer about what, if anything, a theory of cognitive development can contribute to epistemology, about the conceptual framework needed to account for the development of physical and moral concepts and for the motivation of cognitive development, and about the relevance of developmental theories for the understanding of adult cognitive behavior (see T. Mischel, ed., *Cognitive Development and Epistemology*, 1971).

Since the participants in this enterprise believed that our discussions had been highly stimulating and useful and that we were achieving a degree of mutual understanding and relevance that is very unusual in attempts at interdisciplinary discussion, we were encouraged to proceed. After consultation with colleagues in both psychology and philosophy, the topics for the next conference and the list of participants were planned by the editor in collaboration with David Hamlyn, Richard Peters and Stephen Toulmin. Several considerations suggested that it might be useful to focus next on issues relating to our understanding of other persons. For one thing, as became clear in our discussions of Piaget, psychologists often tend to assume that 'person-perception' develops out of 'object-perception' and is not essentially different from it; thinking about persons has a different and more complex 'object', or content, but does not differ in structure or form, from thinking about other things. But some philosophers, e.g., those who have stressed some form of 'Verstehen', have argued that there is a radical difference between understanding people and understanding things, a difference connected with the fact that we can stand in personal relations to people but not to things. In order to come to grips with these issues we have to get clearer than we now are about how to conceptualize the processes through which persons come to understand each other as persons. That is, we need to understand more clearly the richer set of categories, the more complex set of skills, involved in thinking about persons and the social environment if we are to see how these could interrelate with those involved in thinking about the physical environment. Further, psychologists have themselves pointed to the rather hazy ways in which the whole area of person-perception has been conceptualized in their investigations, and Warr and Knapper even call explicitly for co-operation with philosophers on the ground that 'the statements about "minds" and "persons" with which philosophers work and the perceptual responses about people with which we have dealt seem to have quite a lot in common' (*The Perception of People and Events*, 1968, p. 386).

Finally, a clearer conception of what is involved in understanding other persons seemed important in view of the now wide-spread questioning of traditional formulations of the nature, scope and methods of psychology. For with the rejection of formulations based on a questionable model of natural science provided by logical positivism, psychologists have come to raise new questions about behavior, questions which are not strictly 'psychological' in the behavioristic sense (or even in the earlier Wundtian-introspective sense), but overlap into anthropology and sociology, on the one side, and into linguistics on the other. But this raises the further question of whether this newly developing science of human behavior can profit by adopting any model that is suitable to the natural sciences, or whether it might do better to develop its own distinctive model. For a common feature of the cognitive, social and linguistic behaviors that are now at the focus of theoretical interest is that they are all in some way rule-guided; this seems to be a feature that distinguishes these behaviors from those studied by the natural sciences and requires some consideration of the explanatory role which 'rules' can play in a science concerned with understanding these complex behaviors of persons.

A conference dealing with these issues was held at the State University of New York in Binghamton on 13 through 15 December 1971, with the support of Grant GS–31335, from the National Science Foundation. In addition to those who have contributed to this volume, the following people participated in these discussions: William Alston (University of Michigan), Max Black (Cornell University), Jerry Fodor (Massachusetts Institute of Technology), Lawrence Kohlberg (Harvard University), Charles Taylor (University of Montreal).

The papers published here are addressed to three related issues. First how are we to conceptualize the processes through which one person comes to understand another? David Hamlyn formulates three conceptual principles that bring out factors involved in the concept of knowing something, factors which have not been sufficiently recognized in philosophical accounts of knowledge. Hamlyn develops the implications of these principles for real interpersonal understanding and what psychologists call 'person perception', as well as for the origins and development of such interpersonal understanding. Part of Hamlyn's thesis is that there can be no understanding at all of people without knowledge of what a person is, and that complete or full understanding of a person is impossible without standing in personal relationship to him. Richard Peters then examines the extent to which entering into personal relationships may be constitutive of, rather than just providing conditions for, knowing and understanding persons. His essay explores the meaning of 'personal relationships' and distinguishes the sorts of relationships in which people can stand to each other in a way that throws light on our understanding of ourselves and others. Peters also suggests a connection between levels of personal relationships and levels or forms of understanding that have been sketched by Piaget and other cognitive-developmental psychologists.

Second, what are the conceptual features and empirical contributions of current psychological investigations into the genesis of our understanding of other persons? Flavell's paper reviews current empirical research on the child's growing ability to recognize that other people have thoughts, feelings, motives, visual percepts, etc., and the processes through which the child comes to know the 'psychological insides' of others. The significance of an adequate understanding of adult social cognition for such developmental investigations is brought out by Flavell, who presents both a general information-processing model for the development of interpersonal understanding and a more specific model of levels of development in the ability to represent and predict the visual experiences of others. The relation of these investigations to Hamlyn's thesis about our understanding of persons is considered in the Postscript of Hamlyn's paper. In the paper by Secord and Peevers we get an empirically based reconstruction of the processes through which the child develops person concepts. Through an analysis of forms of attribution, of the types of descriptions of persons characteristically used by people of different ages, from young children to adults, they attempt to trace stages in the development of the child's conception of himself and others as responsible agents. These two papers high-light some of the interesting empirical research currently being done in this area.

The form of explanation appropriate to a science of interpersonal behavior, a science that seeks to account for the actions of persons who perceive each other as persons, is examined in the third group of papers. Harré argues that human social behavior is an essentially cultural phenomenon generated in the following of rules, rules which are used by intelligent, plan-making and self-monitoring agents to achieve their goals and manage their affairs. His essay outlines the ways in which the concepts of 'rule' and 'rule-following' may be used as the major explanatory tools for the scientific analysis of those behaviors in whose generation conscious awareness can play an indispensable role. The methodological implications of this 'new paradigm', exemplified in work like that of Erving Goffman, and the types of models it uses—as contrasted with the methods and models of the behavioristic paradigm which seeks to account for regularities in behavior in terms of the conditioning of responses by environmental contingencies, without assigning any role to consciousness—are made clear, and the 'scientific' status of the rule-following, intentionalistic paradigm is defended. Harré's 'ethogenic' approach assumes an unbroken continuum between thought and action, and attempts to bridge the gap between individual and social psychology through the role assigned to rules in the generation of interpersonal behavior.

Toulmin's paper presents an analysis of a spectrum of cases in which rules are invoked to account for human behavior, cases which range from those in which there is nothing conscious or rational about the behavior to highly sophisticated performances in which there is a self-conscious and self-critical application of intellectual procedures. His analysis is designed to show that recognizing important distinctions between explanations of the actions of persons that appeal to rules, and explanations of the movements of things that appeal to natural laws, does not commit us to another form of the mind-body dichotomy. Toulmin also discusses the relation of his analysis to Harré's 'ethogenic' approach and points up its implications for our understanding of persons and personal relationships.

This approach to the understanding of persons is extended, in Mischel's paper, to behaviors that arise from unconscious intentions. Through an examination of the development of Freud's thought he tries to show that, while Freud began by supposing that the scientific understanding of persons requires that they be conceptualized as complex biological structures whose behavior is brought about by various 'mechanisms', the germinal discovery Freud made in his clinical practice—that symptoms, which were previously regarded as having causes but no sense, do have sense because they are brought about intentionally but unconsciously by the agent himself—required a very different conceptualization of persons as thinking, social beings who act intentionally in a matrix of personal relations with others. Freud's account of defense in response to anxiety, developed in the nineteen-twenties, and the psychoanalytic ego-psychology that grew out of it are used to defend the claim that the dynamically unconscious and driven character of neurotic behavior, as well as its social and cognitive rather than merely biological nature, can be made intelligible in the framework of intentionalistic concepts that informs our normal understanding of persons.

T.M.

Person-perception and our Understanding of Others

D. W. HAMLYN

I

The term 'person-perception' which has come to be used to mark off one province of social psychology must seem an odd one to the layman. Why should people, *qua* objects of perception, raise any questions that do not arise in considering perception in general? Some of the problems here arise from the familiar internal/external, or private/public distinction—from the fact that not all or even much that is the case about a person may show on his face or even be evident in his external behavior. Much of the work discussed in the psychological literature about the recognition of emotions or attitudes in people on the basis of such things as facial expressions bears this out. But to put this kind of thing at the centre of any investigation of what it is to know or understand another person seems a strangely intellectual, not to say artificial, way of construing the situation. We may in our everyday lives have to form judgments about other people on this kind of basis to some considerable extent, but we should surely admit that when we do so we are not in the position of knowing much about the person concerned. If we have to have resort to such 'external judgments' it is because we really do not know the person concerned. If we did, those very externals might take on quite another appearance, we might be able to see things in a quite different light. For this reason it seems to me a useful prolegomenon for any attempt to investigate person-perception so-called to inquire also into what is entailed by knowing a person.

What I have been saying in effect could be put by saying that the cases in which we derive knowledge or understanding of

another person through what we see of external expressions, whatever form these may take, are to be viewed as degenerate cases and
not the basis for a general understanding of our knowledge and
understanding of other people. They are degenerate in the sense
that if those expressions make sense to us they normally do so on
the basis of further knowledge of what a person is; the expressions
are not to be taken as data on which all the rest of our knowledge
of people is built. Nor is that knowledge to be construed as the
response to the stimuli provided by those external expressions. If
the external manifestations were such data we should in effect be
confronted with the classical 'other minds problem', so well known
to philosophers, but in a way that makes the problem impossible
to solve. For the data, construed as data on which knowledge of
the other person is to be constructed, would be totally inadequate
for the purpose. In order to construe a facial expression as one,
say, of joy one would have to know first that the expression was
one manifested by something that could indeed manifest joy—by,
that is, a person. And that fact could not be derived from the data
themselves. The same applies even to the construal of bodily
movements as actions; for them to be taken as actions we have
already to know that we have before us a person.[1] (The inadequacies
of the so-called argument from analogy here are well known to
philosophers; the argument fails for similar reasons. To use an
analogy between ourselves and others we have to presuppose that
those others are fitting recipients for the analogy—and that is the
whole point at issue.) Thus a classical empiricism that tries to
derive knowledge of other persons from perceptible data must fail,
and short of an appeal to innate ideas of persons (a suggestion which
certain remarks of Chomsky in *Language and Mind* (1968) might
lead one to assume he would espouse) one must seek another
approach.

But all this is, as I hinted earlier, a curiously intellectual approach
to the problem, a curiously intellectual attitude to what is involved
in interpersonal understanding. Let me for a moment try to
approach the matter as it were from the other end. If I am asked
to try to understand another person with whom I am confronted

[1] Cf. J. Cook (1969).

the best way to start may well be for me to attempt to put myself in his place. This requires imagination, so that some people are better at it than others; but in any case it may be that in many situations there is little enough on which imagination may get a purchase. What of course may help it to get a purchase is knowledge about the person concerned. And putting oneself in his place is not necessarily a sufficient condition of getting the understanding in question, however much it may be necessary. What I have in mind here is the point that people do not always see themselves aright, so that even if we manage to get ourselves into the position of seeing things and them as they do we may not have got all the way. That is why I would not wish to repudiate in any way that form of knowledge of people which may be obtained by general inquiries into, for example, the motives that people have in certain sorts of circumstances. There is plenty of knowledge of people, their motives, their behavior in certain sorts of circumstances, and so on, to be obtained by purely empirical inquiries. That is not in the least in dispute; nor is the fact that such knowledge may be of considerable use in the attempt of one individual to understand another. The question is simply *how* it gets a use, *how* the general knowledge of people gains an application to one man's understanding of another. It may be that, in some instances at least, this kind of knowledge may be another necessary condition of getting such understanding. But this does not entail that putting oneself in the other person's place may not be just as necessary. It is just that in some cases, if not all, I shall not be able to put myself in the other person's place without some knowledge at least of this other kind. Alternatively or in addition, my putting myself in his place may be insufficient for a true understanding of him; where I fail may be just where he fails in understanding himself. This may be due to an inability to get a proper perspective, and this in turn may be due to my not knowing sufficient facts about him, just as he may know insufficient facts about himself. Failure to understand oneself may come about in many ways and for many reasons; another may acquire a better understanding because he knows more about me than I do or because he has a better view of the facts, a better perspective than I do. Hence, by putting myself in another's place in the imagination I may or may not obtain a better understanding of him. I wish to make no claim that such a procedure is sufficient, merely that it is necessary. If it fails it may be because of my ignorance of crucial facts, which may be of differing kinds. But it *may* be because I do not really know him, and for that reason cannot really put myself in his place.

There is a very subtle difference if any between really knowing someone and really understanding them. Some people might wish to claim that we cannot ever really know our fellows, and this point of view has been reflected in certain metaphysical theories that claim to present a view of the nature of man and his place in the world. I have in mind here, for example, the views of Sartre, in whose philosophy it is something of a necessary truth that one man cannot really know another. I do not want to go into this in detail here. It is however worth noting that the origins of Sartre's point of view are Cartesian in the sense that there is presupposed a radical division between consciousness and what is bodily. Hence one is confronted with the impossibility of getting to another's consciousness through his body. This is another version of what I have already described as a curiously intellectual approach to the issues. Is the attempt to understand or know another adequately represented as an attempt to get at something between which and us there is necessarily a veil? Whatever the metaphysical basis of Sartre's view, the picture that results surely fails to fit the facts. If we fail to know or understand another person it is because the task is just too difficult, not because it was doomed to failure from the start through some kind of metaphysical necessity. Some people are no doubt inscrutable, and some people are no doubt impercipient, but whether they are or are not is a matter of empirical fact, not a necessity. There are certain philosophical models of human beings which, as we have begun to see in the Sartre case, turn this into a necessity. The Cartesian model is very much with us in one form or another, and the assumption that a person is fundamentally a centre of consciousness has its hold on many approaches to a variety of psychological issues. Certainly it generates the over-intellectual attitude to our present problem which I have already referred to, since it promotes the idea that in getting to know a person we have, as it were, to penetrate beyond the veil constituted by a person's bodily expressions to the inside him; or it promotes instead by reaction the idea that there is nothing but the outer expressions, the bodily movements, or whatever. And it is on one or other of these models that person-perception, so-called, tends often to be construed. But if, as I have suggested already, we are to have person-perception at all, we have to have some prior understanding of what a person is. If we are to understand person-perception therefore we must be clear about that understanding, an understanding which must surely be based upon what we might call natural reactions of persons to persons.

One way of doing this is to investigate the question what is conceptually necessary for a person's standing to us as an object of knowledge and therefore of understanding. I say '*therefore* of understanding' because the sense of 'object of knowledge' that is in question is one which implies the 'really knowing' that I have already mentioned. There is of course a sense of 'know' in which to know something is merely to recognize it or to be able to recognize it. Thus we might say 'You know Edward, well the girl I was talking about is the one sitting next to him'; and we may imply little else when we talk on occasion of knowing certain people. But we may accept such a usage without being concerned with it in the present context. For we might equally go on to say that we do not really know the people concerned; and we could not be said to know someone really if we did not have any understanding of him. If there are degrees possible in our knowledge of people there are equally degrees of understanding, though whether the two are correlated is another matter. It is possible and legitimate for us to say 'I know him very well, but I don't really understand him; indeed I doubt if I understand him at all.' If the last is probably an exaggeration it may not be totally false. Yet the conditions necessary for knowledge of a person in the sense in question overlap, if they are not identical with, those necessary for understanding that person. I wish at all events to approach the matter from the side of knowledge, and on the broadest front, by considering what is necessary for something to be an object of knowledge in general; in the course of my inquiry certain differences between knowledge of persons and knowledge of other sorts of thing will emerge. I wish to consider certain principles, viewed as conceptual principles, statements of what is necessary to something's being properly considered as an object of knowledge. I shall mention four principles in all, the first three of which I consider valid; the fourth, which is, I think, invalid, I mention because some things that I have to say may tempt people to think that it too is valid.

II

(a) The first principle (which I shall call Principle A) is that *a necessary, but not sufficient, condition of our being said to know X is that we should understand what kind of relations can exist between X and ourselves*. This principle is by far the least problematic, except that in relation to a large number of possible objects of knowledge it hardly seems to arise and may therefore seem otiose. What I mean is this. The principle has its origin in what seems quite obvious—that in order to be said to know something we must at least understand what it is for something to be the thing in question, we must have the concept of that thing, or, if it is in one sense or another a complex object, the concepts involved in understanding what it is for it to be what it is. If I am to be said to know my car I have to understand what it is for something to be a car, and this will comprise a complex piece of understanding, which will involve knowing certain facts about cars, knowledge which will presuppose the understanding of other concepts and so. I am not concerned here to set out the relationships between knowledge and concepts in detail, but that there is such a relationship is clear. Given this, the question that Principle A raises is whether, if knowing something involves having the concept or concepts in question should involve in turn an understanding of the relations that can exist between that thing and ourselves (and *a fortiori* the relations that cannot exist). I suggest that the answer to this question is 'Yes'. What this answer implies is that we cannot have a proper conception of a possible object of knowledge unless we understand what relations can and cannot exist between it and ourselves.

It might be asked why a conception of a thing should necessarily involve a conception of its possible relations with us. Whatever may be said about that issue it is not to the point in the present context, since we are concerned only with the conception of a thing as a possible object of knowledge. How could something be a possible object of knowledge if it stood in no relations to us? Indeed it seems reasonable that its status as an object of knowledge turns on what these relations may be or perhaps even are. The relations that can exist between myself and another person are quite different from those that can exist between me and physical things. The relevant considerations are the following. The relationship that exists between me and another person can be in a very real sense reciprocal; the relationship that I have with him may have a reflection in that which he has to me. It does not of course have to be so; there are such things as one-way relationships, though even here reciprocity must be possible. But nothing of this kind can be true of relationships to physical bodies except via the relationship of my body to them; there may be reciprocal spatial relationships, and causal relationships, between my body and other bodies, but does this amount to a relationship between me and other bodies? If it does, it is in some way a derivative sense. Being a person involves being more than just a physical thing; it involves having all that philosophers have come to speak of, rightly or wrongly, under the heading of 'privacy'. For present purposes, I think that the important thing to stress is the feelings that one person can have with another, since it is on these feelings that personal relationships are based, and these can clearly be reciprocal. Moreover, I suggest that these, in one way or another, provide the basis for moral relationships that can exist between one person and another, but not between a person and a thing as long as the latter is taken in independence of persons. To understand what a person is, therefore, involves understanding what sorts of relationships can exist between mere things or between persons and things.

One might ask how much of this applies equally to animals. It is not to be doubted that relations of some sort can exist between me and my dog; the dog can exert influences of one sort or another on me, and I on him, apart from the obvious spatial relations that exist between us. The question is whether these influences amount merely to the causal relations that can exist between material things and my body. I can have feelings towards my dog; can these be reciprocated or is the relationship necessarily one way only? To put the matter in another way, can animals share our form of life? Some philosophers would rule out of court an affirmative answer to this question, or say that to attribute to animals anything like the kind of things that we attribute to humans is, as it were, a courtesy attribution only (this presumably on the grounds that the ability of human beings to use language creates a great gulf between them and other creatures). My own view is that such a view flies in the face of the facts. Something like rudimentary personal relationships *can* exist between humans and certain animals. And it may be that to the extent that we are willing to contemplate such a possibility with an animal to that extent are we willing to consider it as a conscious being with states of mind in some way akin to ours. I say 'akin', since I do not of course wish to claim that animals can share all our states of mind. Yet when Wittgenstein (1953) asks the question whether an animal can hope, I think that the answer is 'Yes'. (Much of course depends on what the hope is; a quite different answer would be pertinent with regard to a hope for something 'the day after tomorrow' since this would imply complex temporal concepts presupposing ways of distinguishing temporal intervals, like a day.) In sum, I suggest that some animals can share our form of life in part, and that this makes them, as far as this goes, possible objects of knowledge in something like the sense in which other human beings are. (I should perhaps say finally on this matter, that this does not merely apply to those animals which we call domestic. Something like an embryo personal relationship can exist between a human and a wild animal, and in saying this I do not have in mind *Born Free* or anything of that kind. My point is that personal relationships are not based merely on feelings of, say, affection or respect, feelings that might be thought to exist in some rudimentary way between ourselves and domestic animals. Hatred is just as possible a foundation for a personal relationship, and it may be in some cases the only appropriate foundation. However that may be, an encounter between a human being and an animal which is in effect a moment of pure hatred can be construed as a personal encounter.)

What follows from all this is that knowing a human being, and in some cases an animal, may be a quite different matter from knowing a merely material object, to the extent that it is intelligible to speak of knowing merely material objects. To know a person (and an animal to the extent that an animal can have relations to us akin to those which we have to people) presupposes at least that we have a conception of what kind of relations can exist between us and him; if we had no conception of this we should not be in the position to have knowledge of him. But I have said very little so far of the relations in which we can stand to merely material objects of knowledge. The truth is, I take it, that there are many material objects in respect of which it would be very odd to say that we do or can know them. Is there any sense in which we might be said to know, for example, a pebble on the beach? I suppose that if we were on holiday somewhere and went regularly to a certain part of the beach we might be struck by the appearance of a certain pebble. On seeing it and recognizing it on the nth time we might say, 'I know that pebble.' Such a remark would be an expression of recognition of the familiar, but perhaps not just this; the pebble has also become an old friend, so to speak. The background story that I have provided gives sense to the remark 'I know that pebble', and a similar story might be given for remarks in the second and third persons. The story might suggest that knowing a thing is a kind of pseudo-case of knowing a person—that to know a thing we have to conceive it as capable of standing to us in ways which are reminiscent of personal relations. I do not think that this would be a correct conclusion. I do not in this wish to deny that people do sometimes treat things in ways which are akin to that in which they might treat people; the things are to them 'old friends' or even 'old enemies'. A gardener, for example, might treat a tree or a weed in this fashion, and if we say of him 'He knows that tree well' it might be this kind of thing that we have in mind. This applies particularly when the objects of knowledge have, as it were or indeed in truth, a life of their own. In that same sense I might know my car very well, and in a way that the garage mechanic does not know it; for he may not know what it is like to live with it.

Yet I may know things which do not have a life of their own in this way, e.g. my desk or my house. Yet these again are things that figure in my life; they are part of my life in a way that any old pebble on the beach is not, and they can for that reason stand as objects of knowledge in a way that the pebble never can unless, of course, it is made to do so for a special reason. So perhaps while it is not true that for a thing to be an object of knowledge it must be capable of standing in quasi-personal relations with us, it may yet be true that it must be capable of playing a part in our life in some way. There is thus an important sense in which for something to be an object of knowledge it must be capable of standing in relations to us, even if not personal or what I have called quasi-personal relations. And by the latter I mean the relations that things may have to us when we treat them as having a life of their own, so that we can view them as, say, old friends or old enemies. But of course to treat things in this way is not to treat them as they actually are, and one who insists on treating a material thing as a kind of person in all circumstances does not have a proper conception of that thing, whatever else may be said about him. Thus it would seem that the relations in which a thing can stand to us do enter into a conception of that thing, and a person does not have an adequate conception of a thing if he does not know what relations it can have with him. Thus he would not have an adequate conception of a material thing if he did not know that while he can in certain circumstances treat it as a person, he cannot without absurdity do so in all circumstances. Similarly, he would not have an adequate conception of a person, if he did not know that he cannot without absurdity always treat people as things.

It might be thought that I ought to have said something stronger here; that is, that a person would not have an adequate conception of a person if he did not know that he can *never* treat people as things, in the sense that it is morally inappropriate that he should do so. It might also be said that when I have in this context spoken of what a person can and cannot do in this connection I have really meant that it is appropriate and inappropriate *in this sense* that he should do. I do not think that this is correct, but it is well that I should go into this matter, since this is the first occasion in my discussion in which there has been reference to the notion of appropriateness, which figures to a considerable extent in my remaining principles. It would, I think, be correct to say that someone does not have an adequate conception of a person if he does not know that it is inappropriate to treat people in all circumstances as things. But to say this is to say simply that if he did do this his behavior would not match his putative understanding. Such a person might still treat some people as things and the question whether this would be morally appropriate is a quite separate question. My question is concerned with how far he could go along these lines before we should say that his behavior was not just morally wrong but crazy in the sense that he had no understanding of what he was up to. The point is that if a man is to have an adequate conception of, say, persons that conception must be reflected in his behavior towards people in an adequate way. What will count as adequate it is impossible to lay down with any definiteness, but to speak of what it is appropriate that he should do is to speak of ways of behaving which are proper expressions of an adequate conception of a person; and whatever counts as appropriate it is certainly inappropriate to treat people as things in all circumstances. Furthermore, if a man is to act out of the conception in question and not merely conform to it he must know the sort of thing that is appropriate and inappropriate in this sense. This is to say that if he treats people as things in all circumstances, and in doing so acts out of his conception of a person it may be inferred that he does not know that it is inappropriate for one with a proper conception of a person so to behave and that he does not have such a proper conception. The inappropriateness of treating people in all circumstances as things that I have in mind, therefore, is an inappropriateness to one who has a proper conception of a person. Part of that proper conception must of course be the recognition that people are moral agents and therefore capable of standing in moral relationships with ourselves. But that does not entail that we must *never* treat people as things.

With this said, we can, I think, turn to my second principle,

Principle B, which will in consequence of all this discussion of
Principle A require a less extended treatment. I hope that I have
shown that the claim that a necessary condition of our being said
to know something is that we should understand what kind of
relations can exist between ourselves and it can be justified in a way
that leaves it fairly unproblematical. I hope that I have also shown
the special relevance this has to knowledge of persons.

(b) Principle B states that *a necessary condition of being said to
know X is that the one should know through experience what it is
to stand in appropriate relations to things of the kind that X is*. This
principle adds to what was stated in Principle A that we should
have had experience of what it is to stand in relation to the objects
of knowledge of the kind in question, and that our understanding
of what it is so to stand is thus based on this experience. Given
what has been said about Principle A, one might wonder how one
could have such understanding in any other way. It might be
argued, however, that we might deduce what it would be like to
stand in certain relations with a certain kind of thing from our
knowledge of those things, knowledge which was in no sense based
on acquaintance with the kind of thing under consideration. Our
knowledge of the kind of thing in question would then be something like the knowledge which we might have of a given
individual person on the basis of a dossier of information about him,
although we had never met him personally. In science fiction there
sometimes occurs the conception of superior intelligences who
acquire this kind of knowledge of human beings in general. They
do not share much that is human, and in particular they do not
share human feelings and emotions. While in consequence they
have never had the experience of standing in relation to human
beings in ways that one human being might stand to another, they
are supposed to deduce what it is like so to stand from what they
learn of human beings by watching them from outside. I think
that such a conception is in fact nonsense. If we can make any sense
of such a being—which is itself doubtful—it must be clear that he
could not deduce what it is like for one human being to stand to
another in characteristic human ways from a study of their

behavior. Or rather, that behavior itself would make no sense to such a being, so that there would be nothing to deduce the requisite conclusion from.

Let us however look briefly at a case which does not involve knowledge of people. There may be people—indeed there presumably *are* people—who have had no experience of cities. Such a person might however acquire a lot of information about, say, London, from reading things about it, hearing accounts of it, and so on. Such information would not be entirely irrelevant to his own experience, which might be confined to life in villages or small towns. Such a person might come to feel that he knows London very well, and others might be surprised that he had never been to London when hearing his accounts of the city. What he knows about London would certainly include things that he had inferred from what he had read and heard; yet in a very real sense he would have had no experience of the kind of thing that London is. All this is certainly possible, but it should be noted that there is no radical break between what he has had experience of and what he has come to know about, as there was between the knowledge possessed by the putative superior beings and the human beings whom they were supposed to come to know about by inference. There is at least an analogy between villages and cities, an analogy which is quite missing in the former case. It is this which makes it feasible to say of our villager that he knows from experience what it is to stand in relation to the kind of things that cities are.

I do not say that our villager does in fact know London. The principle which we are considering is concerned only with one necessary condition of being said to know something, not a sufficient condition. There might be some justification in saying of the villager that however much he feels that he knows London, he does not do so in fact. If he were brought to London, and if the difficulties of practical adjustment to new ways of life were surmounted with aplomb, someone might say of him that it was as if he had known London all his life. But one who did not know of his circumstances might say that he obviously knows London very well indeed, and I am not sure that the correct reaction on being told of the circumstances is to say that after all he did not really know London; it was only *as if* he did. Here much depends on what we expect of one who is supposed to know a city, and it should be noted that we do not expect the same knowledge of everyone. We do not expect of ordinary inhabitants of London who might justly be said to know London the kind of knowledge to be expected of, say, a civil engineer, any more than we expect of the driver of a car who may justly be said to know it knowledge of the kind possessed by his garage mechanic, or of the householder all the knowledge possessed by the builder of his house. To be said to know something a person need possess only that knowledge which is appropriate (in the sense already discussed) to the relation in which he stands to the thing—provided that he does stand in some relation of a pertinent kind. Thus perhaps our villager does have all the knowledge that is appropriate to the relation in which he stands to London, and might therefore justly be said to know London, before he has had any personal experience of it. If we feel some reluctance to agree to this it is because his case is an unusual one, it is not one that we normally feel obliged to allow for, not because there is any logical objection to the villager's being said to know London.

Whatever may be the right conclusion on this matter the case is very different, as I have already said, from the earlier one. It remains true that someone who has no relevant experience of something of a certain kind could not be said to know something else of that kind (and we can stretch the term 'kind' to cover experience of things only in a fairly remote way similar to the putative object of knowledge, as long as there is a relevant connection). The question that I have left open is whether it is a necessary condition of being said to know something that one should have had experience of *that* thing. It is a pertinent question whether I can be said to know a certain *person* if I have not had personal experience of him in some way, and not merely of people in some way like him. In other words, we may grant that we must have had experience of what it is to stand in appropriate relations to the kind of thing that X is if we are to be said to know X (and I have hinted at what is involved in the notion of 'appropriate relations' in what I have said above about what might be expected of ordinary inhabitants of London in relation to London etc.); but do we require another necessary condition—that we must have had experience of standing in appropriate relations to just this thing?

Whatever may be said about our villager in relation to London, can we properly be said to know people whom we have never met —even people whom we have seen much of, such as those who appear repeatedly on television? We can certainly feel that we know them, just as the villager felt that he knew London. But it may be that in this case it is a definite illusion, for knowing people seems to involve a reciprocal relationship, which does not apply to knowledge of cities. This fact may make all the difference between the two cases. With material things, even with such things as cities and cars, a reluctance to admit that we might be said to know a thing of this kind without having had experience of it itself may be due just to the rarity of such possible cases. We might find it difficult to imagine *how* a person could have come to know a city without having experience of it, and on this basis come to insist that such a person only has the feeling that he knows it, without actually knowing it in fact. In most cases there might be reason for such an insistence; but I still think that it would be wrong to elevate this into a point of logic, into something that follows from an aspect of the concept of knowledge. With knowing people, however, the situation seems different. If we had learnt an immense amount about a given person, so much that other people say in a surprised way that it is just as if we had known him all our life, there must still be an 'as if' about it if we had never in fact met him. This does not affect the truth of Principle B, since this gives a necessary condition for knowledge of people, not a sufficient condition. But the case suggests the need for an additional necessary condition, since in it the reason why there is not even the *possibility* of our knowing the person in question (let alone its actually *being* the case that we know him) is that we stand to him in no sort of personal relationship. This in effect takes us to Principle C.

(c) This says that it is *a necessary condition of being said to know X that we should actually stand to X in relations which are appropriate to the kind of thing that X is.* I have said earlier that there is not one way, nor indeed any one class of ways, in which a

man should have stood to a car, a city, or a house in order to be
said to know it—not, that is, *qua* man. And I took it to follow from
this that there is not one set of items of knowledge that a man, *qua*
man, should know about if he is to know a car, a city, or a house.
In cases of this kind much depends on the kind of role that he
plays in relation to the object in question. These roles determine
what has to be satisfied if he is to be said to know the thing in
question. Once given this it may seem obvious that to know X a
man must actually stand in relations to X which are appropriate
to one conforming to such roles in relation to X. This, it might be
said, is what I meant in specifying Principle C as saying that to
know X we must actually stand to X in relations that are
appropriate to the kind of thing that X is—appropriate, that is,
for one of a certain kind playing a certain kind of role in relation
to a thing of this kind. Thus, for a builder to know my house, he
must stand in relations to it which are appropriate for a builder
towards a house, i.e. he must have built it, or otherwise been
involved in the details of its construction or reconstruction and
repair. For me to know my house I do not need to stand to it in
those relations, but what I know of it must be based on familiarity
of another kind—from which it follows that I do not need to know
all that my builder knows nor he all that I know. Here the roles
determine the relationships, and these determine what must be
known about X if X itself is to be known. If I do not stand towards
my house in the kind of relationship appropriate to it as a building-
construction (i.e. if I did not build it or repair it, and am not
interested in it as a building) then I cannot be said to know it as
that; but the role that I do have in relationship to it does imply
that I may know it as something else, e.g. as a home.

It is, I think, analytic that if a man's relation to a thing is determined by the sort of role that he plays in relation to it he must
actually stand in that relation if he is to know it as the sort of thing
that fulfils that role. Suppose, however, that a man's relation to a
thing is such that it could never properly play the part that he gives
it in the role that he plays. A man's relation to his car may, we are
told, sometimes be like that of a man to his mistress. The question
is 'How like?' 'Surely we may say that if it is really like that he

does not really know his car. It cannot after all respond in all the appropriate ways. But if it were really like that as far as he is concerned, what sort of mistake would he have made? If a man treats his wife entirely as a mistress, then whatever else he is doing, he *is* making a mistake about his role in relation to her. But if he treated his car in this or some analogous way, the confusion would go well beyond anything that could be called a 'mistake'.

Two further points need to be made. The first is that the relationship of one person to another, to the extent that that relationship can be specified in terms of roles, must be one that is two-way if it is to be a condition of knowledge. This is the point about reciprocity that I have made before. The second point is that the relationship may go beyond any roles into which they have entered. This gives a vast complexity to the question of what counts as a mistake in this context. Neither of the points applies, however, to the relationship of the man with his car; for whatever one says about that relationship it depends ultimately on the fact that he stands in relation to it as user to used. And as I said earlier, one who thinks that he can stand in this relation to people in all circumstances does not have an adequate conception of a person. But conversely if a man really did treat his car as a mistress, he would not have an adequate conception of a car, and must therefore be at least confused. Thus if a man's relation to a thing is such that it could never properly play the part that he gives it in the role that he plays, he must lack an adequate knowledge of that thing in that he is confused about the sort of thing it is. He fails to stand to it in the relationship that is appropriate to the kind of thing that it is.

I spoke earlier when discussing Principle A of the point that for something to be a possible object of our knowledge it must be capable of figuring in our life in some way. This point is connected with the second point that I mentioned just now—the point about human relationships going beyond roles. One way in which something may figure in our life is, it is true, that it plays a part in connection with certain roles that we perform in relation to it. This could be applicable both to material things, and in some respects persons, as I have indicated. But as far as persons are concerned, it could not be the whole truth. For people do not figure

C

in our lives simply in respect of the part that they play in connection with our performance of roles, nor simply in respect of the roles that they play in relation to us. Nor have we got very far when we attempt to construe our knowledge and understanding of people in terms of roles. For people are not just role players; they can feature as objects of more personal and emotional attitudes on our part, and the relationship can be reciprocal. Can it be maintained, therefore, that a necessary condition of our knowing people is that we should stand in this kind of relationship to them? For, after all, this is a relationship which is appropriate to things of this kind, i.e. to persons. I am not here saying that the relationship should be one of any specific attitude, not for example love. Hatred may be the appropriate attitude towards some people, although this would be a case of moral appropriateness and we are not here concerned with that. All that I am asking is whether if a man did not stand to another person in some relationship that involved one or other of those feelings which we might call 'personal' he could have any claim to be said to know that person. I am not asking, for example, whether the more involved he is with the other person the more he is entitled to claim knowledge of him. That might well not be the case. On the other hand the absence of any feeling towards the other person does seem to prejudice the possibility of knowing him; it prevents one getting close enough for the purpose, so to speak.

In connection with knowledge of persons, too much feeling is blinding, too little inhibits personal relationships, such that one is in danger of being concerned with externals only, and eventually perhaps in danger of treating people merely as things. I do not mean to imply by this that one might not have feelings towards things as distinct from people. Indeed some of them—pride, affection, dislike, boredom, for example—might be the same. But with people there must be the reciprocity that I have emphasized all along. I do not mean by this that they must have the same feelings towards you that you have towards them. This need not be so at all. But suppose someone had a passionate interest in another person in a personal way but received nothing of this kind at all in return, being treated if anything somewhat as a thing. Would there be any possibility in this case of the person concerned being said to know the other in any real sense? For one thing, he would not have had experience of the other's personal side, as one might put it. But it might be argued that this merely reduces to the considerations adduced under Principle B—he must have had experience of the other's personal side, have had experience of standing in personal relations with him at some time; he need not so stand now. But it should be noted on the other side that we do tend to say things like 'I used to know him very well, but I haven't seen him for a long time; I cannot really claim to know him now, not personally at any rate.' It is the current relationship that is important in this respect; for people change in their attitudes and relationships as much as in everything else. But the important point is that whether or not one has met a person lately and whatever feelings one has toward him currently one must have some attitude to him which is the sort of attitude one has to a person.

Some may think this something of a minimal claim, and I am happy to acknowledge this fact. Others may be worried that a story about attitudes, feelings, and the like should be thought to be part of an account of what knowledge consists in. What of this sort of thing is involved in an account of what is to be count as knowledge of facts? Accounts of knowledge that something is the case in terms of such notions as justified true belief have come under considerable attack lately, and rightly. If knowledge of this kind implies belief, and I think that it does, the knowledge that p will imply the belief that p because p is true and not for some other reason. I do not put this forward as a sufficient account of the place of belief in an account of the concept of knowledge, but it is sufficient for my purposes. For to believe that p because p is true implies a certain attitude towards truth or fact. Thus even in this case there is involved some attitude and relationship to the object of knowledge, which ought to be mentioned in any adequate account of the knowledge in question. To be said to know a fact a person must stand in a relation to the fact that is appropriate to the kind of thing in question, i.e. to facts in general. The relationship is simply stated —it is appropriate that he should accept it as such. Thus knowledge of fact falls under my principles and is not to be thought of as an

exception to my account of knowledge. The man who knows that
p must stand to the fact that p in the relation appropriate to facts—
acceptance. When it comes to objects of knowledge of other kinds
the relationship that is appropriate will depend on how the object is
construed. If the object is construed in terms of the part that it plays
in connection with roles that we perform in relation to it, then, as
we have already seen, the relationship is prejudged. But where
this is not so, as is the case with knowledge of persons as such, then
the relationship has to be determined independently, and this I have
been trying to indicate. It remains true that the relationship to the
thing in question exists in virtue of its being a *kind* of thing, e.g. a
fact or a person; and it is our understanding of what that kind of
thing is that determines what relationship is appropriate to it.
Indeed what is meant by an appropriate relationship here is simply
one that is involved in an adequate understanding of the kind of
thing in question. If Principle D were valid more would be suggested than this, and I must therefore turn, finally, to a brief
consideration of this.

(d) Principle D, the invalid one, is that *a necessary condition of my
being said to know X is that I should stand to X in relations which
are appropriate to X.* This principle states that a condition of being
said to know something is that I should stand in relations to that
thing which are appropriate to it, i.e. that the relations that should
exist between me and it should be of a kind that should exist
between me and it independently of the fact of knowledge, and
independently of the thing's being construed as an object of knowledge. It is perhaps difficult to know what that would mean in
connection with a material thing. What relations should exist
between me and a thing of that kind independently of its being
construed as an object of knowledge of a certain kind for me? But
the situation might be thought different in connection with knowledge of people. Could it be the case that for me to know my wife I
must stand in relations to her which are appropriate not just to a
person or to a wife, but to her? I think that if any sense can be
given to this suggestion it will have to be in terms of *moral* relations.
For it could certainly be maintained that certain moral relations

are appropriate between me and my wife, and it might even be held, that the relations in question might go beyond anything that turns simply on the fact that she is a person or a person of a certain sort or kind, e.g. a wife. Again, to take a very different example, the moral relationships that would be appropriate between me and a man who was positively evil in a certain way might well go beyond anything that turned on the fact that he had other relationships with me or that he was in other ways a person of a certain kind. Whatever be the case on this point, it would be very difficult to maintain that having appropriate relations of this kind is a necessary condition of being properly said to know the person in question.

Suppose for example that there were someone towards whom the only morally appropriate attitude for me to adopt was complete sympathy. Suppose also that I just could not bring myself to this attitude—something that might be due to certain factors in me. Would it be right in this case to say that I cannot then know that person—or at any rate not properly? I cannot think so, for I might know the person in question very well indeed and know that my attitude should be the sympathy in question, but still not be able to bring myself to that attitude. This kind of thing is a familiar occurrence with human beings, and must be reckoned with, in any account of them, as a possibility at least. We do sometimes say to someone 'You cannot really know him or you would not take that attitude towards him', and in some cases the remark may be quite just. But it need not always be so. Normally indeed we expect what a man knows to show in his behavior; but this is not to say that one who knows someone cannot behave towards him in ways that we feel to be morally inappropriate. The behavior may in such circumstances require explanation or justification and we may feel that the man in question is being unreasonable. But this does not amount to the claim that there is an absurdity in someone who knows another behaving towards him in ways that are morally inappropriate, let alone ways that we simply *feel* to be morally inappropriate.

The way in which knowledge of something has been connected with attitudes towards that thing, throughout all the principles until this last one, has been that the thing *construed as an object of knowledge* brings with it kinds of attitude towards it in being construed in that way. The attitudes that are morally appropriate to someone are not a function of how he is construed in the same way. My failure to take towards someone the appropriate moral attitude is not, or not necessarily, the result of a failure of understanding. Hence, I do not think that Principle D can stand. The other three principles remain, I think, valid.

III

What are the implications of all this, perhaps boring, detail for our present concern? They are surely these: In order to know someone we must know what personal relations are, we must know from experience what it is to stand in personal relations, and we must stand in some kind of personal relationship to the person in question. It seems clear that in one sense of 'understanding' at least, the same applies to understanding a person. The question before us is 'How are we to conceptualize the processes through which one person comes to understand another?' If anything else emerges from my discussion it must be that we cannot conceptualize those processes as if the understanding of a person was no different from the understanding of any other kind of thing. Moreover it matters whether we stand in any kind of personal relationship to the person and this must be taken into account in an attempt to set out what it is for one person to understand another and how that understanding comes about. It might be said that we can sometimes stand outside any such relationship with another person and seek to understand him in an impersonal sort of way; indeed it might be maintained that just this must be involved in any scientific and objective attempt to understand people. My claim would be that if what I have said in discussing my third principle is right there are limits to what understanding of people can be derived in that way. For without standing in a personal relationship to the other person we cannot be said really to know him, and while some understanding of him may be possible without so knowing him, complete understanding, if this is in any sense feasible, is not possible. Hence

the fundamental importance in any adequate treatment of interpersonal understanding of interpersonal dynamics.[2]

In the first two principles that I have discussed as giving necessary
conditions of knowing another person, I have made reference to
knowledge or understanding of other things—what relations can
exist between the other person and ourselves, and what it is to stand
in relations appropriate to a person. This could be put in other ways
by saying that the two principles in question state the conceptual
underpinning of knowledge of persons—what is involved in having
the concept of a person. The third principle demands something
more than this, and it is this principle which must be relaxed if
we are to allow the impersonal knowledge and understanding of
people to which I made reference just now. I insist here only on the
recognition that there are limits to what can be known or understood unless application is given in a particular case to this principle.
But it may be that further questions arise in connection with the
first two principles. If, as I said at the beginning of this paper, it is
necessary in order to see what is in front of us as actions, behavior
which has sense,[3] that we should already understand that we are
concerned with a person, and if a condition of this is that we should
understand what it is to stand in personal relations with another,
how does *this* understanding come about? From experience, yes,
but how? Secondly, in what sort of ways do these necessary
conditions get translated into sufficient conditions? In what sort of
ways, in other words, does the actual understanding and knowledge
of another develop? I spoke earlier of putting oneself in the other's
place; but clearly much else must have gone on before this is possible
at all.

I have said something on the former question elsewhere.[4] It

---

[2] I was interested to see that in Philip Vernon's book *Personality Assessment* (1964), person-perception and the like is discussed under the heading
'naive interpretations' of personality. This categorization is right if person-
perception is thought of independently of personal relationships.

[3] Cf. for this way of putting it Franz From (1971).

[4] In my paper 'Human Learning' which was a contribution to the Royal
Institute of Philosophy Conference on the Philosophy of Psychology, at
Canterbury, Kent, September 1971—to appear in the proceedings of the
conference (*The Philosophy of Psychology*, ed. S. C. Brown).

would be wrong to think that a child comes to understand what a person is by asking himself what relations are appropriate between himself and other people. It cannot be, that is, a question of the child having to decide just what is the difference for him between people and other kinds of thing. The animism of children which Piaget and others have emphasized is more than understandable if one thinks of the child having to come to see what is *not* a suitable object for a personal relation rather than what *is* a suitable object. I have in the paper referred to spoken of the crucial role in the development of the child's understanding played by what it is put in the way of by others, and I have claimed that without so being put in the way of things there would be no possibility of there arising an objective understanding of an objective word (something that brings in social considerations). Whatever be the truth on that matter it remains a fact that the child's relationship with his mother (or in other cultures than our own whatever other human being is responsible for the child's nurture) takes up a considerable part of his early life. Such relationships are not to be construed as, so to speak, transactions between the child and adults, nor indeed a matter of stimulus and response unless this is viewed in a far from orthodox way. I mean by this that while it would be quite inadequate to think of the child reacting to stimuli provided by the mother in the usual mechanical way that is implied by talking of stimulus and response or reaction, it is more feasible and perhaps indeed vital to see how crucial emotional responses and attitudes are in this business. It is impossible to construe such attitudes and the responses to them merely as the presentation of, say, pleasurable stimuli which the child then reacts to in a positive way (with negative reactions to painful stimuli, of course). To adopt such a simple-minded hedonism does not do justice to what human beings, even very young ones, actually are. Hedonism of this kind, in which it is supposed that human behaviour is built up from positive and negative responses to what is pleasurable or the reverse have, in the history of thought, generally gone along with attempts to construe human beings along mechanist lines (cf. Hobbes). The idea that human beings are rather more complex than this does not imply a kind of mysticism; we need suppose only that certain emotional attitudes and reactions (by which I mean not simple mechanical reactions but complex forms of response to e.g. love and concern) are part of our genetic inheritance, thus forming the basis of what I spoke of in Part I as the natural reactions of person to person (cf. here, in opposition to my previous reference to Hobbes, Bishop Butler's view of man as something possessing a set of particular propensities, among which might be benevolence). What may be the physiological basis for such propensities is another matter, but we need not suppose that, on the psychological level, human beings are to be viewed simply as governed by hedonic pushes and pulls.

One might put the matter in other ways by saying that a personal relation is a natural thing for a person whether it is recognized as such or not. There is no need to find the notion of personal relations either puzzling or mystical. Rather, it would be more adequate to think of the child's view of the world around him developing out of what he is put in the way of in the course of relationships of this kind. Hence the animism; it is likely in these circumstances that the child will see personal agency in inappropriate places, since he will see all sorts of things as suitable recipients of personal attitudes and not just persons themselves. Hence it is no puzzle that the child should, to go back to my second principle, come to know through experience what it is to stand in relations which are appropriate to persons, since standing in such relations is what he is from the beginning and the fact is continually pressed upon him. It may well be doubted whether a baby could possibly stand in such relations to anyone from the beginning. I mean simply this. The possibility of being aware of other people as people and of oneself as a person among others depends on the ability to receive what is offered as, for example, love *as love*, and on the ability to respond with analogous expressions of affection. I do not mean by this that the child has to have any deep understanding of what love is; I mean only that the child is genetically determined to respond with whole patterns of behavior, emotional expression and feeling to certain forms of treatment. It learns what it is appropriate so to respond to in terms of whether the patterns of response so released fit in with subsequent treatment, whether the whole pattern of behaviour and response by others is one that fits in with its needs and interests. It is important to distinguish this sort of account from one which says that stimuli call out certain reactions which produce further stimuli etc., such that those reactions which are rewarded are repeated, those which are not rewarded not repeated. If the child construed as a physiological mechanism can be thought of as subject to stimuli which produce physiological reactions (and whether a child can be so construed and so thought of is in the end an empirical matter of a kind) this is not the level at which I intend my account to apply. To receive a certain form of treatment as love involves engaging in a complex form of emotional and other kinds of behaviour, which may develop in certain ways according to what fits in with what happens. To learn what is appropriate to certain kinds of object of that behavior is to learn what fits in this way. But in so far as the child, for genetic reasons, responds and can respond in a human way to human forms of treatment so it stands in embryo personal relations with others. It is only to be expected that it may stand in bogus or inappropriate relations of this kind to things that are not persons, and a proper development includes the recognition that this may be so. Hence the possibility of recognizing others and oneself as persons, and of acquiring the concept of a person proper, depends on the natural tendencies that a child has as a human being, on, to use Wittgenstein's phrase, what is part of its form of life. The understanding of what it is for something to be a person rests on what is in effect the facility for *being* a person and for reacting to the world in ways that are appropriate if this is to be encouraged. Without being treated personally and as a person by others no such development would be possible.

I have in this tried to say something (no doubt inadequately) about the conditions for the development of an understanding of what it is to stand in relations appropriate to persons. Once given this the child must be given *eo ipso* a rough knowledge of the sort of thing that counts as a person, an ability at least to distinguish in most cases between what is a person and what is not. This does not of course amount to any real understanding of people; it amount only to that rough understanding which makes person perception possible, which makes it possible to see certain things in the world in the light of what is to be expected from persons. In this light a facial expression, for example, is not just a pattern, a physiognomy, but a complex reaction from a person which may or may not fit in with whatever else that person is taken to be. I suspect that the negative results of many experiments on the recognition of facial expression are due to the fact that the operation is divorced from the living context, so to speak. A physiognomy is just one aspect, and perhaps a minor aspect of a person, and it may not loom very large in a personal relationship. Within a personal relationship there may be much less uncertainty about the other's moods than the undoubted ambiguity of facial expressions might suggest.

This in effect takes me on to my second point—what else has to be added to the necessary conditions for knowledge of persons, of which I have spoken, to give the sufficient conditions? No *general* answer to this question can be given, since what will be sufficient will depend on the people concerned, the circumstances, and how deep the knowledge and understanding has to be. I wish here only to give some pointers, and some suggestions as to how it *cannot* be. Given what I have said it cannot be the case that we have to gain our understanding of others *via* inferences from their outer expressions in behavior etc. I mean here just what I say—it cannot be the case that we *have* to do this. I do not wish to deny that this is how it may sometimes be, although it would not be possible in this way did we not have other understandings of people, other understandings of what it is to be a person. But we do of course sometimes have to gain our understanding of a person from external observations. I doubt, as I have said before, that this can take us all that far, even if it may be in some cases essential as a basis for other kinds of knowledge. Nevertheless this cannot be the way it is in every case or even perhaps normally.

One other suggestion that might be made by way of reaction to the failure of inference from data as a general method of coming to know people is that our knowledge and understanding of others may be a matter of skill or knack. I do not think that this will do either. Such a suggestion would reduce our relationships to other people to one of craft. Once again this may be how it is on some occasions, but it cannot be how it is in general. To suppose that it might be would be to present a false, indeed a corrupt, picture of what humans are like. This is not to say that knacks or skills may not enter into those transactions with others in which we seek understanding of them. A diagnostic session of whatever kind must involve such things. But to confine oneself to this entirely would be to stand outside a relationship with the other, and thus fail to fulfil the necessary conditions which I have stressed.

I spoke in Part I of the place that a general knowledge of people and their motives etc., can play in the understanding of a particular person. It also needs to be stressed that a direct experience of relationships with other people can also be vital for the understanding of one particular person. For what may be vital to such understanding may be the ability to see the person in a certain way in terms of relationships of this kind. In any account of understanding the notion of 'seeing' in an extended sense ought to play an important role. I say 'extended sense' though I am not at all sure that this is a correct way of putting it. How we see things can often enough have little to do with any properties of the strictly visual experience. One way, for example, to describe what is involved in the experience of being happy is to say that we can see the world as, say, a glittering place. That we see it in this way may be determined by our mood, our understanding of certain things, what we know to be the case, and so on, but our seeing things in this way is not to be identified simply with our mood, our understanding or our knowledge. Analogously, how we see a given person may be determined not simply by what we know of him in a way that we could express, but by various things that have entered into our experiences, including feelings that we may have towards him or that he may have towards us. Nevertheless the growth in our understanding of a person may be viewed as an increase in our vision of him; we may see him from a wider point of view, from more aspects. It is easy enough to see that closer relations with a person may well present us with more aspects, even if a too great degree of closeness may sometimes be blinding. We need sometimes to stand back and take a more detached view. The point might be put by saying that the only general thing that can be said about how knowledge and understanding of other people is to be attained is that it comes by way of increased experience, general knowledge of people, and above all perhaps by way of an imaginative approach to them. We could not do this without experience of and insight into the relationships that we have with others. Hence the concept of a personal relationship plays a crucial role in any conceptualization of what is involved in one person coming to understand another, and this is the central point that I wish to make.

IV

Postscript and Commentary

The principles that I have set out and discussed in Part II are meant to be *conceptual* principles; they are meant to bring out factors which are involved in the concept of knowing something, and these factors have, I think, been overlooked or under-emphasized in philosophical accounts of knowledge. They seem to me to apply to knowledge of objects of all kinds, even facts, though they may assume a role which is more important in connection with certain objects than with others. With facts in general, for example, it is important to recognize that an understanding of what it is for something to be fact involves certain attitudes on our part to it. Someone who had no regard for and saw no reason to accept facts could scarcely be said to know what facts are. Here perhaps, however, the importance of what I have said about our relationship to the object of knowledge goes no further; but in the case of other objects of knowledge, particularly persons, there are further implications and ramifications.

The principles that I have discussed are progressive in the sense that starting from the proposition about the necessity for understanding the relations that can exist between a putative object of knowledge and ourselves, they move to the proposition that we must actually stand to that object in relations appropriate to things of that kind if it is really to be an object of knowledge. As far as

concerns persons this means that the notion of something like
personal relations enters into an account of what knowledge of
persons involves. It may do so in different ways and to different
degrees according to the extent of the knowledge. Since understanding a person implies knowledge of him, or does so if that
understanding is to be an adequate understanding or something
approaching a complete understanding, the same principles apply
here too. I have no wish to deny that there can be certain kinds or
degrees of understanding of people which may be arrived at through
a kind of impersonal observation or analysis of them and their
behaviour. Even so I believe that such understanding presupposes
the application of my principles A and B. But I also believe that
there are limits to what is possible in this way. Hence for complete
or fully adequate understanding and knowledge of people, for real
knowledge of them, my principle C must be taken seriously and
the point of principle D is in effect to make clear the limits of
principle C.

My concerns, when it comes to the application of my principles,
are, therefore, fundamentally twofold—the conditions for *really*
knowing and understanding another person, and the conditions
for having knowledge and understanding of persons at all. The first
concern brings in all three of principles A, B and C, the second
principles A and B only, although it is scarcely conceivable that
someone should have come to know what it is to stand in relation
to persons without so standing to some person or persons. Thus in
effect my concerns cover (a) person-perception so-called, and real
interpersonal understanding, and (b) the genetics and development
of such interpersonal understanding. In each case my concern is
with necessary conditions, since I believe that little can be said of a
general kind of what is sufficient for such knowledge and its development, although Richard Peters (below, pp. 37–65) has attempted to
do something along these lines. It is clear, on the other hand, that John
Flavell (below pp. 66–116) is very much concerned with what I have
listed under (b). Yet, it could be said that he and I pass each other by
in our concern with genetic considerations. I am very much interested
in how the business gets off the ground, so to speak; his interests start
two or three years later in the life of a child. On the other hand, my

interest under (a) is with the kind of knowledge and understanding that a fully developed adult might hope to have. Thus, in the lifetime of the child I am concerned with issues that arise either earlier or very much later than those with which he is concerned. I think that this point requires emphasis.

Professor Flavell's model for the child's coming to see another's point of view (and it is more often than not a very literal point of view) is described as a model of interpersonal inference, and his account relies heavily on the notion of inference. I have two sorts of comment to make here—comments which arise out of my own paper:

(a) Inferences of this kind, which undoubtedly play a large part in our and children's coming to understand others, could not, so to speak, stand on their own feet. They must have at their back other forms of interpersonal contact, and in this respect Flavell's account seems to me based very much on what one might call 'externals'. I would emphasize again that I am not denying the fact that inference enters into our understanding of others to a very large extent, just as I have no wish to deny that knowledge of facts about a person plays a very large part, or may do, in our knowledge of him. I am simply denying that this can be all that there is. William Alston has put it to me that, once the concept of a person has been acquired, inferences may always be involved in knowledge of others, for all my account has shown to the contrary. I do not know how to assess such a claim without reference to arguments in support of it. All that I can say here is that if this kind of account were generalized it would have the implication, as I think Flavell's model also implies, that we have to stand back, as it were, from other people and try to infer what is going on in their minds. This would be, not something that may happen sometimes and contingently, but something that is a necessity. But it certainly cannot always be like this, for, as I have said in Part I of my paper, the view saddles us with the other-minds problem in a particularly vicious form. To put the matter in a direct and crude way, which has special relevance to Flavell's view, how do children come to see others *as* others (others indeed who may have different points of view from theirs, whether they initially see this or whether, as

Piaget's egocentricity thesis implies, they do not). What is it to see something as a person so that there can be a question of what their point of view is? I would suggest that Flavell's model is *too* cognitive, *too* much concerned with 'intellectual' questions about others, and needs some supplementation at least by some reference to what relationships exist between the children in question, to, if you will, a context of interpersonal dynamics.

(b) We need also, I think, a story about how the child can even get to the stage of making such inferences. This is my problem of how the business gets off the ground. What I have suggested is that we need to bring in something like the notion of personal relations at the beginning. Knowledge of others would then have for its foundation something like relations between the child and others based on feeling. This could be summed up by saying that the child comes to have understanding of others as persons if and only to the extent that it is itself treated as a person rather than a thing. It is the relations so established that are all important. I have tried to say something about this in Part III of my paper, but I am conscious of the inadequacy of what is said there. The attempt to get back into the child's mind at the very beginning of its life is in one sense an impossibility since success would mean sloughing off all the features of adult understanding without which an *account* of the child's mind would be impossible anyway. Thus the very features that are necessary for such an account—the concepts and terms in which the account is and must be expressed—make the success of the account impossible. Here, however, as in some other contexts, I believe that there is every virtue in trying to do what is impossible.

I said something in Part III about the inadequacy of trying to explain the way in which the child comes to behave to other human beings in terms of what it finds pleasurable and painful in the treatment that it receives, particularly of course from its mother. Satisfaction of hunger cannot, for example, consist merely in the receipt of what is pleasant to the child, the hunger itself being unpleasant or even painful. I do not think that this is an adequate account of what it must mean to the baby to have its hunger satisfied. In discussing this issue lately Mr. R. K. Elliott said to me that such satisfaction might be more like grace and salvation to it, and I am much indebted to him for this observation. Some may find such theologically-derived terms too high-flown for these purposes. But there is something apt about the description. It is not of course claimed that the child sees the food, the mother's breast, or what have you, in these terms; *that* would be an impossibility. It is that such terms do greater justice to what must inevitably be the child's experience on such an occasion. Indeed the process of development and learning about the world must involve learning that this satisfaction is not, as it were, a gift of heaven, but due to another human being who stands to him in a complex relationship within which love, it is to be hoped, figures prominently. I do not think that this is mere sentimentality; I think that such an account, if it could be developed, would be the only realistic one, even if it would require much imagination on the part of the theorist.

For these purposes, the child must be granted a fairly rich genetic equipment, and a consciousness which can be educated by experience. Such an education will involve the turning of an awareness which has a formal object only (an awareness, perhaps, of everything in general and nothing in particular) into an awareness of different and particular things. For this to happen the child must be able to come to see things as belonging together and other things as different, if and to the extent that things are brought before the focus of its attention. That is why, again, it is so important how the child is treated and what it is put in the way of. But to think of the child as a simple classifier and distinguisher would be far from doing justice to the facts; for this would be to confine one's attention, once again, to the purely cognitive aspects of its life, and I think that these would be nothing without the background of feeling and emotion which constitutes the foundation of the relationships with others within which alone its development could thrive.

That is why the fact that the child stands in relations to other persons is so important for a general account of how it comes to have an understanding of the world. But it might be thought that this presupposes that an answer has been given to a prior question —'How does the child come to recognize persons as such?' For how can the child stand in relation to persons without having some

D

idea of what it is standing in relation to? And how does it come
to have that idea? It is perhaps interesting that Chomsky (1968,
p. 64) includes human action under suggested topics for a theory
akin to his generative theory of linguistic competence. The point, I
take it, is that just as there is, given his premises, a problem how the
child comes to recognize the noises made by other humans in its
presence as language unless it already has the idea of what language
is, so there is a problem how it comes to recognize the movements of certain bodies as actions. Those movements would, of
course, be in the running for identification as actions only if they
were made by persons. Hence the problem specified amounts to
the problem how the child recognizes certain things as persons
unless it already has the idea of what a person is. I do not think
that an appeal to a putative innate idea of a person will do, although
I cannot discuss this issue here (I have discussed it in a general way
in Hamlyn 1971, forthcoming). But I do not think that we have a
need for such a solution any way, for what is really wrong lies in
the premises of the argument. It is not a question of the child
having to come to recognize persons as such in this way. The child
could come to have the idea of what a person is only *via* and in
the context of *being* a person; and for this to have any real sense
the child must, as I have said, be treated as a person. Thus when I
said in Part III that the child must stand in personal relations from
the beginning, I did not mean that the child had from the beginning
to be aware of this as the case. *That would* presuppose an understanding of what a person is and the problem that I have been
discussing would immediately ensue. Rather the child must be
thought of as being the recipient and progressively the source of
attitudes and behaviour which is of the kind appropriate to persons,
whether or not the child is initially aware of this as such; all this is
the product of what I have spoken of as natural reactions of person
to person. It is this human context which provides a basis for, and
eventual substance to, the understanding of what it is both to *be*
a person and to take other persons *as* persons. For this is the sort
of concept that the concept of a person is. (It is perhaps worth
noting that, although they may not provide exact parallels, there are
numerous concepts the acquisition of which is dependent on partici-

pation in activities and possible relations; consider—to take what some may think a highfaluting example, but one which may well have some pertience in the present connection in the light of the theological conception of a personal God—the concept of prayer and the correlative concept of a God to whom prayers may be addressed.) At all events, to think of the child's recognition of persons as merely a function of its classification of some things as persons and other things as non-persons in virtue of characteristics possessed by the first and not by the second is a most unrealistic account of the situation, and one which fails to take proper account of what sort of concept that of a person is. If what I have been saying is right it is no surprise at all that knowing what a person is implies knowledge of what it is to stand in personal relations, and hence that understanding people implies this too. Such a conclusion indeed seems inescapable. Hence my answer to the question 'How does the child come to recognize persons?'

Let me return finally and by way of summary to the general thesis of my paper. My position could be put as follows:

(1) Any understanding of other people, any person-perception, presupposes an understanding of what people *are*. This implies knowing what it is to stand in relations to people, and implies also, if I am really to understand another person, standing in a personal relation to him or her. The child has somehow to enter into relations of this kind, if only in a rudimentary way, if he is to develop any understanding of what persons are.

(2) There is, even without the 'real understanding' which I have mentioned under (1), the possibility of *some* degree of understanding of people. Coming to understand people in this way may, *provided that one has a prior knowledge of persons in general*, involve such things as (a) putting oneself in their place, (b) inferring things about them from 'externals', (c) applying to them knowledge that one has about what makes people tick in general, and other things of this kind.

(3) Hence, what I have had to say implies limits at two ends of a scale, so to speak.

(a) Complete or full understanding of a person is impossible without standing in a personal relationship to him (and to say this is not *merely* to say that without this I should not have sufficient information about him, if that information is construed in an impersonal way, nor is it to say that without this I should not have the tacit knowledge how to cope with him and things of that kind).

(b) Understanding of people is impossible altogether without knowledge of what a person is, and this implies a foundation in what Wittgenstein would have called features of our form of life, and what I have referred to as 'natural reactions of person to person'. It is on this basis, as I see it, that interpersonal understanding develops, and without it it would never get off the ground.

One final and dogmatic point: I argued in relation to my principle C that one cannot fully know or understand another solely in terms of the roles that either of us plays. The view that a human being can be summed up in terms of a collection of roles seems to me not only an inadequate view of human beings, but, if I may so put it, a corrupt one. It leaves out of account those features of human beings which give morality a real content and reduces personal relations to something at the best artificial and at the worst inhuman.

REFERENCES

Chomsky, N., *Language and Mind*, Harcourt, Brace and World, Inc., New York, 1968.

Cook, J., 'Human Beings' in *Studies in the Philosophy of Wittgenstein*, ed. P. G. Winch, Routledge and Kegan Paul, London, 1969.

From, F., *Perception of Other People*, trans. by B. A. Maher and E. Kvan, Columbia University Press, New York, 1971.

Hamlyn, D. W., 'Human Learning' in proceedings of Royal Institute of Philosophy Conference on the Philosophy of Psychology, 1971, forthcoming as *The Philosophy of Psychology*, ed. S. C. Brown.

Sartre, J-P., *Being and Nothingness*, trans. by Hazel E. Barnes, Barnes and Noble, New York, 1956.

Vernon, P. E., *Personality Assessment*, Methuen, London, 1964.

Wittgenstein, L., *Philosophical Investigations*, Blackwell, Oxford, 1953.

Personal Understanding and Personal Relationships

RICHARD S. PETERS

Introduction

It is a commonplace in the literature about understanding other people that there is a radical difference between this sort of understanding and the understanding which we have of the behavior of things, which is connected in some way with entering into personal relationships with them of the sort that we do not and cannot enter into with things. We can, of course, know about people in the way in which we can know about things. We can know that man is six feet tall and that he will fall rapidly to the ground if pushed from the top of a cliff, just as we can know that a piece of wood is of the same height and will behave in the same way if dropped. But we also know and understand people in ways in which we do not know and understand pieces of wood. This form of knowledge is often connected with the peculiar vantage point that we occupy in relation to other people; for we ourselves are people and enter into special sorts of relationships, namely personal relationships, with the objects known. This special kind of relationship, making possible a special kind of vantage point, is the basis of the special kind of knowledge or understanding which we enjoy.

David Hamlyn's paper deals with this general type of claim and attempts to specify more precisely the ways in which personal relationships provide conditions for knowledge of other people. I do not disagree with his general thesis. Indeed I wish to take over more or less at the point at which he leaves off. I think that, in a way, his thesis is not radical enough, for he does not examine the extent to which entering into personal relationships with others is constitutive of rather than just providing conditions for knowing and understanding them. So this will be the first thought that I wish to explore in my paper. This will lead me, secondly, to try to get a bit clearer about what is meant by 'personal relationships' in this and other contexts. In my view there are distinctions here which need to be made which throw light on the understanding of ourselves and others. Thirdly I shall advance the suggestion that there are levels of personal relationships which are connected with levels of personal understanding and personal attraction.

1. *Explanation and initiation*

The usual way for a philosopher to approach problems of personal knowledge is to set out possible conditions of 'knowledge' and to see whether knowing people can be fitted into some pattern of 'knowing how', 'knowing that', 'knowing how to', and so on. I do not propose to follow this track, partly because it has been traversed by David Hamlyn, partly because I am more interested in 'understanding' than in 'knowledge' and partly because there is another approach which is likely to be of particular pertinence in a conference between psychologists and philosophers. I refer to the sort of approach pioneered by William Dilthey who was impressed by the methodological differences between the natural sciences and human studies. He thought that the sciences of man would get nowhere if the methodological paradigm of the natural sciences was copied. His objections to the natural science approach need not detain us (cf. Hodges, 1944, Ch. III). Indeed many of them are based on some of the misconceptions of the natural sciences which Popper tried to make explicit in *The Poverty of Historicism*. His positive conception of the epistemological basis of human studies is more important and interesting.

(a) THE PSYCHOLOGY OF VERSTEHEN

Dilthey claimed, first of all, that psychology is a descriptive science whose principles can be extracted from what is given to the individual in his inner perception. Secondly he claimed that inner perception reveals not isolated units of mental life such as sensations, feelings or intentions but a unity of conation, affect and conation in 'a total reaction of the whole self to a situation confronting it' (Hodges, 1944, p. 43). This unitary reaction constitutes the ground-rhythm of mental life, and is called the 'structural system'. Psychology is an elaboration of this system which is given to us in 'lived experience'. Thirdly our understanding of others is not, in essence, an inferential process. We are able to understand the expressions of the mental states of others because of the psychological law that expressions have the power, under normal conditions, to evoke corresponding experiences in the minds of observers. We feel in ourselves reverberations of grief, for instance, when we see another human being in a downcast attitude, with his face marked by tears (cf. *ibid.*, pp. 13–17).

Some of these assumptions about understanding others are shared by Michael Scriven (1966) who regards the claims of the Verstehen psychology as one example of a general type of explanation. He distinguishes between two types of understanding. Firstly, he claims, there is the usual type employed by the natural sciences in which descriptions of particular events are subsumed under general laws. Secondly there is the analysis of a structure into its components, to see how these components are related to each other as parts of a system. When, for instance, we understand how a clock works there is very little in the way of subsumption under general laws which does much explanatory work and so aids our understanding. The weight is carried by tracing the relationships between the particular springs and levers. Simple mechanics can understand how such systems work without any knowledge of the underlying physical laws. Understanding others is a particular case of this latter sort of understanding; for we extend to others the understanding which we have from our own case of the system which is our own personality. 'Now when we understand a person's behavior in terms of his attitudes, goals, perceptions of the situation in which he finds himself, etc., in short in terms of the phenomenology of the situation—what we are doing is, so to speak, attaching the facts of the particular case to the terminals of our own response system, i.e.

our own personality' (Scriven, 1966, p. 60). We attempt to do this
without crediting him with any of our own idiosyncrasies. In brief
it is our own knowledge of the system constituted by our own
general human characteristics that enables us to understand the
behavior of others. This is similar to the way in which we understand how other machines work if we are familiar with a machine
which is like them. And general laws are not necessary for understanding in either case. The special feature of explanation in human
studies is that we rely on the human model with which we are
familiar through our own possession of general human characteristics.

There is much to be learned from these two versions of the
psychology of Verstehen. Certainly in understanding other people
we make use of concepts in which cognitive, affective, and conative
components are structurally related. Certainly the notions of fitting
particular forms of behavior into a system is helpful, though it is
questionable whether this means abandoning general assumptions.
And certainly in relation to understanding human beings we occupy
a special vantage point which we lack in our understanding of the
natural world. But, in my view, neither Dilthey nor Scriven makes
this point in a radical enough way. Indeed the way in which they do
make it results in their position being vulnerable to attacks of the
sort which have been launched against views of understanding other
people which gives some sort of priority to knowledge of our own
case (e.g., Malcolm, 1964). Knowledge of others is made either a
matter of inference based on analogy, which is Scriven's position, or
of non-inferential empathy, as in Dilthey's thesis, which can only
be defended, surely, as a way of knowing a limited number of
things about other people, e.g. that they are angry, afraid, or in
pain.

(b) UNDERSTANDING AND INITIATION

The more radical thesis which I wish to propose is that we are
indeed at a special vantage point in understanding others (or at
least some others) which we do not enjoy in our understanding of
the natural world. This comes about because in learning to *behave*

as human beings we are, ipso facto, being initiated into the concepts, rules, and assumptions without which we could make no sense of the life of others. Our minds, in other words, are mainly social products. In making sense, therefore, of the behavior of others we rely on concepts, rules, and assumptions which both they and we have internalized in the early years of our initiation into human life; these structure our own *behavior* as well as our *understanding* of the behavior of others. The level of understanding of which we are capable is largely a function of the type of social life which we have enjoyed. There is no mystery about our understanding or failure to understand others. For it depends largely on the extent to which we have been, to put the matter crudely, programmed in the same sort of way by our early social experiences. We understand people well with whom we have been in close contact from early childhood not just because we are familiar with all the particular circumstances and life history of individuals which play such an important part in understanding people as distinct from the behavior of things, but also because we, like they, have been initiated into the same rules, concepts, and assumptions which give structure and coherence to the thought and behavior of both of us.

This may sound rather like a crude version of Marx's aphorism that 'It is not the consciousness of man that determines his existence —rather it is his social existence that determines his consciousness.' Some qualification must be briefly sketched to make the thesis sound more civilized. The first type of crudity is conveyed by the image of programming. Man's consciousness cannot be solely dependent on his social existence because he differs from a machine in his capacity to understand and make something of the purposes, rules, and concepts which he internalizes. There are many things that can be meant by 'following a rule' which can almost be arranged in a continuum as Max Black (1967) has indicated. But most of them presuppose consciousness. The Marxist thesis can be taken as a dramatic way of making the point that man's 'social existence' is constituted by various forms of learned behavior. But most forms of learning at the human level presuppose consciousness.[1] The same sort of point can be made about language, which is

[1] See, for instance, Peters (1970) Section 3 and Hamlyn (1970).

the medium through which a great deal of socialization takes place; for there is the prior problem of how the child comes to take noises as symbols. The development of thought cannot be accounted for entirely in terms of the development of language; for language has to be understood *as* language in some embryonic way from the start.

A connected difficulty for the Marxist type of thesis is that presented by the evidence relating to the development of categoreal concepts such as causality, thinghood, means-to-an-end, and so on. These are the most fundamental categories of the understanding; yet, it is claimed by followers of Piaget (cf. Kohlberg, 1968) that they cannot be taught. They develop in the process of the individual's interaction with his environment. Piagetians, however, admit that development can be accelerated by what they call 'cognitive stimulation' which includes social transactions such as asking children leading questions, getting them to engage in games with other children, and so on. There is evidence, too, that these concepts develop very slowly in cultures in which children are socially discouraged from manipulating the environment and finding out things for themselves (cf. Greenfield and Bruner, 1969). A similar point could be made about the development of reasoning by means of which the range of the understanding is extended. It would, I think, be fanciful to suggest that principles like that of non-contradiction are just social products. But there is evidence to suggest that the tendency to rely on generalizations, the imagining of consequences in the distant future, and the general tendency to transcend a sense-bound, concrete, myopic sort of existence depends to a large extent on the type of language available in the home and on predictability in child-rearing practices (cf. Klein, 1965). Obviously, too, the tendency to be critical, to develop an individual viewpoint, depends enormously on the prevalence in society of a critical tradition (cf. Popper, 1963).

It would be rash, therefore, to suggest that the *form* of understanding which we employ in making sense of the behavior of others is entirely a social product. Much more work would have to be done in answering Chomsky-like questions about the genesis of concept such as 'purpose', and 'taking means to ends', which are the relevant categoreal concepts in this sphere. But from the point of view of my general thesis these speculations would not much matter provided they were developed to account for the fact that the categories for structuring our own behavior and for making sense of that of others are universal, though people reach different points in culturally invariant stages of developing them. For, whatever the explanation, both our behavior and our understanding would be programmed in terms of these universal categories. Such a cautious thesis about the *form* of our understanding would be quite consistent with a much more thorough-going thesis about social determination of its *content*. For the particular purposes and rules in terms of which we make sense of the behavior of others are basically those into which we have been initiated and which are, therefore, constitutive of our own purposive, rule following behavior. We know why people arriving at a strange golf club are looking for the secretary or the steward because we too have been in the situation of looking for the recipient of a green-fee as a preliminary to playing. Reference to rules about punctuality or to motives such as ambition are obvious enough to us as explanations of behavior because we have been initiated into a society in which time and individual self-assertion are taken for granted. But they would not be obvious explanations to members of a society which placed no value on them. The content of our understanding is certainly a social product whatever the status of its form.

Not all behavior, however, is of this highly socialized form, and thus initiation cannot be the source of all our understanding of it. There are some emotions, for instance, such as fear and anger which have natural expressions, of which Darwin gave a biological type of explanation. There is evidence, too, that, at least amongst the higher primates, they are contagious. A snarling ape sets other apes snarling by some kind of associative mechanism. There must be some kind of mechanism, more primitive than imitation, by means of which the mother's smile activates similar expressions in the baby, together with the inner states that accompany such expression. So, at a certain level of reaction, there is probably much truth in Dilthey's contention that the expressions of the mental states of others tend to evoke corresponding experiences in the minds of observers which form the basis of empathetic understanding. We have all felt, surely, the contagion of aggression. Even the stomach responds in a queer sort of way. And does not a sudden intake of breath, quickened breathing, wide opening of the eyes, or the slight slobbering of the greedy person contemplating food convey itself insensibly to the observer and stir up a similar sort of state in him? I am not arguing, of course, that there is anything infallible in this form of understanding. Like anything of an intuitive sort it may be mistaken. I am only making the point that, at a basic, scarcely socialized level of reaction, a mechanism which is more primitive than imitation plays a crucial role. At this level, to revert to my previous crude analogy, we are not programmed with a common system of rules; we are rather wired up in a similar way.

There is, finally, another crude kind of explanation of why people who have shared a common life together over a long period understand each other so well that they often know just what the other is thinking even though no overt sign is given. For not only will familiarity with a person provide the common life which is constituted by the rules and purposes which render his behavior intelligible; it will also provide a rich source of associative cues which will lead another to be right about what he is thinking or feeling without any proper basis for inference. People who have been very close to each other over a long period, and who have a fund of shared experiences, develop all sorts of common associations. X knows what Y is thinking or going to say, not because he has evidence on the basis of which he can infer it, but because similar associative tracks are activated in the two people concerned. Cues rather than clues provide the basis of understanding. X knows what Y is thinking in the sense that he is right about this and in that this is no accident (cf. Griffiths, 1967, pp. 12–14). But he has not really any proper grounds for his conviction. It is not like the cases when he knows, on the basis of inductive clues, that a look on the other's face will lead to a certain type of remark or behavior. Rather exposure to similar experiences has established similar associative tracks. A particular cue activates both of them in a similar way and, because of associative tracks, they both find themselves thinking about the same thing even after quite a lapse of time, during which their thoughts have proceeded along similar lines.

My basic assumptions about understanding others can therefore be summarized as follows; I assume that, with the development of the sort of conceptual apparatus which was mapped by Piaget, children gradually come to make sense of the behavior of others in terms of categoreal concepts such as 'purpose', 'means-to-an-end' and in terms of rule-following. Their understanding of others proceeds pari-passu with their ability to structure their own behavior by means of this type of conceptual apparatus. There are difficult problems about how this form of understanding is acquired, but its content, the particular rules and purposes which they attribute to others and which they exhibit in their own behavior, is largely dependent upon the particular society in which they grow up. This way of understanding others is, however, not the only way. More primitive empathetic and associative mechanisms are also operative.

These crude epistemological assumptions give rise, of course, to a number of problems about the meaning of 'internalization', about empathy and inference, and about the relationships between association and inference, which it is not my business to pursue in this paper. But obviously the operation of all these types of understanding is dependent upon having 'personal relationships' with people. This notion is a very cloudy one which shrouds many important distinctions embedded in the different levels at which it is possible to understand or to misunderstand others. The rest of my paper, therefore, will be concerned with trying to pin-point some of these important distinctions.

2. Types of relationships

The thesis that the mind of the individual mirrors the society of which he is a member is, of course, as old as Plato. Plato, however, was interested in this parallelism because of his interest in social change and social policy. He did not link it with any theory about understanding people. The distinctions which he made were therefore closely related to problems of social control and individual regulation of conduct. Not that these preoccupations are irrelevant to the understanding of people; for one of the key concepts in understanding people is that of 'motive'. And most of the motives which we ascribe to people such as envy, ambition, greed, benevolence, and the like are also regarded as virtues and vices. But, in spite of Ryle's (cf. 1949, Ch. IV) tendency to regard almost any explanatory term for human behavior as a case of 'motive', there does seem to be a radical difference between explaining what a person is doing in terms of his conscientiousness, his ambition, his interest in symbolic logic, and his aims as a university teacher. How do these types of explanation differ from each other? How are they connected with social life? In what ways are personal relationships with others necessary to or constitutive of these types of explanation?

Let us begin with a very general point about the notion of having personal relationships with people. There is a sense of 'personal relationships' in which almost all explanations of human behavior presuppose them; for most of the concepts which we use pick out various ways in which we can be related to people as distinct from to rivers, boulders, or trees. So, in this general sense, the appeal to a persons's aims as a university teacher will involve reference to personal relationships just as much as speculations about his motives of benevolence or ambition. The concept can be used in this very general way, but, of course, at the expense of its doing any work; for some account must be given of the fact that we often say that a role relationship, such as that of being a teacher, is essentially an impersonal one. There is also the point that it is quite intelligible for a teacher to say that he fulfills his role as a teacher and, in addition, he shows benevolence and respect towards his pupils but has neither the time nor the inclination nor the energy to enter into personal relationships with them. Obviously some important distinctions are being made here which are connected with a more specific concept of 'personal relationships'. So I propose to try to elucidate what might lie behind this more specific concept rather than use it in a very general sort of way.

In attempting to get clearer about these types of distinctions I will concentrate on the case of a university teacher trying to make sense of the behavior of one of his colleagues; for this is an example with which we are all familiar and which should reveal most of the basic distinctions which we need. It is, of course, possible that concentration on one type of example may bias the analysis in some respects. It may lead us to ignore distinctions which might be important if a wider range of examples was taken. And certainly, if my basic thesis is correct, distinctions will emerge that probably have no application if I were to concentrate on a simple tribe whose social structure and consciousness is far less differentiated than ours. But a start must be made somewhere and my brief is not to write a complete prolegomenon to the social sciences.

(a) ROLES AND SHARED ACTIVITIES

We, like policemen, may have had all sorts of idiosyncratic motives for joining our profession, and these may influence the way in which we discharge the various duties which are incumbent on us. But there are presumably some unitary aims which give coherence to our institutional lives in the same sort of way as a concern for preserving law and order give some kind of unity to the lives of policemen. Many, like Popper, have argued that it is vain to search for essences. That may be so if we are thinking about the natural world. But in considering the social world the enterprise might not be so vain. For human institutions are constituted largely by the conceptions of men and it is possible that men might band together with some single, unambiguous aim in view, such as the preservation of the blue whale, and their institutional duties might be all clearly related to the pursuit of this aim, which would express the essence of the institution. Most institutions, however, do not present such a rational ideal. There is usually more than one aim which most members conceive themselves as forwarding, and these aims often pull them in different directions. The duties, too, which define their roles, are not always so rationally related to the aims of the institution. Maybe they are precipitates left by the past. Maybe the roles have developed a life of their own which has made them non-functional in relation to the dominant aim. And may be, as most institutions have not been determinately instituted, the demand to get clear about the essence of an institution is a way of trying to rationalize an institution that has accumulated all sorts of odd traditions and practices in a period of unplanned historic growth. All sorts of qualifications of this sort have to be made if we are to talk realistically about institutions. But, nevertheless, there is something that fits the appearances in this type of analysis of institutions. As university teachers we do conceive of ourselves as concerned with the advancement of understanding and with the initiation of others into this activity. Whether we also conceive of ourselves as concerned with the more general education of students or with pressing problems of the society in which we live is much more a matter for debate. But at the moment, at any rate in Great Britain, whatever university teachers think about educating students and about 'relevance', they would at least subscribe to the first type of aim and would think that any concern for education and for 'relevance' must be understood in the context of an institution which is essentially concerned with the advancement of understanding. If this ceased to be the case, if the dominant aim became the provision of occasions for discussing what students found to be 'relevant' issues in their lives, then universities would become very different types of institutions. This type of change would affect our lives very much but would not affect the conceptual point which I am making; for the new race of university teachers would then have a whole range of their activities structured by a different type of aim.

Given then, this dominant aim which is more or less definitive of a university as an institution, we are able to explain much of the individual's dealings with others in the light of it. In particular his dealings with his pupils will be structured in the light of his view of them as learners. This view of them provides a rationale for rights and duties which are constitutive of the teacher's role (cf. Downie, 1971). He has, for instance, the right to criticize his students' thoughts and writings, which might be resented outside a role relationship. He has, also, the duty of taking trouble over the work of students whom he does not particularly like, of meeting students whose company he would avoid if free play were given to his inclinations. Much of a university teacher's behavior could be made sense of in terms of this over-all aim and the rights and duties that are connected with its implication. But it could only be made sense of by those who understand from the inside what 'teaching' is and who have been initiated into the concepts and rules which are constitutive of the appropriate rights and duties. Peter Winch (1958) has developed this sort of point in so much detail that it would be otiose for me to labor it any further. But, to revert to my search for 'personal relationships', the point about the relationships in terms of which we give explanations at this level is that, though they hold between persons, there is an important sense in which they are impersonal. Let us call them interpersonal relationships.

'Impersonal', too, might be applied to other interpersonal relations in shared activities which have aims but not of sufficient generality to co-ordinate wide areas of life or to generate elaborate systems of duties. Examples would be activities such as gardening, singing in a choir, or playing golf. We might have a feeling of fraternity towards others who shared these activities with us of the sort that Marx hoped that the workers of the world would have for other workers; but this would be consistent with saying that the interpersonal relationship between the people concerned was rather an impersonal one.

A much stronger sense of 'impersonal' is when someone is treated, whether within or outside of an institutional context, as an object rather than as an individual who is a person in his own right, who has purposes, aspirations, and a point of view of his own. He might be regarded just as somebody who could be simply used by another for his own purposes, or manipulated for the sake of forwarding some social ideal. Or he might be considered purely as an occupant of a role without any consideration for his point of view as a human being. In such situations lack of respect for persons would be shown and 'impersonal' would almost be too weak a word to do justice to the depersonalization involved.

E

(b) INTERPERSONAL RELATIONS AND PERSONALITY

Respect for persons introduces a whole range of interpersonal relationships which are not role relationships, but which still might not be called personal relationships in a full sense. Suppose, for instance, that a student fell down and broke his arm. It is possible that a teacher might go to his aid because he viewed this injury as likely to be detrimental to his potentiality as an essay-writer. But, more probably, he would act towards him in a way in which he would act towards any other human being, irrespective of his special role relationship. He would act out of benevolence or sympathy. And a great deal of his behavior both towards his pupils and towards others, with whom he was not in some sort of role relationship, could be explained in terms of rules and purposes which are constitutive of relationships with people but not within the confines of any particular role or structured type of activity.

There would be, first of all, that body of internalized rules which we call 'character-traits'. Examples would be honesty, punctuality, tidiness, thrift, selfishness, and so on. Such terms, like all trait terms, are primarily adverbial in significance (cf. Peters, 1962). They do not, like terms for motives, such as benevolence, ambition, greed, and the like, indicate the sorts of goals that give unity to a person's behavior. Rather they draw attention to the rules which he follows, or the manner in which he pursues his goals. The connection with regulation is fundamental for distinguishing character-traits from other sorts of traits—for instance those which we connect with a person's temperament. Character-traits are regarded as virtues or as vices. There would be no point in marking them out in this way if there did not exist, in general, inclinations which they regulate or canalize. And there are some character-traits, which are connected with the will, or with what we call 'having character', which *have* to be exercised in the face of counter-inclinations. Examples are courage, integrity and determination. (By that I mean that virtues such as honesty and punctuality, which represent internalized social rules, would be pointless if there did not exist, in general, inclinations to say what is false or to take no account of time. To explain a person's behavior by reference to such traits does not necessitate the existence of such inclinations in the person when he acts. But with courage or integrity the case is different. For these higher-order types of traits can only be ascribed to a person if it is thought that he is sticking to some course of action in the face of fear, temptation, and the like.) Most character-traits of the first sort are constituted by interpersonal rules that are internalized. This is not the case, however, with the character-traits that are connected with the will; for though very often temptations take the form of bribes or approval from others and though fear can be of social ostracism or disapproval, counter-inclinations need not be social in character. They can come from consciousness of heights or from the stomach.

There are other traits which people exhibit, which are closely connected with their interpersonal relations, which seem more indicative of their personality than of their character. (I am using 'personality' here in the way in which it seems to be used in ordinary speech, not in the omnibus way in which it is used in psychological textbooks.) Examples are friendliness, cheerfulness, shyness, awkwardness, alertness, and so on. We would think of such traits as developing or flowering rather than as being built up by decision or by the internalization of rules. They are connected much more with our perception of others and of ourselves than with codes of conduct. They are very closely connected with ways in which we impinge on others in our dealings with them. Hence their connection with our personality. For, whereas our character bears witness to the choices which we have made and suggests some sort of personal effort to make something of ourselves, our personality is very much the mask or appearance which we present to others. A man with a strong character is a man who has made efforts with himself and who exhibits virtues such as courage and integrity that are connected with the will. But we do not naturally speak of a man having a strong personality. Rather we speak of personality as being forceful, dynamic, and hypnotic. These terms draw attention to his influence on others.

Underlying these character and personality traits are the wants, inclinations, motives, and emotions which are constitutive of our natures. Some of these, such as hunger and thirst, which derive from deficit states, have little to do with interpersonal relations. But most motives and emotions are very closely connected with a form of social life into which we have been initiated in which we view ourselves and others in a certain light. It is only possible, for instance, to feel jealous and to recognize it in others if we are able to see another as possessing or making advances towards something or someone to which or whom we think that we have some sort of special claim. This presupposes the understanding of social concepts such as 'rights', 'claims', 'possession', and the like (cf. Bedford, 1956–7). Some attitudes, like respect, for instance, mean different things according to the difference in the social context. Respect can be felt for someone who is superior in a social hierarchy; it can be felt for someone who is good at something, as when we speak of having a healthy respect for an opponent in debate or in a boxing ring. Respect, too, can be used in a generalized sense when we talk of respect for persons, and are only viewing another as a center of choice and of evaluation. Other emotions, such as pride, ambition, guilt, and remorse imply a certain view of ourselves. They are probably not felt in cultures in which little importance is attached to individual effort and responsibility.

Fundamental to the analysis of motives and emotions are the general dimensions of liking-disliking, love-hate, pleased-displeased. Some, like Hobbes, have tried to bring this out by postulating a general tendency in human beings to move towards or away from objects. Others have tried to construct a kind of chemistry, rather than a dynamics, of the emotions in which complex emotions are represented as compounds of simple ones such as fear, anger and love. It is not my intention to discuss, or to attempt to improve on such accounts of this dimension; for this would involve a lengthy examination of the relationship between the concepts built into the cognitive components of the various emotions. My concern with it in this paper is only in the context of its relevance to questions about personal relations. And it does seem relevant in this context. For if questions were asked about a teacher's personal relations with his pupils answers would be given which revolve round this axis of his personality. By that I mean that we would not think about whether he was honest or fair in his dealings with them, or whether he was punctual, conscientious, or even unselfish, though these terms in fact pick out ways in which he deals with them as persons. We would be interested in facets of his personality rather than of his character in so far as it impinged on them. Of relevance would be whether his manner was friendly, or defensive, relaxed or stiff. Of relevance, too, would be whether he aroused feelings of insecurity or confidence in his students, whether they liked or disliked him, were afraid of him or sorry for him. We would not take account of whether they admired him for his competence as a teacher, felt respect for him as a man or even had a feeling of fraternity for him as a fellow learner. In brief the question would draw attention not to what he was like as a teacher, or as a moral agent but to how his personality came through to them, and how they reacted to it.

(c) PERSONAL RELATIONSHIPS PROPER

Ordinary language is not very determinate in the area which is being investigated. Nevertheless it sounds perfectly meaningful to say that a teacher's personal relations with his students are very good but he does not believe in having personal relationships with them. What would he be avoiding? Immediately what comes to mind are situations in which some kind of reciprocal knowledge of private matters is built up as distinct from matters connected with the public institutionalized context in which they encounter each other. By this is meant some knowledge of the details of the private lives of the people concerned as well of their motives, attitudes, and aspirations. This is surely an obvious feature of a developed personal relationship, but is it a distinguishing feature? Surely not; for examples can be produced in which we would say that a personal relationship existed without this exchange of confidences. Examples can also be produced in which a great deal of personal knowledge is exchanged but we would be disinclined to say that there was a personal relationship.

Let us consider both types of counter-example in the hope that something more fundamental will emerge. Suppose that, in the middle of a seminar, a student starts thumbing through a *Good Food Guide* during a rather boring exchange between two other members of the group. He looks up guiltily and is aware of a knowing look from the tutor who passes him a note with the name of a restaurant written on it. The student acknowledges the note with a grateful nod. Surely we would say that this exemplifies a personal relationship, though a minimal one, even though nothing further develops in the way of private disclosures. Conversely suppose that in the course of a literature class, those participating in the discussion of a novel contribute much of their private experience to a common pool in order to arrive at a better understanding of the novel. Suppose that the tutor also reminisces about his own private life in order to illustrate a point, just as lecturers in psychology often regale their students with stories about their own children. This would not be described as entering into a personal relationship. What is present in the first example and absent in the second is a certain aspect under which the other is viewed. In the second example private matters are revealed to others but under the aspect of their role as learners. In the first example only a minimum of information is disclosed of a not very private sort, but it is not disclosed to another as a learner or in any type of role capacity.

What seems to emerge from these counter-examples is that a personal relationship involves some reciprocal response of individual to individual, which often does but need not take the form of the disclosure of private matters, but which involves a view of the other under some aspect other than that of his occupancy of a role. What is this aspect? Respect does not seem to be right; for it can be argued that one can have a personal relationship with someone whom one despises. Respect, also, can signify a rather negative attitude—just a refusal to treat another as a means to one's own ends. It need not issue in any positive sort of outgoingness which seems characteristic of entering into a personal relationship. It is too moralized, too much connected with a view of another as a subject of rights, as a chooser. Does liking, then, provide the required aspect? Surely not. Women often meet and, within minutes, are swapping notes about their confinements and maladies with great animation. They may, when they meet again, begin where they left off and build up quite a relationship. But they may not particularly like each other and yet, surely, they are not just passing the time of day. Liking is, of course, a frequent occasion for people developing a personal relationship. But it is not necessary to it. Many personal relationships develop through force of circumstances. One of my previous colleagues, for instance, maintained that his personal relationships with fellow philosophers were occasioned, at one time, through meeting them so often outside rooms where committees were interviewing people for jobs. He was just left alone with people in situations which made them prone to some kind of mutual openness or outgoingness. Sympathy is suggested by this last example as the appropriate aspect. It fits also the case of the student with the *Good Food Guide*. It signifies an outgoingness issuing in responses below the level of morality, custom and institutionalized roles. It does not necessarily imply liking, either. It suggests only receptivity and outgoingness towards another at an affective level, as someone, like ourselves, who has wishes, wants, and emotions, who is sensitive to pain and other such passive states. Sympathy, however, is not quite the right word; for it is usually associated with seeing another only as a sufferer. If it could be extended to cover also a responsiveness to the joys and pleasures of another, it would be the right word. This is a case, I think, where we have the concept but not just one word to make explicit what we mean. The point is that the response must be to another *simply* as an individual human being who is subject to pleasure and pain and the usual gamut of emotions and desires. The other person must not be viewed in the context of any extraneous purpose, whether individual or shared. He must not be thought of as a means to one's ends or just as a co-operator or competitor in a common pursuit. Moralization is not necessarily involved as in benevolence when there is thought about his interests, or in respect when he is regarded as a subject of rights. There is simply a receptiveness to him and outgoingness towards him as an individual human being. This can take place in institutionalized situations, such as the seminar case, when an individual steps out of his role and responds to another just as a human being. Or it can happen in an unstructured type of situation as when two people meet in a park.

Usually, of course, when we talk of personal relationships we mean a development of the minimal type of relationship that I have sketched. Receptiveness and outgoingness towards another usually takes the form of receiving another's confidences and self-disclosures. In this way a common world is built up which the individuals share. This is constituted not simply by their shared experiences but by the common stock of knowledge which has developed as a result of being kept informed about a whole variety of private matters. When they meet they keep each other up to date, as it were, about the details of the private worlds that intersect on such occasions. Friendship is an extension of such a relationship. For it requires extra conditions.[2] Firstly there is the condition that the individuals concerned should share some pattern of activities, e.g., reciprocal services, leisure time pursuits. Secondly friendship requires that the individuals concerned should like each other and desire each other's company. Thirdly, there is the requirement that this special sort of relationship should be acknowledged. There is some sort of reciprocal commitment.

3. *Levels of relationship and levels of understanding*

So far I have sketchily distinguished the sorts of relationships which people can enjoy with other people in order to get clearer about what is distinctive of personal relationships. This analysis was necessary because of my original suggestion of the close connection between having personal relationships with people and understanding them. Even at this juncture it would be possible to say a few things about this connection which are developments of what has already been said.

(a) *The vantage point of personal relations.* It could be said, firstly, that explanations in terms of roles and general social rules and purposes presuppose initiation into a common form of life. So for these types of explanation the content of our understanding presupposes, in general, having entered into these sorts of relationships with others. This applies to our explanations of our colleagues'

[2] These suggested conditions are taken from Telfer (1970–1).

behavior in terms of their conception of themselves as university teachers, of character-traits such as punctuality and selfishness, and countless other socialized purposes which structure smaller segments of their lives. In other words, what I have called interpersonal relationships would be constitutive of the content of our understanding. But personal relationships, in the specific sense, would not be necessary even as an epistemological condition for understanding particular people. For little face to face contact with the particular individuals concerned would be necessary to give explanations of this type though, of course, we might be wrong in particular cases because of the impersonality of these explanations in terms of generalized content. A similar point, secondly, could be made about low-level types of explanation, grounded in expressions of someone's personality, which give rise to judgments about his personal relations. We can like or dislike people because they are friendly, shy, dynamic, domineering, etc. We have to share a common life in order to learn how to apply these descriptions; but we do not have to enter into personal relationships with the people concerned in order to make such judgments. We can say that we loathe a politician because of his obsequiousness, aggressiveness, charm, or stiffness. We can also note simple generalizations about him. But we can do this on the basis of seeing him answer questions on television.

In both such spheres, however, it might be said that our judgments are too quick or superficial because we do not really know enough about him. And, indeed, we can work with a colleague for years and make sense of countless things that he does or says in the above terms, and yet we can say that we feel that we really do not know him. We do not really understand what makes him tick. What is lacking is a glimpse of the store he sets by his various roles, his underlying motives and aspirations. Shrewd observers of people can often glean these from observing others in their public lives. Messages can be picked up from their frowns and hesitations, from noting the general drift of their conduct over a period, and from confrontations with them in public situations. But personal relationships proper provide more reliable clues. This is for three obvious reasons. Firstly, personal relationships proper usually involve close personal contact with others, though such contact is possible in role relationships as well. This contact provides a context in which people reveal themselves most; for they respond to the constant pressure on their privacy exerted by others. Indeed many responses indicative of people's motives, aspirations, etc., are only possible if another person supplies the appropriate stimulus in such an interactive situation. As observers of other individuals we find out a great deal about them by eliciting responses from them in this way. This cannot be done with a person on a television screen if we are sitting at home. This type of interaction is likely to reveal more if the people concerned are emotionally involved with each other in ways which are characteristic of personal relationships —in those colored by hate as well as by love. For in role relationships there may be contiguity but each individual may, figuratively speaking, be wearing the appropriate mask. But, as was argued before, personal relationships proper, even at a minimal level, involve some outgoingness and spontaneity of response. This unguardedness suggests authenticity and an absence of role-playing in the pejorative sense, and hence indications of a person's nature.

Secondly, developed personal relationships and friendship are characterized by mutual disclosures of private matters and by the laying bare of motives, hopes, fears, and aspirations. These are fundamental for discerning the main threads which determine the pattern of a man's life. Thirdly, a great deal of detailed information is necessary to understand how another person sees the world. It is necessary to know how much he knows, what he takes for granted when he faces any situation, as well as some details about his past history which predisposes him to respond in certain ways. This kind of information can only be gleaned by being with a person over a long period and in the different areas of his life—at home, at work, in his leisure time pursuits. This sort of information is far more important for understanding another person than any generalizations about human nature suggested by psychologists. In cases of married couples, friends, etc., it often leads to the rich source of associative cues, already referred to at the end of Section 1b, which lead people to be right about what others are thinking or feeling without any proper basis for inference.

(b) *Personal relationships as constitutive of understanding others.*
So far having personal relationships, in a specific sense, has only
been considered as providing epistemological conditions in the sense
of a favorable vantage point for understanding particular individuals. There is a question, however, about the extent to which this
individualized type of understanding is itself constituted by the
capacity to enter into personal relationships of the specific sort. It is
interesting to speculate about the extent to which this individual
kind of understanding of people proceeds pari-passu with the degree
of individualization of behavior encouraged in society.

When I spent some time in America many years ago I was
puzzled by the way in which I was treated by some Americans.
They behaved to me in public in a way which made me speculate
about what their private thoughts and motives were behind this
public display. It was pointed out to me, however, that there did
not exist much differentiation between the public and the private
realm. Friends could be changed as rapidly as jobs and dwelling
places, and one behaved to someone in a public role almost in the
same way as one behaved to him privately. Could it then be that
there was actually very little extra going on behind those smiling
faces? Is Behaviorism more or less an appropriate philosophy of
mind in this type of culture? The Americans in question, needless
to say, were not academics! But the speculation which they
occasioned in me suggests one of the main sources of the super-
ficiality of my treatment to date of the connection between personal
understanding and personal relationships. I have not explored the
possibility that there are levels of personal understanding which
are closely tied to levels of personal relationships.

I have only space to make some speculative suggestions here
which are really extrapolations of the Piaget-Kohlberg type
approach to moral development. I wish to suggest that there are
levels of personal relationship which correspond with levels of
understanding of people and levels of affective response to them.
Since my account of personal relationships has been given in terms
of the aspect under which the other is viewed this should not prove
surprising. I shall, therefore, be concerned not with how relationships with others are constitutive of the *content* of our understanding

of people but with how they are connected with its form. This is
why the Piaget-Kholberg type of approach is relevant. For they are
not concerned with the content of morality but with the form of
moral understanding—in particular with how rules are viewed at
different stages of development.

In using the Piaget-Kohlberg approach I do not have space to go
into niceties about whether Piaget's three stages can be broken down
into six. I just propose to use the rough and ready distinctions
between ego-centricity, realism, and autonomy as indicators of very
general types of difference.

(i) THE PRE-RATIONAL LEVEL

It is worth remarking, first of all, that there is a level of experience
and of reactions to others that are pre-rational. By that I mean the
level of experience, in which Freud was particularly interested,
which is not structured in terms of the categories of secondary
processes of thought, whose emergence Piaget studied. Freud
himself was more interested in vicissitudes of sexual wishes than he
was in the cognitive features of this level of experience, but it has
been studied by later theorists such as Arieti (cf. 1967, pp. 109–112).
He noted the connection between this type of experience and a more
primitive, palaeological form of thinking in which classification is
purely on the basis of the similarity of predicates without any
importance being attached to the identity of the object. Some
primitive people, for instance, identify men, crocodiles, and wild-
cats because they have the common property of having an evil
spirit. Very small children think in this way about people. So also
do those suffering from various forms of mental disorder. Classification is based on affectively loaded similarity without regard to
identity. Examples would be a paranoiac who interprets the
behavior of others indiscriminately along the dimension of threat.
A less extreme case is that of a person who reacts violently to
anyone in a position of authority over him. In all such cases no
proper attention is paid to the identity or differentiating properties
of individuals. At this level the concepts of 'personal relationships'

and of 'personal relations' cannot get a grip; for there is no proper identification of individuals.

(ii) EGO-CENTRICITY

The main feature of this stage of moral development is that rules are seen purely as indicating things that have to be done to avoid punishment or to obtain rewards. One would expect a correspondingly instrumental view of people which would develop from a less calculating awareness of the association between a person's company and pleasure or pain. Others would be picked out and named, but would be classified mainly in terms of their frustrating or pleasure-enhancing properties. Children at this level, or adults whose thinking remains stuck more or less at this level, might be able to make quite shrewd appraisals of people in these self-referential terms. They might, too, in their dealings with others with whom they spent a lot of time, rely much on the type of empathetic cues to which reference was made in Section 1. But their thinking about others would be based mainly on association steered by self-interest. They would be incapable of seeing the world from the other person's point of view, of distancing themselves and imagining what sense could be made of the behavior of another in terms of his own purposes and plans. As others would be seen in this self-referential way the type of relationship would be basically an exploitative one. Others would be regarded as objects to be placated, manipulated, cajoled, and, if necessary, eliminated or diminished if they interfered with satisfaction. Friendships could be with people whose presence and reactions enhanced the self of the individual, who, as it were, constantly massaged his ego. There would be sensitivity to personality traits such as friendliness, obsequiousness and charm, but little awareness of character.

(iii) REALISM

At this stage rules are seen much more as entities 'out there' and conforming to them is seen as connected with obtaining approval and avoiding disapproval from peers and authority figures. One would expect, therefore, a much less ego-centric view of others. They would be viewed much more as status holders were viewed in a traditional type of society, as global persons whose attributes were determined mainly by roles. Understanding of others would therefore tend to be in terms of typologies based upon roles—what could be expected from a father, a soldier, or a teacher. Character-traits derivative from socially approved ways of behaving would also be attributed to people and a range of emotional responses towards them would be possible that would be outside the reach of the purely ego-centric man—loyalty and shame, for instance. There might also be a feeling of fraternity towards others as sharing a common role or as engaged in a common pursuit. This might lead to friendships of the 'comrades in arms' type.

(iv) AUTONOMY

The level of autonomy is more difficult to deal with because many different but connected notions are combined. There is first of all the dawning of the notion that rules are alterable, that they can be valid or invalid, and that their content depends upon consent. Secondly there is the notion of the individual as a chooser, as an individual who has responsibility for his actions and who can be, to a certain extent, the determiner of his own destiny. This is connected, thirdly, with the notion of authenticity or genuineness, with the individual choosing activities and codes of conduct that are based on considerations which he appreciates in a first-hand way, as distinct from on extrinsic considerations of rewards and punishments, approval and disapproval.

The individual's understanding of others now parallels the type of life of which he himself is capable. First of all he can view another as an individual existing in his own right, as it were, who has decisions to make about the roles which he has to assume and how he is to perform them. He is capable, too, of thinking about codes of conduct and trying to base his own on thought out principles. Character-traits such as punctuality and tidiness now become superficial indicators of a person's character; for there is now a question about the individual's reasons for conforming to such rules, which derive from the principles which he takes as fundamental. Account must be taken, too, of his long-term aspirations, of the way in which his activities are structured in terms of long-term concerns. Questions of motive now become much more important; for in himself and in others he becomes much more aware of the ways of viewing people and situations which make sense of a whole range of responses towards them. Understanding in depth is now possible.

This more individualized and objective view of others makes possible a different level of response and relationship. He can distinguish between an individual as a person and as an occupant of a variety of roles. He can be drawn towards him in friendship not just because of the enhanced self-feeling which he gets from his company, nor just because of fellow-feeling as a comrade or team-mate, but because he appreciates his qualities for what they are and because he is concerned about his good as a particular individual. He is capable, in other words, of love as distinct from just liking. He can, too, respect him as a person, even if he does not feel much drawn towards him.

The postulation of these different levels of response throws light on some of the theories of friendship and personal attraction that I encountered in reading through the summary of work done in this area provided by Secord and Backman (1964, Ch. 7). I was astonished to learn that the basic assumption is that friendships are formed with those who satisfy some desire or need in the individual. The debate seems to be between those who hold that the individual's needs are best met by someone similar to himself and those who hold that preference is for someone different from himself in a complementary respect. Those views can be unified by an 'exchange theory' of attraction in which it is postulated that the tendency to seek individual gratification by means of friendship works according to a kind of profit and loss estimation. If this theory were universally true of human nature Sartre, of course, would be quite right about personal relationships. The other is basically alien to us, an object whom we can only exploit, possess, or enjoy for our own ends. It suggests, perhaps, that 'liking' and not 'loving' is the only possible basis for friendship. But if my suggestion about levels of personal relationships is valid, these generalizations about the determinants of friendship would be applicable only to certain societies in which the view of others was generally an exploitative one, or of individuals in a less homogeneous form of society who were still stuck at Piaget's ego-centric level of person-perception.

This type of speculation, however, raises wider questions about the concept of 'friendship', which I have only dealt with in a summary fashion, and about the logic of 'liking' and 'loving' on which a great deal more work needs to be done. But this would be a topic for another paper—perhaps even another symposium.

REFERENCES

Arieti, S., *The Intrapsychic Self*, Basic Books, N. Y., 1967.

Bedford, E., 'Emotions', *Proc. Arist. Soc.*, 1956–7.

Black, M., 'Rules and routines', in Peters, R. S. (editor), *The Concept of Education*, Routledge and Kegan Paul, London, 1967.

Downie, R. S., 'Personal and Impersonal Relationships', in *Proceedings of the Philosophy of Education Society of Great Britain*, Supplementary Issue, Vol. V, No. 2, 1971.

Greenfield, P. M. and Bruner, J. S., 'Culture and Cognitive Growth', in Goslin, D. A., *Handbook of Socialization: Theory and Research*, Rand McNally, Chicago, 1969.

Griffiths, A. P. (ed.), *Knowledge and Belief*, Oxford University Press, London, 1967.

Hamlyn, D. W., 'Conditioning and Behaviour', in Borger, R. T. and Cioffi, F., *Explanation in the Behavioural Sciences*, Cambridge University Press, 1970.

Hodges, W. A., *William Dilthey: An Introduction*, Kegan Paul, London, 1944.

Klein, J., *Samples from English Cultures*, Vol. 1, Routledge and Kegan Paul, London, 1965.

Kohlberg, L., 'Early education: A cognitive-developmental view', *Child Development*, Vol. 39, 1968.

Malcolm, N., 'Knowledge of Other Minds', reprinted in Gustafson,

D. F., *Essays in Philosophical Psychology*, Doubleday-Anchor, New York, 1964.

Peters, R. S., 'Moral Education and the Psychology of Character', *Philosophy*, Vol. XXXVII, No. 139, 1962, pp. 37–56.

Peters, R. S., 'Reasons aond Causes', in Borger, R. T. and Cioffi, F., *Explanation in the Behavioural Sciences*, Cambridge University Press, 1970.

Popper, K. R., 'Toward a Rational Theory of Tradition', in *Conjectures and Refutations*, Routledge and Kegan Paul, London, 1963.

Ryle, G., *The Concept of Mind*, Hutchinson, London, 1949.

Scriven, M., 'The Contribution of Philosophy of the Social Sciences to Educational Development', in Barnett, G., *Philosophy and Educational Development*, G. Harrap and Co., London, 1966.

Secord, P. F., and Backman, C. W., *Social Psychology*, McGraw-Hill Co., New York, 1964.

Telfer, E., 'Friendship', *Proc. Aristot. Soc.*, 1970–71.

Winch, P., *The Idea of A Social Science*, Routledge and Kegan Paul, London, 1958.

E

The Development of Inferences about Others

JOHN H. FLAVELL

I. *Introduction*

The aim of this paper is to present some ideas and speculations concerning the development in children of certain types of cognitive activity regarding other people. These ideas are partly based on previous work by other investigators and myself on the genesis of role-taking skills and related forms of social cognition (e.g., Flavell, 1966, 1970a; Flavell, Botkin, Fry, Wright, and Jarvis, 1968; Miller, Kessel, and Flavell, 1970). They have also been shaped by some research data my students and I have recently obtained concerning the early beginnings of the child's ability to make inferences about another person's visual experiences.[1] Thus, while the paper will discuss the growth of social inference making in general, special emphasis will be given to this latter, percept attribution or perceptual role taking type of inference.

The development of inferences about others is a problem area that lies at the intersection of at least two major fields of study, one of them falling within developmental psychology and the other within (adult) personality and social psychology. The first field is cognitive development, and more specifically the small but growing

---

[1] The term 'inference' is used throughout this paper in the epistemologically neutral and nonspecific sense of 'somehow obtaining impressions about' the relatively more inner-psychological acts and attributes of human objects. I am not, by adopting this term, taking a specific and explicit stand on the philosophical question of the immediacy-nonimmediacy of our knowledge of persons ('direct perception' versus 'cognitive inference'). To put it another way, I never knowingly do philosophy rather than psychology, and would at all costs refrain from doing it at a conference such as this one, that virtually teems with keen-eared philosophers!

body of theory and research within it that deals with the growth of the child's cognitions about his social, human world (Flavell, 1970a, pp. 1025–1032). Representative examples would be the above mentioned studies of children's role taking abilities (Flavell *et al.*, 1968), Kohlberg's important writings on the genesis of moral thought and related topics (e.g., 1969), and much Piagetian research on these and other aspects of social-cognitive growth (e.g., the waning of animistic thought). Recent work in developmental sociolinguists might also be included in this category, since it deals with the growth of communicative competence in social situations (Ervin-Tripp, 1969; Hymes, 1970; Krauss and Glucksberg, 1969; Slobin, 1967), surely a bona fide example of social-cognitive development.

The other field is most frequently referred to nowadays as 'person perception', but there seem to be no end of alternative designations for the processes it investigates. These designations include inter-personal perception, interpersonal inference, person cognition, social perception, social cognition, social sensitivity, social acuity, clinical inference, clinical intuition, diagnostic competence, impression formation, naive psychology, implicit personality theory, role taking, role playing, role perception, the attribution (i.e., of dis-positions or intentions) process, empathy, identification, insight, and doubtless more (e.g., Cline, 1964; Flavell *et al.*, 1968; Hastorf, Schneider and Polefka, 1970; Heider, 1958; Jones and Davis, 1965; Jones and Gerard, 1967; Kelley, 1967; Sarbin, Taft and Bailey, 1960; Tagiuri, 1969).

There tends to be something less than adequate interchange and mutual stimulation between the social psychologists who study various forms of adult social cognition and the developmental psychologists who investigate the growth of the same or similar forms during childhood and adolescence. While developmental work is sometimes cited by the specialist in adult social cognition (e.g., Tagiuri, 1969), one suspects that, with occasional exceptions (e.g., Scarlett, Press, and Crockett, 1971) it plays little role in his thinking about the topic. More importantly, perhaps, research on social-cognitive growth is only rarely (e.g., Baldwin, Baldwin, Hilton and Lambert, 1958) explicitly shaped and guided by

research and theory in the corresponding adult field, despite the fact
that some of the recent work in this field (e.g., Hastorf *et al.*, 1970,
chap. 4) presents what appears to be a very rich and interesting
picture of the average adult's tacit hypotheses about other people. I
shall return to this point in the final section of the paper.

What, exactly, does 'social cognition' refer to, for either social
psychologist or developmentalist? What sorts of 'inferences about
others' do we characteristically make? Tagiuri (1969) says it well:

> The observations or inferences we make are principally about inten-
> tions, attitudes, emotions, ideas, abilities, purposes, traits, thoughts,
> perceptions, memories—events that are *inside* the person and strictly
> psychological. Similarly, we attend to certain psychological qualities of
> relationships *between* persons, such as friendship, love, power, and
> influence. We attribute to a person properties of *consciousness* and *self-
> determination*, and the capacity for *representation of his environment*,
> which in turn mediates his actions (p. 396).

From the developmentalist's vantage point, such observations,
inferences, attendings, and attributions with respect to social objects
represent potential 'developmental targets' (Flavell, 1970a). That
is, they constitute sets of cognitive dispositions and abilities which
the child seems wholly to lack at birth, and which he therefore must
acquire or develop—very slowly and gradually, no doubt, and very
possibly according to some regular sequence of steps or 'stages'.
They could represent, in other words, a new chapter in the
cognitive-developmental story, and one that may be well worth
reading (Flavell, 1970a).

Moreover, the major questions here appear to be the same ones
the student of cognitive growth confronts in trying to read all the
other 'chapters' (Flavell and Wohlwill, 1969; Flavell, 1971a,
1972). There are first of all questions of development description.
What social-cognitive skills and dispositions (specify them *precisely*
and in *detail*, perhaps in the form of an information processing
analysis) develop in the 'normative human childhood' (however this
be defined), and roughly *when* (in what typical or invariant ontogenetic *order*, etc.)? The problems associated with the descriptive
enterprise include those of adequate measurement and develop-

mental diagnosis, i.e., of how to ascertain with any degree of certainty that task X dependably measures social-cognitive ability Y, that child A has 'acquired' Y (in exactly what sense? to what level of mastery?) and child B has 'not acquired' Y (not even minimally? not even capable of displaying it under ideal testing conditions, or following intensive training?), and so on. Much as in psycholinguistics (e.g., Fillenbaum, 1971) and other areas, the essential problem is that of trying to infer or construct, from his behavior, a meaningful representation of an individual's underlying 'competence', and of the 'performance' type, information processing activities that realize or instantiate it in various concrete situations— a problem that hardly looks any easier to solve when the individual in question (i.e., a child) keeps changing his design as a cognitive system.

Other questions have to do with explanatory aspects. Exactly what events, conditions, processes, mechanisms, or whatever—both within the child and within his environment—tend to promote (or to inhibit) his social-cognitive growth? In other words, *how* (explanatory aspects) does the individual acquire *whatever* (descriptive aspects) succession of inferential capacities and tendencies we finally decide that he *does* typically acquire? A major corollary question here concerns the extent to which various social cognitive skills and dispositions can be improved through deliberate training, alteration of life experiences, or other interventions, with either the connotation of simply 'accelerating' a developmental progression that is deemed certain to occur spontaneously, or of really boosting the individual's asymptotic, adult level of skill, or both. Parallels in closely related areas of development would include Cazden's (1965) experimental attempt to facilitate grammatical development through systematic expansion of the child's speech, and the seemingly endless succession of experiments (e.g., Brainerd and Allen, 1971; Flavell, 1970a, p. 1042) that attempt to 'train in' conservation and other Piagetian concepts and skills apropos of the nonsocial world. A good case could be made that social-cognitive abilities, together with the motivation to use them actually represent, a priori, a more reasonable object of educational endeavor than those just mentioned. On the one hand, their acquisition might be judged more useful and desirable for the individual and for mankind at large (think of heightened sensitivity or role taking skill with respect to the thoughts and feelings of others, think of better understanding among nations . . .). On the other hand, the average adult level of ability and disposition here, although no doubt far from negligible, may still not be anywhere near as high as we might wish it to be; in contrast, all intact members of our society *do* seem finally to acquire a satisfactory grasp of conservation and a respectable degree of grammatical competence.

Nonetheless, it is that 'far from negligible' qualifier in the preceding sentence that ultimately makes this area of functioning so interesting to the student of cognitive development, as contrasted with the more practical concerns of the educator, the would be reformer and refiner of human nature, and other good people. The reason is that at least some measure of social-cognitive skill must qualify as what might be termed a 'cognitive-developmental universal', and perhaps a species-specific one at that. It is, in other words, a cognitive ability that: (1) seems not to be present at birth (2) must therefore be the product of some sort of developmental process in any organism that displays it (3) has probably developed to some nontrivial level in all biologically intact human adults the world around (can one even *imagine* a nonretarded adult who has *never* made *any* inferences about the thoughts, feelings, etc. of other people?) (4) may not develop to any significant degree in any species but our own. And in my view, the identification, developmental description, and developmental explanation of just such species-specific universals ought to be the ultimate objective of the student of human cognitive growth.

The organization of this paper partly reflects the analysis given above. The overall topic is the development of inferential or other knowledge-seeking processes concerning the 'psychological insides' of other people, such as their thoughts, feelings, intentions, motives, and above all, given the present focus of my research interests, their visual percepts. Accordingly, the next section (III) presents a very general, 'boxology' type, information-processing model of the major things that seem to get acquired in this domain. The section following (III) presents some more specific hypotheses regarding the development of the child's inferences about visual percepts. Both sections are limited to the purely descriptive aspects of the problem, however. Unfortunately, I simply have nothing significant to add at present to what little has already been written about the explanatory side (e.g., Flavell *et al.*, 1968, pp. 217–22; Kerckhoff, 1969; Kohlberg, 1969, and other chapters in the Goslin volume). The paper concludes with that old standby, suggestions for future research (Section IV). Contrary to usual practice, however, I actually plan to follow up some of my own suggestions during the next several years.

II. *A General Model of Interpersonal Inference*

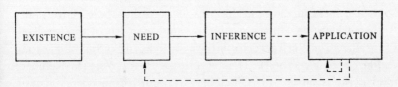

Figure 1. Knowledge and skills involved in making inferences about other people.

Figure 1 presents a global, flow diagram type characterization of what might be involved psychologically in making inferences about others. It represents a revision of an earlier model having to do with the child's acquisition of role taking and communication skills (Flavell, 1966; Flavell *et al.*, 1968, pp. 208–15), and is therefore well adapted to a general developmental account of social inference making. The *Existence* component refers primarily to the subject's (*S*'s) basic knowledge that he or another person (*O*) might possibly possess some particular or, indeed, *any* sort whatever of covert psychological process (percept, intention, ability, feeling, etc.). *Need* means his awareness that the present situation calls for inferential activity about one or more of these properties. *Inference* covers everything having to do with the actual character of this activity. *Application* refers to any subsequent behaviour *S* might engage in (usually vis-à-vis *O*) as a consequence of the new ideas about *O* generated in the *Inference* component. The four components are of course functionally interrelated, as the following example will show. Supposing *S* is about to play chess with an unknown opponent (*O*). He is first of all certain to know the general meaning of such psychological properties as 'chess skill', and 'knowledge of the game', and also that *O* could conceivably possess these properties to a greater or lesser extent (*Existence*). He will also be aware that it would be sensible (*Need*) of him to try to find out (*Inference*) just how skillful and knowledgeable *O* is, so that he can adjust his own game accordingly (*Application*).

I shall now discuss each component in more detail from a developmental-descriptive orientation. References will be cited mainly to illustrate generalizations made, and hence the coverage of the pertinent literature in this area will definitely be selective rather than exhaustive. However, a more complete inventory can be pieced together from such recent sources as Feffer (1970), Flavell (1970a), Flavell *et al.* (1968), Hegion (1969), Izard (1971), Kohlberg (1969), Krauss and Glucksberg (1969), Rothenberg (1970), Savitsky and Izard (1970), Scarlett *et al.* (1971), Sullivan and Hunt 1967), and Tagiuri (1969, pp. 404–6, 427–8).

A. EXISTENCE

In order for *S* to infer that a particular *O* possesses any given inner characteristic, *S* must at minimum be aware (1) of the very existence of that characteristic as a possible psychological property that the self and other human beings may possess, and (2) of the possibility that this particular *O* might possess it in this particular situation, even if *S* himself does not. There is every reason to believe that both types of awareness represent very fundamental, and probably closely interrelated outcomes of social-cognitive development, and also that the age at which they emerge could vary a great deal as a function of the particular *O* characteristic being inferred.

Consider first the meaning of awareness (1), with respect to the most elementary and undifferentiated sorts of O characteristics. The assertion here is that one of the child's initial developmental tasks is to become aware of the mere existence, both in the self and in others, of those basic psychological events and processes we call perceptions, emotions, intentions, thoughts, memories, etc.—i.e., to become cognizant solely and simply of the fact that such entities *exist* and that people *have* them. The correlative type of awareness (2) is the recognition that O's inner events and processes (the existence of which is now at least dimly recognized) *need* not be the same as those of S himself currently or chronically experiences, although of course they may be and often are. Awareness (2) therefore means that S gradually comes to think of his own psychological processes as distinguishable and potentially different from O's; we might describe it by saying that his role, perspective, or viewpoint gradually becomes 'differentiated' from those of others. In practical terms, the developmental attainment of (1) and (2) with respect to these most elementary O characteristics would imply that the child could now (1) be made to understand the general *sort* of answer you had in mind when you asked him what he —and especially what O—'sees', 'feels', 'wants', 'thinks', etc., and (2) would not necessarily be obliged to answer your question about O's current experiences simply by reading off his own.

The absence of (2) is of course exactly what is meant by Piaget's famous concept of cognitive egocentrism (e.g., Piaget, 1926; Piaget and Inhelder, 1956; Flavell *et al.*, 1968). However, there seems to have been less explicit attention given, either by Piaget or others, to the nature and genesis of (1). It would seem logically possible for the child: to be at least dimly aware of the act or experience itself of say, looking-seeing (as contrasted with just being aware of the objects encompassed by that act or experience, i.e., with *what* is seen); to attribute that act or experience both to himself and to other people; and yet not yet be able, in his egocentrism, to conceive or imagine that O would really see anything while S's eyes are closed, that O might be seeing X while S is looking at Y, and the like (Fishbein, Lewis and Keiffer, 1972). At the same time, it is more than possible that this emerging ability (2) to distinguish and contrast one's own and the other's inner experiences does serve to heighten one's consciousness (1) of both sets of experiences, thus promoting, among other things, a sense of differentiated selfhood or self concept. This latter is, in fact, the sort of causal-developmental connection between (2) and something resembling (1) that Piaget always seems to stress, although it is unclear to me whether he would categorically reject the possibility of there ever being at least *some* (1) without there yet being *any* (2).

When do such basic and elemental forms of social-cognitive knowledge first develop, i.e., when does the child first become aware of the existence of psychological processes as such? There is reason to believe that at least some such elemental knowledge of visual percepts (Flavell *et al.*, 1968, chap. 5; Masangkay, McCluskey, Sims-Knight and Flavell, unpublished) and of emotions (Borke, 1971; Izard, 1971) emerges very early, perhaps during the second or third year of life. Other properties on Tagiuri's (1969, p. 396) list, such as ideas, intentions, abilities, memories, etc., probably become potential objects of awareness later than this, although there really is not much good research evidence on the question (DeVries, 1970; Flavell, 1966; Flavell, 1971b; Flavell *et al.*, 1968, p. 209; Meyer, 1971). The advent of such awarenesses represents the developmental emergence of what might be called 'metacognitive' ability, i.e., the ability to have cognitions about cognitions. It should be borne in mind that there is a great deal of formal and informal evidence to support Piaget's early conclusion (1926, 1928) that children of preschool and even early elementary school age *do* not spontaneously reflect much about either their own or other people's psychological processes (a *Need* problem), and are not very skillful at it when induced to try (an *Inference* problem). The present question has rather to do with the most basic and elementary conceptual prerequisite (*Existence*) for such reflection.

It might be supposed that only a developmental psychologist—indeed, only one preoccupied with the earliest years of life—would find reason to put an *Existence* component into a boxological model of social inference processes. Adult subjects are, after all, very clearly —and probably all equally clearly—aware of the existence of these basic categories of human experience and action. The *Existence* component may seem less trivial for the nondevelopmentalist, however, when less global and elementary processes are considered. For example, he may have to contend with the fact that one of his adult subjects includes some subtle and rather esoteric personality trait in his implicit personality theory, whereas another subject is completely unaware of that trait as one of life's possibilities:

While there are significant disagreements among researchers as to the definition and measurement of cognitive complexity, nearly everyone agrees that the cognitively complex [adult] person has more categories and makes more distinctions [than the cognitively simple adult] in his [social] perceptions (Hastorf *et al.*, 1970, p. 57, brackets supplied).

Miller, Kessell, and Flavell (1970) have recently studied a psychological property whose developmental status as regards *Existence* lies between these two extremes. According to their data, there appears to be a marked growth during the elementary school years in the child's awareness of the potentially recursive, self-embedded nature of human thinking, e.g., '*A* is thinking that *B* is thinking that *C* is thinking . . .' (see also DeVries, 1970; Flavell *et al.*, 1968, chap. 2). The emergence of such knowledge would seem to provide the cognitive basis for some of the adolescent's more legendary feats of obsessional social cognition ('I wonder what she thinks I thought of her when she did that?' etc.).

B. NEED

A frequently encountered characteristic of the child's behavior in a wide variety of task situations is his failure spontaneously to bring into play task-appropriate knowledge and skills that we know, based on independent evidence, he actually possesses. I have previously referred to this characteristic as a *production deficiency* when it occurs in memory task settings (Flavell, 1970b), and in more general terms, as a problem in the *evocation*, as contrasted with the *utilization*, of task relevant cognitive abilities (Flavell, 1971a). In the typical case of an evocation failure, an observer would be inclined to think that this child for some reason just did not recognize the need to retrieve and utilize relevant item of stored knowledge X, or that it simply did not occur to him to apply cognitive strategy or process Y to the problem. His conclusion would be that the child certainly could have done these things with at least some degree of effectiveness, if only he had spontaneously seen the need or utility of doing so, or if only someone had suggested the idea to him. It goes without saying that evocation failures are not peculiar to children, but it is the behavior of children with which we are presently concerned.

The *Need* component of the model reflects the presence of this sort of evocation problem in the sphere of social cognition. A child may have some knowledge of the existence and specific nature of, say, the activity of thinking (*Existence*). He may also display some ability, if so requested, to make sensible guesses about a particular O's thoughts in a particular situation, based on the available cues, his knowledge of O or of people in general, etc. (*Inference*). He may, however, not yet have acquired much of an operant tendency to make such guesses on his own (*Need*), either out of idle curiosity (many adults do a fair amount of noninstrumental people reading), or—of most interest to us here—because doing so might provide a useful means to some concrete, practical and involving O (*Application*). In the latter case, where there is some clear interpersonal objective, the problem might be that he simply does not understand the relevance of interpersonal inference to the achievement of this objective; alternatively, he might comprehend its relevance at some level but simply not 'think to' make the necessary inferences on most concrete occasions (because of a high threshold for spontaneous interpersonal inference generally, because the *Need-Inference* response is not yet well enough practiced to be near-reflexive in the case of this particular category of *Applications*, etc.). Whatever the underlying cause, the net effect is a marked gap between our hypothetical child's developed *capabilities* for social cognition (i.e., his developmental level re: *Existence* and *Inference*) and the amount of social cognition he *spontaneously carries out*, particularly in situations where such cognition might serve a useful instrumental function. It is precisely this gap that defines a *Need* problem.

The available evidence suggests that children of roughly early elementary school age and younger evince very little felt need to make spontaneous use of whatever elementary *Existence* knowledge and *Inference* ability they may have acquired, but that there tends to be a very marked increase in this disposition during later middle childhood and adolescence (e.g., Flavell, 1970a, pp. 1026–32; Flavell *et al.*, 1968, chap. 1, pp. 211–13; Tagiuri, 1969, pp. 427–428). For instance (Scarlett *et al.*, 1971), if asked to describe an acquaintance, first and third graders are rather likely to refer to his overt behavior (e.g., 'He gives me things'), whereas a fifth grader is likelier to cite a more abstract, inner-personal property (e.g., 'He is kind'). While granting that fifth graders do undoubtedly understand the concept of kindness somewhat better than third graders, it is rather improbable to suppose that the latter would have been literally *incapable* of appropriately attributing that particular property to an acquaintance—if, say, the experimenter had started them thinking along those lines. The likeliest explanation of the younger child's behavior is that, whatever his *Inference* skills may be, he is at least *less* prone than his elders to automatically conceptualize others in terms of inner, dispositional properties.

The younger child's difficulties with the *Need* component are even more apparent in his performance on certain types of communication tasks (Flavell *et al.*, 1968; Krauss and Glucksberg, 1969). A communication task becomes an implicit social inference problem whenever the speaker's immediate, 'top of the head' message will simply not be adequate to his listeners' informational needs, perhaps because these needs happen to be deviant or exceptional in some way in relation to the data to be communicated (Flavell *et al.*, 1968). In such a situation, the appropriate move for the speaker is to take careful stock of this particular listener's information-processing skills and limitations (*Inference*), and then to try to maintain this reading as a continuous basis for constructing a message that will accomplish the speaker's communicative objective (*Application*). There is much evidence that young children tend to be quite insensitive to this hidden, inferences-about-the-listener requirement of many verbal communication tasks (e.g., Flavell *et al.*, 1968; Glucksberg and Krauss, 1967; Krauss and Glucksberg, 1969). A striking example of this sort of failure to keep the listener's situation in mind is the young child who says, complete with gestures, 'it goes like *this*' (Glucksberg and Krauss, 1967, p. 314) or 'you put *that thing* in the cup' (Flavell *et al.*, 1968, p. 96) to a listener who cannot see the stimulus array the child is talking about. It is not, of course, that the child (kindergarten age and older in the above samples) actively *believes* that the listener can see the stimulus array, and that such verbal pointing would therefore be appropriate. It is more probable that he simply fails to sense the need to pay careful attention to his listener's response capabilities and to keep them continuously in mind throughout his communication. A blind listener, a stupid listener, a cognitively immature listener (Flavell *et al.*, 1968)—unusual audiences like these almost automatically stimulate (*Need*) the more mature communicator to make a careful analysis (*Inference*) of their information reception abilities in the service of constructing an effective individually tailored message (*Application*); immature communicators are simply much less likely to be stimulated in this way. A vital part of what needs developing in the area of social cognition, then, is something analogous to a set of conditioned responses, namely, an almost reflexive triggering of *S*'s inferential activity by the various classes of tasks and situations which tacitly call for it, i.e., for which this kind of activity is adaptive.

C. INFERENCE

The *Existence* and *Need* components warrant special emphasis in a developmental analysis precisely because they would likely be ignored or taken as givens by the specialist in adult social cognition (not wholly justifiably, perhaps). In marked contrast, he devotes an enormous amount of attention to the *Inference* component, forever trying to conceptualize and measure the inferential processes *S* uses, *S*'s level of inferential accuracy, the construct system or implicit personality theory from which *S*'s inferences proceed, etc., and the developmentalist is not likely to beat him at this game. For example, there is almost nothing that this developmental psychologist, at least, could imagine adding to Tagiuri's (1969) elegant account of the overall structure of this component, i.e., all the major classes of processes and variables that seem to be involved in the act of making inferences about others. The following, then, is little more than a reorganization of some earlier conclusions (Flavell *et al.*, 1968) about the nature and development of *Inference*.

First, even children of early preschool age or younger appear to show some limited capacity for veridical *Inference*, provided that the *Need* problem is effectively bypassed (i.e., by clearly instructing them to make a carefully specified kind of inference about *O*), most unequivocally so in the case of inferences about *O*'s visual percepts and affects. In fact, at this level of social-cognitive development, we are likely to be sure that the child has at least some notions about *Existence* only because he *does* demonstrate some minimal but genuine competence for *Inference*. We may be able to show, for instance, that he *can* accurately infer at least some emotional states (e.g., 'happy', 'sad') from *O*'s facial expression (Izard, 1971) or from certain experiences *O* has undergone (Borke, 1971; Masang-kay *et al.*, unpublished), and that he *can* correctly predict the gross content of *O*'s current visual experiences, using very clearcut, almost banal sorts of cues (Flavell *et al.*, 1968, chap. 5; Masangkay *et al.*, unpublished). However, most of the typical adult ability to make rich and varied (although not always accurate) inferences about others probably develops during middle childhood and adolescence. On 'pure' *Inference* tasks—where *Existence* can be assumed, where potential *Need* problems are eliminated through careful instruction, and where no *Application* is subsequently called for—the data virtually always show enormous increases in inferential complexity and ability across this broad age range.

Second, as the seasoned person perceptionist well knows, *what* gets developed here appears to be prodigious in quantity and variety, with no developmental catalog of it all even remotely in sight. Some of it probably consists of general intellectual skills (e.g., logical abilities) which, when pressed into service vis-à-vis social objects, essentially represent a form of 'applied cognitive development':

There are in fact some indications that the 'ontogenetic patterns' which are going to emerge here will turn out to be rather similar to those found in other conceptual areas. It is reasonable that this should be so. The mind of the child at any given level of its development would hardly be expected to change its basic design features when turning from logical-mathematical or physical to social content (Flavell, 1970, pp. 1025–1026; see also Feffer and Gourevitch, 1960).

One implication of the foregoing might be that the child's overall level of attained intellectual growth predicts his *Inference* ability to a limited extent, and there is some evidence that this is true (e.g., Rothenberg, 1970). The bulk of what develops here, however, probably consists of a great deal of highly structured but usually inexplicit knowledge or 'naive theory' (Baldwin *et al.*, 1969) about how various sorts of people are likely to react, internally and externally, in various situations. In contrast to the general cognitive skills just mentioned, this knowledge is more specifically inter-personal in its application, and also undoubtedly more specifically interpersonal in its developmental origin.

Finally, our research experience has suggested that *S* may often be faced with two problems rather than just one when engaged in an *Inference* enterprise, especially if it has an appended *Application* component. The one problem, invariably present, is of course that of constructing a suitably rich and accurate picture of the covert properties of *O* that *S* is interested in. The other is a potential difficulty *S* may have in maintaining this picture intact for whatever period of time is needed or required by the situation (e.g., during an *Application* period). Keeping the picture in pristine condition may be no mean task in situations where there is a natural tendency for *S*'s own inner process to distort and contaminate it, i.e., where *O*'s perspective tends to get assimilated to and confused with *S*'s own. In the sort of communication task mentioned earlier, for example, *S*'s problem need not be that he fails at the outset to notice *O*'s inability to see the stimulus array, nor that he fails to grasp the implications of this fact for his communicative behavior with *O*. Rather, it may be a sheer incapacity to keep *O*'s lack of visual ability firmly in mind throughout the entire message, an incapacity that stems from the unremitting *presence* of this selfsame visual ability in himself; he himself *does* continuously view the stimulus array as he communicates, after all, and it takes a special effort to keep remembering that *O* cannot. There is, in other words, not only the danger of being egocentric right from the outset, for good and all; there is also the danger of lapsing into it later, unconsciously and perhaps only intermittently, under the constant press of one's own (dissimilar from *O*'s) experience. Thus it was that we originally postulated two developmental problems for what the single category of *Inference* now covers:

Prediction—how actually to carry out this analysis, that is, possession of the abilities needed to discriminate with accuracy whatever the relevant role attributes [i.e., inner properties of *O*] are.

Maintenance—how to maintain in awareness the cognitions yielded by this analysis, assuming them to be in active competition with those which define one's own point of view, during the time in which they are to be applied to the goal behavior (Flavell *et al.*, 1968, p. 208; brackets added).

D. APPLICATION

An explanation of the dashed arrows in Figure 1 is a necessary preface here. As indicated earlier, *Application* is a frequent but not inevitable consequence or concomitant of *Inference*, and hence the dashed arrow between these two components. Sometimes we do nothing more with the cognitive fruits of an *Inference* process than merely contemplate them, as when we idly make guesses about the personality structure of the man next to us on the plane. The other dashed arrows refer to two options available to *S* if he should find that his initial *Application* efforts have not been wholly successful. Recall our example of a chess game between *S* and *O*. Supposing that *S*'s early game plan (*Application*), based partly on his estimate of *O*'s chess skill (*Inference*), now seems not to be working out very well. One of *S*'s option would be to retain his initial estimate of *O* and simply continue to plug away at his game (the shorter arrow), either sticking with the original plan or changing it. Alternatively (the longer arrow) he might decide that a reevaluation (*Inference*) of *O*'s overall chess ability, the strategy *O* may be following, etc., is called for (*Need*), given this unexpected turn in his fortunes. The reevaluation may in turn lead to some sort of change in his game behavior, thus completing the circuit back to *Application*.

The *Application* component is not, in itself, of great interest to the student of social cognition, be he developmentalist (Flavell *et al.*, 1968, p. 215) or nondevelopmentalist (Tagiuri, 1969) (for some rather dubious exceptions to this generalization, see Hastorf *et al.*, 1970, chap. 5). We are very interested in how *S* infers *O*'s chess skill and strategy (*Inference*); we are less interested in how *S* translates the resulting information into specific chess moves (*Application*). Similarly with verbal communication behavior that implicitly calls for mediation by role taking (i.e., social-inferential) activity: the former has been of interest to us largely insofar as it reflects the presence or absence of the latter (Flavell *et al.*, 1968). Needless to say, the skills and processes involved in any particular type of *Application*, e.g., verbal communication to *O*, need not be the same as those involved in any antecedent *Inference* that may have occurred. For example, both logical considerations (Flavell *et al.*, 1968, pp. 18–20, 191) and some research evidence (Kingsley, 1971) lead to the conclusion that a child's verbal communication performance would only be partly predictable from the degree to which he is disposed, and able to infer his listener's information processing abilities; for example, there is also the not inconsiderable matter of his level of linguistic development (vocabulary knowledge, verbal fluency, etc.). The skills and processes specific to any given *Application* problem also undergo development with age, of course, but their development is not the subject of this paper.

There may nonetheless be an interesting developmental story in connection with the dashed arrows shown in Figure 1. One of the variables that is known to affect an adult speaker's communication behavior is audience feedback (Mehrabian and Reed, 1968). There is evidence, however, that younger children are less likely than older children and adults to modify and alter their communication behavior the second time around upon learning that their initial message to *O* did not achieve its communicative objective (Flavell *et al.*, 1968, chap. 6; Glucksberg and Krauss, 1967). A recent study (Peterson, Danner and Flavell, 1972) illustrates the sorts of problems young communicators may have in coping with various kinds of noncomprehension signals from the listener. Four-year-old (nursery school) and six-year-old (first grade) children first demonstrated in pretest the ability to think of at least two alternative ways of characterizing each of a series of simple line drawings suggestive of real objects, e.g., indicating that an igloo-like figure looks like a 'house', and also like a 'bridge', or a 'tunnel', etc. Subsequently, they were instructed to describe each line drawing to an adult confederate so that he could pick it out from among a number of drawings set before him. After each characterization (six in all), the confederate acted conspicuously uncertain as to which drawing the child had been describing. His uncertainty was conveyed by means of one of three types of negative feedback, each child having a total of two consecutive experiences (messages) with each of the three types: (1) after making sure that the child was watching his face, the confederate looks exaggeratedly puzzled and unsure as to which picture to pick (scratching his head, frowning, etc.), but says nothing to the child (2) he says, 'I don't understand', followed after a rather lengthy pause either by 'I don't get it' or 'I don't think I can do it' (3) he says, 'Look at it again and tell me something else about it' (pause) 'What else does it look like?'

As would be expected, all subjects at both age levels said something new and different about the drawing ('recoded' it) following feedback (3). In contrast, few at either level recoded in response to purely gestural feedback (1). Finally, most of the first graders, but only a few of the preschoolers, responded to (2) as they did to (3), i.e., as if it were a tacit instruction to recode. (Not surprisingly, a group of adult subjects tested with the same experimental procedure invariably recoded in response to all three types of feedback, i.e., on all six trials.) Observation of the children's behavior suggested that feedback (1) may have communicated virtually nothing to them. They seldom looked or acted as if they understood it to signify a communication failure; indeed, most first graders would probably have recoded if they had so interpreted it, in view of their behavior in response to (2). On the other hand, the preschoolers usually acted as if they really *did* know that feedback (2) meant listener incomprehension and even that this incomprehension called for some sort of response on their part. However, they simply did not seem to understand *what* sort of response was appropriate, despite their recent experiences in the same experimental situation (e.g., pretest) with *precisely* that sort of response. Additional preschoolers were given trials in which the listener indicated that he did not understand (feedback 2) and also added the question, 'Is there *anything* you could do to help me?' They, too, did not think to recode. In the language of Figure 1, we might conclude that feedback (1) induced the adult subjects to loop back through *Need* and *Inference* (i.e., they correctly read the listener's inner state from his nonverbal gestures) and thence to a new *Application* (i.e., they correctly interpreted the implications of that reading for their own behavior); no such recycling was possible for most of the children in the case of (1), however, because the confederate's puzzled gestures were apparently not interpretable as such. In contrast, feedback (2) did lead most of the children back to *Need* and *Inference*, but only the older ones were generally able to complete the circuit by going from *Inference* to *Application*. It appears, then, that young communicators, in their egocentrism, may appear relatively inattentive to signs of listener incomprehension, unable to understand all the signs they attend to, and unable to see the communicative implications of all the signs they understand.

III. *Inferences about Visual Percepts*

A. BACKGROUND OF THE PROBLEM

There now exists a fair number of developmental studies dealing with the child's ability to infer the perceptual activities and experiences of another person (for reviews of most of the literature on this topic published prior to 1967–8, see Flavell, 1963, pp. 330–332, 388–9; Flavell, 1970a, p. 1027; Flavell *et al.*, 1968, pp. 34–5 and elsewhere). One of these studies concerning the child's growing sensitivity to the possible listening-hearing activity of others (Moore, 1958). All the rest, however, have dealt specifically with his knowledge and inferential ability regarding *O*'s visual experiences. Their point of departure has in all cases been Piaget's well known theory and research on the development of the child's representational or symbolic, as contrasted with his purely perceptual or sensory-motor, knowledge of projective space (Piaget and Inhelder, 1956). In interpersonal inference terms, this largely means S's growing knowledge concerning O's visual perspective, e.g., S's ability to imagine or represent to himself how an object array might look to O, from O's position with respect to the array, as distinguished from how it presently appears to S himself, located in a position different from O's.

Despite the rather substantial volume of research done by Piaget and others, the overall developmental picture concerning this type of social inference is still far from clear. Notwithstanding Piaget's insightful analysis of the problem (Piaget, 1954, pp. 364–9; Piaget and Inhelder, 1956), there remain numerous uncertainties and ambiguities as to just *what* develops here (one basic skill? several basic skills? different 'levels' of the 'same' skill?), and *when*. Different tasks, all purporting to measure the 'same' perspective-taking skill, exhibit wide and unexplained differences in difficulty level or average age of mastery. Accordingly, the aim of this section is to try to order and clarify the developmental picture a bit. I shall begin with a concrete illustration of just how wide these differences in age of task mastery can be. Next will come a brief presentation of those aspects of Piaget's theory of the development of spatial representation that are most pertinent to the present topic. I shall then offer a tentative model of just what development in this area might comprise. While this model owes a great deal to Piaget's theoretical analysis and actually incorporates whole segments of it, the two are by no means identical. The section will then conclude with an attempt to reinterpret the available research evidence in terms of the model.

At the high end of the task-difficulty continuum is Piaget's famous 'Three Mountains' task (Piaget and Inhelder, 1956, chap. 8) and its more complex variations (e.g., Flavell *et al.*, 1968). In the Piagetian original, the child views a scale model of three mountains and is tested in one or another way for his ability to imagine or represent the mountains' visual appearance from various positions or perspectives other than his own, e.g., by being asked to select from among several alternatives, that photograph which depicts what O sees from a certain position, or by having to reproduce O's view with a set of duplicate mountains. Piaget and Inhelder found this to be a challenging task for children as old as 9–10 years. Laurendeau and Pinard (1970) later replicated their study, using what was probably a somewhat more demanding and 'conservative' version of the same testing procedure, i.e., one that would be expected to yield fewer 'false positives' (correct responding mediated by cognitive skills of a lower developmental level than those the task was intended to tap). Under these conditions, only 14 out of 50 twelve-year-olds (the oldest group tested) demonstrated full mastery.

Flavell et al. (1968) used what appears to have been a still more exacting variation of the Piaget and Inhelder task (p. 56, Display 4). Display 4 consisted of an irregular (nonlinear) arrangement of three wooden cylinders of different heights, each painted red for half its circumference and white for the other half. The subject's task was to reconstruct a given view of these cylinders, using a duplicate set. To solve this perspective-taking problem, he must compute such facts as, for example, that when the display is viewed from the side opposite his own, the middle-sized block will present its white side full face and will appear to be located leftwards and frontwards of the other two. Only 8 out of 20 sixteen-year-olds achieved maximum scores on that percept-inference problem.

The other end of the task-difficulty continuum appears to be defined at present by two tasks, called Picture and Eye Position, used in a recently completed study by Masangkay et al. (unpublished). These tasks were designed to have two characteristics: (1) they both looked like genuine tests of visual-percept inference (2) they were the least demanding, least encumbered by 'performance' problems (in Chomsky's sense), 'lowest level' tests of percept inference we could devise.

The Picture task is a variation on one that nursery school children appeared to find easy in a previous study (Flavell et al., 1968, pp. 169–70, Task IIID). It consisted of six subtasks. A description of one of them will serve to illustrate their general character. The child is shown a piece of white cardboard with a cut-out picture of a dog pasted on one side and a cat on the other, and is asked to name what is shown on each side. He then holds the cardboard vertically between himself and the experimenter, so that he sees the dog and the experimenter sees the cat, and the experimenter asks first, 'What do *you* see?' and then, 'What do *I* see?' Of the remaining five subtasks, two could be correctly answered on a noninferential, purely egocentric basis, because both S and O have identical visual inputs on those subtasks (e.g., a cut-out of a duck mounted on a piece of transparent plexiglass rather than on cardboard). These 'control' subtasks were included to test for any possible set simply to give different responses to different questions, and also to lend variety and flexibility to the procedure. In each subtask the child was of course able to look at the experimenter's side if he should forget what was on it (since he himself held the card); few children did so, however.

The second, Eye Position task was administered as follows. Four toy objects familiar to young children are suspended in various positions around the subject, who is seated on a rather high chair: an airplane from the ceiling above and a bit to the front of his head, a boat and truck on the walls to his right and left, respectively, and a block on the floor just in front of his feet. The experimenter is seated about four feet directly in front of the child, at about his eye level. She first pointed to each object in turn and asked the child to name it. She then said: 'Now this time, instead of pointing to the toys with my hand I'm going to look at them with my eyes and you tell me which one I'm looking at'. As soon as she was certain the child was watching, she closed her eyes, moved them *while still closed* (thus, the child never saw any eye *movements* in an object's direction) to the appropriate upwards, downwards, or sidewards position, and then opened them again, maintaining visual fiixation on the object until the child responded. Her eye fixations were randomly ordered, with a total of two for each of the four objects.

These two tasks were administered to 16 two-year-olds (2:0–2:11 years) and 9 'young' three-year-olds (3:0–3:7 years). Since some of the younger children had very minimal linguistic skills, at least on the production side, subjects were allowed to respond by pointing to what the experimenter was looking at rather than naming it; most of the responses were verbal, however. Great care was taken to secure and maintain the child's interest and attention, and to ask questions only when these were engaged.

The children did surprisingly well on these two tasks. On the Picture task, all 25 answered correctly on the two control subtasks; more importantly 8 of the 16 two-year-olds responded correctly on all four of the remaining, more clearly and unequivocally percept-inferential subtasks, and 8 of the 9 three-year-olds did the same. The Eye Position task proved to be of roughly comparable difficulty: 6 out of 16 two-year-olds and 7 out of 9 three-year-olds responded correctly on 6 or more of the 8 trials (with each trial of course presenting four options).

The Masangkay *et al.* Picture and Eye Position tasks thus proved to be just about as easy for two-year-olds as the Flavell *et al.* (1968) Display 4 was for sixteen-year-olds, and that is surely an age gap or *décalage* that calls for explanation. To be sure, we cannot rule out the possibility that the two-year-old data are ridden with false positives (or that the older subjects' data are full of false negatives, for that matter). Some or all of the young children's correct responding on these two tasks might, after all, have been mediated by something other than an awareness *that* O, like S himself, does see things (thus, *Existence* knowledge of some sort) plus some ability to estimate *what* O sees, when provided with obvious enough cues (thus, *Inference* skills of some sort). The behavior of at least one of our two-year-olds would be hard to dismiss in this fashion, however, i.e., as a case of what I shall shortly be referring to as Level 0 (pre-inferential) versus Level 1 (primitively but genuinely inferential or percept-attributive) responding. On the duck-on-plexiglass control subtask of the Picture Problem, this child's answer to the experimenter's second question was 'me', and then, after the question was repeated, 'duck'. As additional anecdotal evidence, one of my colleagues resports having seen his 22-month-old daughter 'showing' a picture book to her doll, saying 'See—apple', etc., while pushing the doll's face toward each picture. It seems plausible to believe that such findings may in fact reflect the presence of primitive *Existence* and *Inference* capabilities 'of some sort', and that our problem is rather to make educated guesses as to just *what* sort of capabilities they might be, to do the same for those enormously more difficult tasks of the mountains and cylinders variety, and then to try to tell a coherent developmental story that somehow connects the one with the other.

Let me preface the story with a very brief sketch of what I understand to be Piaget's developmental analysis of the problem (Piaget, 1954, pp. 364–9; Piaget and Inhelder, 1956; see also Laurendeau and Pinard, 1970, pp. 8–17). By the end of the sensory-motor period (1½–2 years of age, on the average), the young child has achieved a well coordinated objective, and in a sense 'non-egocentric' *practical* knowledge of objects and of the space in which both he and they exist and move. That is, he possesses an essentially nonsymbolic and nonrepresentational, concrete and pragmatic, knowledge-in-action sort of understanding of objects and space. For example, he 'knows' in this special, purely behavioral sense, that the same object looks different in different orientations and at different distances from him (thus, a size and shape constancy type of 'under-standing' of perspective). Similarly, he now 'understands' that previously experienced objects can sometimes be reexperienced by taking the appropriate action (Piaget's famous object concept, or concept of object permanence); for instance, he knows what to do when he wants to retrieve a hidden object, or to view once again the picture shown on the other side of the page.

But, according to Piaget, this practical, perceiving-and-doing kind of understanding is to be carefully distinguished from a symbolic-representational understanding of the same phenomena. In fact, many a post-infancy year will be required for the child to achieve the same measure of objectivity and nonegocentrism on this new plane, the plane of symbolized, imagined, and reflected upon space as opposed to that of experienced and acted upon space. Conse-quently, throughout the preschool period at least, the child is believed to be profoundly egocentric and incompetent with respect to the representation of visual perspectives and also, one might suppose, of any other visual phenemenon. He cannot yet represent (imagine, contemplate, take as an object of thought) either his own or another's visual acts and contents, and hence 'as seen from a certain perspective' and similar concepts are simply not yet part of his cognitive repertoire. Unaware of such concepts, his own point of view continually dominates his judgments, since of course he vividly and continually *experiences* that point of view, while not yet being capable of *representing* either that or any other. Consequently on the Three Mountains and similar tasks, he has the unwitting tendency to reproduce his own point of view when asked to reconstruct or identify another's. As certain concrete-operational skills get perfected in late middle childhood (Piaget and Inhelder, 1956, pp. 469–74), however, he finally becomes fully cognizant of the idea of visual perspectives and also begins to master the main rules and principles governing their reconstruction. For instance, he eventually understands that perspectives form a coherent, integrated system, that a given position in relation to object array defines one and only one view of it, that right becomes left when seen from the opposite side, and other relevant facts. In Piaget's terms, the child gradually becomes capable of 'differentiating' and 'coordinating' visual perspectives, and these capabilities largely define his 'conception' (versus 'perception') of projective space.

Piaget's developmental account is undoubtedly correct in the main, and seems at least roughly consistent with a good deal of the available research evidence. At the same time, there seem to me to be some gaps and ambiguities in his analysis, at least with specific regard to the ontogenesis of inferences about visual percepts, as contrasted with the development of spatial representation in general. The problems lie not so much in his description of the final outcome of development here, that is, in his account of what the mature individual knows and can do that makes him a successful differentiator and coordinator of perspectives on such problems as the Three Mountains task. They rather lie in his characterization of the younger subject's cognitive assets and liabilities, particularly those of the preschool and early school age child. What, precisely, do children at various younger ages *lack*, when contrasted with mature perspective-takers? What—and again *precisely*—do they *have*? For example, just what do Masangkay *et al.*'s two- and three-year-old subjects know about their own and others' visual experiences that a late sensory-motor period child would presumably not know? And what do they, in their turn, not yet know that, say, a five-year-old does, or an eight-year-old, or one of Flavell *et al.*'s (1968) perfectly-responding sixteen-year-olds? Are findings such as those of the Masangkay *et al.* study really compatible in some way with Piaget's developmental account, or do they genuinely contradict it? As a careful comparison of the first three with the last two of the following excerpts from Piaget and Inhelder (1956) will show, one is not always quite certain, from that account, just what the younger child is and is not supposed to know about visual percepts and perspectives:

In short, due to the lack of any conscious awareness or mental discrimination between different viewpoints, these children are unable to to represent perspective ... (p. 178).

The children belonging to both groups from which we drew our examples all really imagine that the doll's perspective is the same as their own, they all think the little man sees the mountains in the way they appear from where they themselves sit (p. 220).

Compared with Substage IIA, the present level is a definite step toward true relativity, to the extent that there is some awareness that things will look different to an observer stationed elsewhere (p. 233).

Now in the present case there are a number of indications which suggest that at Substage IIA the child is already perfectly well aware that the appearance of the group of mountains changes together with the observer's point of view. This is what might be expected considering that from their second year babies are perfectly capable of turning things round to co-ordinate the different perspectives, or if the object cannot be moved, turning their heads or their entire persons. Admittedly, this is only a matter of successive perception and not yet a series of visual images as in reconstructing or anticipating a situation (p. 216).

It is not easy to determine right away the real nature of the difficulties which prevent these children [of Substage IIA] understanding how a variety of possible perspectives may result from displacement of an object. On the perceptual plane they clearly realize, and are able to to say so, that the appearance of the object changes with its orientation [this particular task involved perspective-taking on but a single object]. Thus, Nic immediately declares that the doll, when confronted with the pencil point first, will 'see it differently' and when presented with the watch in profile 'doesn't see the whole watch' (p. 177, brackets added).

B. A DEVELOPMENTAL MODEL

The distinction between *Existence* and *Inference* (or some similar, competence-versus-performance type of distinction) must always be kept in mind when trying to make a developmental analysis of percept inference. For example, an individual may be perfectly well aware (and on the symbolic-representational, not merely the sensory-motor level) of the fact that an *O* located on the opposite side of our Display 4 will necessarily see the three cylinders differently than he does (*Existence*), and yet not be able in actual practice to make a precise reproduction of *O*'s viewpoint (*Inference*). Moreover, he may even know all of the basic rules and principles that govern how the appearance of a set of objects should change with changes in an observer's position (more *Existence* knowledge?—a 'competence' form of *Inference* knowledge?—it matters little for the moment how we classify it), and *still* not be able to compute *O*'s visual experience perfectly. The individual might, for instance, forget to take the colors of the cylinders into account when trying to reproduce *O*'s view, so preoccupied is he with getting each cylinder into its proper front-back and right-left position in relation to the others; he might also, no matter how exalted his level of cognitive development in this area, momentarily lapse into spatial egocentrism and unwittingly insert a bit of his own perspective into his reproduction of *O*'s. We must be careful to distinguish, in other words, between a subject's achieved level of development with respect to, say, the fundamental *idea* of perspective and perspective differences, i.e., that they exist, and his level with respect to the actual *computation* of specific perspectives in real time, especially when presented with multi-object, complex arrays; his 'in competence' type knowledge of specific perspective transformation rules, his habitual strategies and operating procedures for constructing a desired viewpoint— these and other cognitive entities presumably stand somewhere between the bare idea and the final, detailed computation.

The model I shall now present deals primarily with the *Existence* side of percept attribution, although some attention will also be paid to the more computational, *Inference*-like skills and knowledge.

The model postulates a developmental sequence of four steps or levels in this area of social cognition (o, 1, 2, 3). Of the four, Levels 1 and 2 probably represent the acquisitions of greater interest and importance. Level o does not actually entail any percept attribution to O (hence its name), and is roughly synonomous with Piaget's concept of practical, sensory-motor knowledge. Level 3 is really only a logical extension or elaboration of Level 2, although its explicit postulation may make for some interesting research possibilities. Piaget and most other researchers in the area (myself included) have been almost exclusively preoccupied with Level 2, and particularly with the *Inference* side of it. A case can be made, however, that the acquisition of Level 1 knowledge represents a cognitive-developmental milestone of at least equal significance.

1. *Level o*

Level o knowledge consists largely of well-developed, sensory-motor type expectancies on the child's part as to what he will find as he moves from here to there in his everyday, object-populated environment. Some of these expectancies undoubtedly have to do with how an object or a group of objects will look or appear as he changes his position with respect to it or it to him, thus a tacit, practical, knowledge-in-action of perspective and perspective variation. However, I suspect that the most ecologically significant expectancies, those which are most salient and important to the child, have to do with *what* object or objects a given change of position will make accessible to him, not with the various possible visual *appearances*, in the perspective sense, of that object or objects once contact is attained. He is, in other words, generally more interested in what real object he has just retrieved than in what that object looks like from any given angle, the latter representing information of little functional significance for him.

I will assume, therefore that the prototype of Level o knowledge is largely knowledge of the Piagetian object concept variety. For instance, the Level o child is capable of anticipating (through his own memory, by means of communications from others, etc.) that object X will be contacted if he goes around to the other side of some interposed object. While he probably does have some tacit expectations, e.g., based upon innate or early acquired size and shape constancies (Pick and Pick, 1970, pp. 774–81), concerning how the appearance of X will change from first sighting to final, close up recontacting, by far the most important anticipation from his point of view is simply that X will be there. The adaptive function of the various perceptual constancies is, after all, to permit us to identify and attend to real objects as such, in their invariant, visual-context-free objecthood, while ignoring such (usually) ecologically irrelevant features as perspective relations and retinal size.

These anticipating skills notwithstanding, the Level o child has as yet no conception or symbolic representation of any sort of visual act or experience, with or without regard to perspective, in either self or others. While able to anticipate that he will reencounter object X if he goes around to O's side of a barrier, he is still quite incapable of representing either his future or O's present visual experiencing of O. Internal psychological processes like seeing are simply not yet objects of cognition. In the Masangkay et $al.$ Picture task, for instance, a Level o child might, if he had sufficient language, be able to understand and correctly answer the question, 'What picture is on this (the experimenter's) side of the card?' He should not, however, be able to make any sense out of the question, 'What picture am I (you) looking at?' except perhaps by somehow reconstructing it as the former, purely object-orientated and subjectless sort of question. In summary, the Level o organism anticipates objects seen and, probably of less importance to him, visual perspectives seen, but cannot as yet anticipate or otherwise represent to himself anyone's seeing activities and experiences as such. He readily attributes nonvisible objects to locations, and probably nonvisible appearances to objects, but no invisible percepts to people (Flavell et $al.$, 1968, pp. 222–3).

2. *Level 1*

The child now shows at least a minimal capacity for symbolically representing certain visual acts and experiences, for attributing them to others as well as to the self, and for distinguishing between these two attributions (at least in some situations). What is represented and attributed, however, is as yet only the looking at and the seeing of real objects per se, not the having of a certain view or perspective vis-à-vis one or more objects. Presumably because things as such rather than particular views of things are what the child knows and cares most about, it is the seeing of things rather than the seeing of views of things that first becomes an object of consciousness. The question, 'What picture am I looking at?' is now at least minimally comprehended in terms of an experience or act on O's part whose object or objective is a (depicted) thing. 'Show how these three mountains appear to me, from where I am sitting' would *not* be properly comprehended, however, since it refers to *how O views* those three objects that *both* S and O currently *see*, rather than, say, to *what* objects O *sees*, from his position, that S, from his position, does not. Just as we said that the Level 0 child could conceivably assimilate the question, 'What object is seen?' to the question 'What object is over there?' we might also expect the Level 1 child to misconstrue the question 'What view of this object is seen?' as simply meaning 'What object is seen?' and answer accordingly (more on this possibility later).

It should be emphasized that, while still unable to represent perspectives, the Level 1 child *does* understand something more than 'What object is over there?' In the Masangkay *et al.* Eye Position task, for instance, all four objects were equally 'over there', in relation to either S or O, but most of our young subjects could readily single out the 'object seen' from among them. Recall also the two-year-old who spontaneously included himself in the experimenter's visual experience, as well as the young child who spontaneously provided her doll with visual experiences. A task from one of our earlier studies (Flavell *et al.*, 1968, pp. 170–2,

Task IIIE) is perhaps even more unequivocally a test of Level 1
Existence knowledge, although it probably also requires more in the
way of *Inference* type, computational skill than either of the
Masangkay *et al.* problems. In IIIE, the experimenter holds a card
vertically between herself and the child. The card presents an
identical appearance on both sides, namely, three pictures of
common objects arranged from top to bottom. The experimenter
first lowers a wide piece of cardboard (wider than the card) down
her side until it obscures the topmost object from her view, and then
lowers it further to obscure all but the bottom object, each time
asking the child to tell her what she, the experimenter, sees on her
side *now*. Clearly, all three objects are 'over there', on *O*'s side, but
on any given trial only one or two are 'seen' by *O*. At the same
time, no representation of perspective is required to solve the
problem, since the child's task is only to determine *what* objects *O*
currently sees. Children as young as four years of age were found
to perform quite well on this type of percept inference task.

3. *Level 2*

The Level 2 child can represent the fact, not only that he and *O*
see things, but also that they have particular, position-determined
views (perspectives) of the things they see. Unlike the Level 1 child,
he can represent differences in visual experience between himself
and *O* even when exactly the same objects are visible to both, and
can thus grasp what for the younger child would presumably be a
mind-boggling possibility: an *S-O difference* in visual experience
embedded in an *S-O similarity* in visual experience. Level 2
Existence and *Inference* capabilities have thus far virtually defined
the subject matter in this area of social-cognitive development.
These are the capabilities that Piaget and Inhelder (1956) and most
subsequent researchers have been primarily interested in studying,
at least implicitly, and, these are the capabilities that the Three
Mountains and similar tasks seem to measure.

There is a sense in which Level 2 knowledge may be regarded as a
clearer and more ambiguous case of percept representation and

attribution than Level 1 knowledge. While it has been argued that the Level 1 child, unlike the Level 0 child, really *can* attribute visual acts and experiences to persons, it must be admitted that the main focus of his attention in the person-object relation is still on the object rather than on the person. In all probability, his representations decrease in salience and articulatedness as they go from the more external to the more internal aspects of that relation, that is, from object seen, to O's visible looking gestures (movements and positioning of head and eyes, 'intent' expression, etc.), to O's covert visual experience: In contrast, Level 2 knowledge seems unquestionably to be knowledge of precisely these latter, purely internal and phenomenological aspects. In the case of our Display 4 array, for example, S must explicitly represent to himself (although not necessarily in the form of a visual image) O's *visual experience* of the three cylinders. It will not suffice to represent just the three cylinders themselves, in their abstract, orientationless objecthood, nor even just to comprehend that O is currently in a specifically looking-seeing kind of interaction with them (versus no interaction, a touching-handling interaction, a 'thinking of' type of interaction, etc.).

It seems reasonable to suppose that, here as elsewhere in the domain of cognitive development, there are numerous intermediate and transitional sublevels (Flavell, 1971b). One can envisage, for instance, a very immature form of Level 1 in which the child does little else than dimly sense a functional connection between O and the object seen (as contrasted with a *completely* subjectless, Level 0 type knowledge), and also a very mature form in which the child clearly and explicitly represents the fact that O is having a visual experience of the object, but with that representation still containing no perspectival or other information regarding the particular *quality* of that experience. Similarly, as will be shown, it is not difficult to imagine types of representation that lie between this most mature form of Level 1 and the more prototypical cases of Level 2 perspective taking; the same can also undoubtedly be said for the Level 2-Level 3 interface. A more serious objection to the present model, and one that I simply cannot credit at present, would be that there really are no intermediate steps at all between unambiguous Level 0 and unambiguous Level 2—that the child has literally no notion (*Existence* type) of the psychological process of seeing until he acquires the notion (again, *Existence* type) of seeing different views of the same objects. I rather think that something akin to a Level 1 acquisition will have to be inserted to describe adequately the beginnings of that giant cognitive-developmental advance from no percept attribution whatever to genuine and unmistakable percept attribution; it is, in any case, just the kind of acquisition that would reasonably fit into what is currently an empty age period in this area of development—that of the early post-infancy years.

4. *Level 3*

The meaning of Level 3 can best be introduced by examining the usual operational definition of Level 2 competence on tasks like the Three Mountains one. In all research administrations of these tasks of which I am aware, the subject is judged to have mastered the problem if he can construct a purely qualitative, and still quite 'real object' oriented, representation of O's perspective. In the Laurendeau and Pinard (1970) replication of the original Piaget and Inhelder study, for example, the following was accepted as a completely correct representation of an O's view of an arrangement of red, yellow and blue mountains:

4(12:0): *Problem 1* (position F). Immediately points to picture F, saying: '*He sees the red one on his right, the yellow one on his left, and the blue behind the red and yellow ones, in the middle.*' (p. 392).

No metric quantification of exact relative positions is called for on such tasks: purely qualitative designators like 'right', 'left', 'behind', and 'middle' are perfectly adequate (and for some views in the Laurendeau and Pinard set up, a quasi Level 1 type assertion like 'He can't see the yellow mountain from there' would also suffice). Similarly, the child is not required to reproduce the *projective* (versus *real*) sizes of the three mountains. The occasion never arises on such tasks where, in order to be judged correctly, the subject must explicitly represent the fact that, for instance, although mountain X is in reality larger than mountain Y, it will appear smaller from O's point of view because it is farther away from him. Problems demanding a representation of O's perspective at this level of accuracy could readily be devised, but they have not been so far as I know.

Level 3 representations add what Level 2 representations omit in their qualitative, imprecise, real-size-centred characterizations of points of view. A Level 3 representation would thus be a literal and precise, Norman Rockwell type reproduction of O's retinal image of the object array: an image that, knowing no size or shape constancy and having no depth perception, reproduces apparent (projective) angles, lengths, and distances with perfect accuracy. Just as Level 2 representations are more abstract and ecologically unrealistic than Level 1 representations (because, unlike the child, they are view-oriented rather than real-object-oriented), so are these Level 3 retinal reproductions even more abstract and remote from everyday visual activity than the informal and qualitative perspective-taking of Level 2. Two facts should convince us that even a purely *Existence* type command of Level 3 reperesentation must require a rather abstract, reflective-contemplative conceptualization of visual acts and experiences. The one is that children younger than about 7–8 years of age frequently seem unable even to *understand* an instruction to judge the retinal rather than the real size of objects (Flavell, 1963, pp. 355–6); one can only guess how comprehensible Level 3 type instructions would be to children of various ages in an appropriately modified version of the Three Mountains task (such a developmental study might be worth trying, by the way). The other fact is of course that perspective drawing, far from being a natural way to represent visual reality, was a relatively late invention in the history of art and normally requires formal instruction for its skillful execution.

It is apparent that Levels 0 and 2 are intended to correspond quite closely to Piaget's sensory-motor and representational forms of knowledge about projective space. So far as I can determine, however, neither Level 1 nor Level 3 finds any explicit and articulated counterpart in his developmental model (Level 3 would probably be catalogued under the heading of projective or projective-plus-Euclidean representational knowledge, and Level 1 might somehow be assimilated to some aspect of the genesis of topological knowledge). Assuming its psychological reality, this series of four levels may well constitute a regular, possibly invariant, developmental sequence of cognitive acquisitions. On the one hand, each level seems to reflect a more abstract, internal-percept-oriented versus external-object-oriented, form of knowledge than its predecessors. The higher the level, in other words, the more clearly and unambiguously one is dealing with inferences about *percepts* rather than about *objects*. On the other hand, each higher level appears to include, but yet go beyond or add to, the information cognized at all lower levels: Level 1 includes the fact that O has visual contact with object X in addition to knowledge of X's physical whereabouts (Level 0); Level 2 includes this fact and adds to it some fairly rough, qualitative data as to how X appears to O; Level 3 represents these same data but attempts to bring them to the precision and fullness of detail of the retinal image itself.

It is, unfortunately, much easier to theorize about developmental sequences than to verify them empirically (Flavell, 1971a). Nothing in the formal description of these four levels, or of any sublevels thereof, tells us much about just *when* each might be expected to begin to conclude its period of acquisition relative to the others (big age gaps between some adjacent levels? small ones between others?). In all probability, lower levels would continue to undergo development for some time after higher levels have made their début. Neither do we know how to obtain really precise and valid developmental assessment data on such questions (how much does a given test confound *Inference* skills with *Existence* knowledge? how comparable, with respect to this sort of diagnostic sensitivity, are various existing or imaginable tests of the different levels?) What follows, then, is really little more than a kind of ordered juxtaposing of existing research findings with what appear to be the corresponding segments of the model. While doing this will hopefully add a little credibility to the model, it could hardly be said to 'validate' it in any serious sense.

The studies I would like to cite pertain mostly to Levels 1 and 2. As indicated above, there seem to have been no studies that have explicitly assessed the child's knowledge and skill as regards Level 3 representations of O's perspective. The voluminous literature on the drawing skills and dispositions of children of different ages might provide some useful clues here, but I simply have not looked into it as yet. As for Level 0, there is, of course, research evidence concerning the infant's capabilities in the areas of size and shape constancy, depth perception, and Piagetian object permanence, but I would also prefer not to cope with that literature in a paper that is already too long. I cannot, however, quite resist citing an ingenious recent study by Shantz and Watson (1970) that seems definitely relevant to Level 0. They tried to measure indices of surprise on the part of three to five-year-old nursery school children in response to a 'trick' condition whereby an object array was caused to have exactly the same visual appearance no matter which of two sides (0° versus 180°) the child viewed it from. About half of their subjects did indeed show overt evidence of surprise but, significantly, I think, the older ones showed no more surprise than the younger ones. It would be interesting to see how 'old' sensory-motor infants would respond to an appropriately modified version of this task; they also should have acquired some tacit visual expectancies (Level 0) as to how object appearances change with position.

Let us begin with Level 2. As indicated earlier, the most frequently used task here requires S to predict O's view of an array of three objects, most commonly three mountains. In addition to the studies already mentioned (Piaget and Inhelder, 1956, chap. 8; Laurendeau and Pinard, 1970, chaps. 14–16; Flavell *et al.*, 1968, pp. 55–70), three-object problems have been used by Dodwell (1963), Masangkay, Feenstra, and Tayag (1971), Neal (1966), Shantz and Wilson (1971), Sullivan and Hunt (1967), and no doubt many other investigators. The results are fairly consistent in suggesting that children do not usually perform even passably well on most three-object perspective tasks until late middle childhood or so, with improvement in performance normally continuing to occur throughout the adolescent period. The accurate computation of three-object perspectives is obviously an advanced cognitive-developmental skill.

What is more difficult to assess is when the child first achieves *any* measure of Level 2 understanding of such problems, e.g., a purely *Existence* type representation of the mere *fact* that O may not see the set of mountains quite as S himself does, or that their visual appearance is likely to change in some way with one's position. A child capable of such representation might nevertheless even have trouble correctly identifying a photograph of his *own* view of the mountains, let alone O's; might systematically but unconsciously select purely egocentric reproductions of O's point of view; might think that any photograph could be correct, perhaps because he mistakenly believes that the task calls for a purely Level 1 representation ('What does O see?'—'Three mountains'); or might otherwise show an almost complete ineptitude at the more computational, *Inference* or mixed *Existence-Inference* end of the problem (all of the above-mentioned error patterns are frequently encountered in children's response records, by the way). He might do any of these things, I would maintain, and *still* have *some* minimal but genuine intuitions as to what perspective might mean for an array of three objects.

Some of Laurendeau and Pinard's (1970) normative data may be helpful here: 90 per cent of the four and a half-year-olds, 68 per cent of the five-year-olds, 52 per cent of the six-year-olds, but only 16 per cent of the seven-year-olds were judged to be at the stage, 'during which even the meaning of the questions and the nature of the task are totally beyond the subject's ability' (*ibid.*, p. 346). From the way the behaviour of these subjects is talked about in the text, it seems likely that they all were able to represent the fact that O looks at and see three mountains (Level 1), but unlikely that they had much of any conception of his seeing them in particular ways, from particular points of view (Level 2). Many of them seem to have acted as if they had, in fact, misconstrued the task as a Level 1 problem (i.e., any photograph will do, because all show 'mountains'). Most of the children of seven years and older, however, seem to have done *something* that suggests an at least minimal, *Existence* type comprehension at Level 2, despite a very high frequency of egocentric and other errors in actual performance. For example, they often tried to lean over towards O, or even walk around to his side of the array, seemingly in order to find out first hand how the mountains looked to him. It is difficult to see why a strictly Level 1 child would want to do that, since 'the mountains' as such are already visible to him from where he sits; indeed, no mention is made of this behavior in the author's discussion of stage 0 performance. While stressing the extreme egocentrism of their stage 1 children (about half of their seven-year-olds fell into this stage), Laurendeau and Pinard (1970, pp. 353–4) also seem to imply that they may possess as least some beginning awareness of the basic idea of perspective variation. The data from Piaget and Inhelder (1956) and Flavell *et al.* (1968, pp. 65–7) are also compatible with this picture of the 7 + year old's understanding of three-object problems.

Not surprisingly, nascent intuitions about perspective appear to surface earlier when the array viewed contains only a single object. Piaget and Inhelder (1956, chap. 6) had children try to imagine the apparent shape that single objects, such as a needle or a disc, would present when viewed from different perspectives (cf. the experiments described in their chap. 7, concerning the projection of shadows, are also somewhat relevant here). My reading of their reported results indicates that some *Existence* level understanding of these single-object problems was present at least by age six, and probably a bit earlier. Lovell's (1959, p. 113) conclusions from his replication of the Piaget and Inhelder study reinforce this impression.

A few other studies (Fishbein, Lewis and Keiffer, 1972; Lauben-gayer, 1965; Lewis and Fishbein, 1969) have used one-object perspective tasks, but involving objects that differ in a crucial way from Piaget and Inhelder's disc and needle. These investigators used complex, highly meaningful objects (in all cases but one, a human or animal doll) displaying four highly distinctive sides, each of which could itself be labelled or else contained parts ('subobjects') that could readily be labelled. One of the objects used in the Lewis and Fishbein studies, for example, was a toy soldier holding a candy cane in one hand and saluting with the other. A subject could there-fore represent to himself that O 'sees the back of the soldier' (a nameable side) or that he 'sees his face' (a nameable 'subobject'). Laubengayer (1965) actually seems to have had such considera-tions in mind when she devised her task materials:

The first hypothesis was that children will demonstrate their ability to take the point of view of another person at an earlier age than Piaget proposes if the test 1) involves simple objects with which the child is familiar, 2) if test objects have clearly discriminable sides, which would allow the child to respond as unambiguously as possible ... (p. 3).

When asked to predict O perspectives with respect to objects like this, children as young as *four* years of age were found to perform quite well. It may be instructive to try to explain such apparent precocity.

One possibility is that these experimenters may have taken more than usual care to reduce to a minimum all unnecessary performance obstacles to the child's underlying competence by careful pre-training on task requirements, by doing their best to secure the child's attention and interest, by supplying the child with explicit feedback as to the correctness of his response, and so on; Lauben-gayer's (1965) study even included a systematic training component. An additional possibility, however, is that at least some of their problems may have been soluble by a purely Level 1 type strategy, virtually never the case when three-object tasks are used. If O is situated face to face with the toy soldier, for example, a subject could represent the situation by imagining that O sees him 'from the front', or has a 'face-on view' of him (Level 2). He could instead, however, simply represent the fact that 'O sees (that object called) his belt buckle' (Level 1, or at most, transitional between Level 1 and Level 2). In this latter case, the toy soldier becomes very like the cardboard used in the Masangkay *et al.* Picture task, but with a belt buckle rather than a cat 'depicted' on O's side. In fact, one of our own earlier tasks (Flavell *et al.*, 1968, pp. 167–9, Task IIIC Revised), which *clearly* calls for Level 1 rather than Level 2 knowledge, utilizes an object even more reminiscent of the Lewis and Fishbein soldier; namely, a cardboard *cube* (thus, like the soldier, *three*-dimensional) with a different object depicted on each of its four vertical faces, the subject's problem being to indicate, using a duplicate cube, which object O sees when situated on the opposite side of the cube. Of 10 five-year-olds tested on this problem, 6 responded perfectly, and unpublished data from a similar study has yielded comparable results (Dr. Justin Aronfreed, University of

Pennsylvania, personal communication). Similarly, one task used in the Lewis and Fishbein studies (Fishbein, Lewis and Keiffer, 1972; Lewis and Fishbein, 1969) actually required the child to display an object to O so that O would see *specific objects*, e.g., 'Show me the mouse so I can see the tail and the ball on his cap, but not his face' (p. 7). Four-year-olds did it with ease. As indicated earlier, the boundary between Level 1 and Level 2 knowledge is hard to define, despite the fact that there appear to be well marked differences between the clear cut, prototypical cases of each; this is a state of affairs, however, with which developmental psychologists are all too familiar.

Finally, there are data that may make the acquisition of some sort of Level 2 knowledge look still more precocious yet. The task in question (Flavell *et al.*, 1968, pp. 163–4, Task IIIA Revised) is to Level 2 what the Masangkay *et al.* Picture or Eye Position task is to Level 1, i.e., an *extremely* elementary but still genuine-looking measure of some form of the knowledge in question. After the necessary preliminaries (clarification of terminology, etc.), a full length picture of a man is placed on the table between S and O in a sideways position (so that both see the man lying down), and O asks S to show the picture to O so that O sees the man 'standing on his head'. Six out of 10 three-year-olds and 9 out of 10 five-year-olds displayed the picture in the correct orientation, i.e., upside down to O and rightside up to himself. In a recent replication, Marvin (1971) obtained almost identical results with a group of three-year-olds (7 out of 14 responded correctly), although none of his 14 two-year-olds seemed able to cope with the task. It is hard to be sure that this task demands no knowledge whatever of perspective—that it could be negotiated on a purely Level 1 basis (e.g., by S deciding that O needs to be shown the 'head side' of the picture?). Whether the apparent ease with which children this young manage this particular task should be regarded as evidence against our postulated Level 1—Level 2 developmental sequence must remain an open question at the present time. However, it should at least make us chary about claiming, in a generalized, task-independent way, that children of such and such an age 'know nothing of perspectives', are 'wholly incapable of imagining another's point of view', etc., a point that is well supported by the results of the Fishbein et al. (1972) study. The dependence of the child's apparent level of cognitive maturity on the specific properties of the tasks presented to him is also, sad to say, a state of affairs with which developmental psychologists are all too familiar.

In most would-be measures of Level 1 knowledge, the child's task is to infer, on one basis or another, that O currently sees some real object that he himself does not. The Masangkay et al. Picture and Eye Movement tasks were of this kind. Flavell et al.'s (1968, chap. 5) tasks IIIC, IIIC Revised, IIID, and IIIE were essentially variations on (predecessors of) the Picture task. Some of these seem to have been just about as easy as the Picture task (IIIC, IIID), while others were clearly more difficult (IIIC Revised, IIIE). One of the least demanding Level 1 type problems, undoubtedly, is that where the child himself is free to provide O with some new visual input rather than being constrained to identify the input O already has. Task IIIA Revised would constitute just such a problem if only a *particular* O view of the main were not required, i.e., if all the subject had to do were to turn the card so that the picture side faced O—turned it so O could 'see the man', orientation ignored. My best guess is that *all* of our three-year-olds (Flavell et al., 1968, pp. 161–4) could do *that* much; the data reported in the two Lewis and Fishbein papers and my colleague's observation of his daughter's doll manipulations also suggest the extreme precocity of this sort of behavior. This ability to reorient pictures or objects 'in order to' (insofar as we can determine) make them visually available to others is the only one of several primitive, Level 1 or Level 1-like skills, the early development of which would be well worth plotting.

IV. *Some Research Problems*

A number of suggestions have already been made (Flavell et al., 1968, pp. 216–26) concerning researchable problems in this area, and there is no need to reiterate those here. I would, however, like to underscore a very general suggestion alluded to at the beginning of this paper, namely, that those of us interested in the ontogenesis of interpersonal inference dispositions and skills would do well to pay more attention than we typically have to the sorts of models the social psychologist has made of the end products of this onto-genesis, i.e., the inferential dispositions and skills characteristic of adults. The logic of such a research strategy is easy to see, and the strategy itself is of course very generally applicable within the field of psychological development:

Our conception of the development of anything is always partly determined by our conception of what that something is like in the mature organism. For example, when we changed our ideas about the basic nature of adult language behavior, with the advent of the Chomskyan revolution in linguistics, we also had to change our ideas about the basic nature of language development (Flavell, 1971c, p. 272).

In the words of the generative grammarian, any developmental study in this area would be scientifically 'well motivated' to the extent that it incorporated some clear and detailed vision of just what the development in question was proceeding towards.

One research topic that merits more attention than it has so far received is that of the trainability of social-inferential and related abilities. Earlier studies by Fry (1966, 1969; see also Flavell *et al.*, 1968, pp. 191–206) had been largely unsuccessful in demonstrating significant training effects on the communicative behavior of fifth-graders, i.e., making that behavior more responsive to the listener's specific informational needs. In contrast, Shantz and Wilson (1972) have recently had considerable success by modifying Fry's training procedures and applying them to second- rather than fifth-graders. It remains to be seen whether subsequent training efforts involving communicative and other social-inference-related skills will sustain the optimism generated by her findings. It should be mentioned that good training studies could also serve a useful developmental-diagnostic function here. That is, training procedures may alternately be conceived as experimental techniques for uncovering (eliciting, 'awakening') a subject's newly developed and largely still latent capacities—his basic, underlying 'competence', in a sense. We might be inclined to think, for instance, that a child must have already (i.e., pre-experimentally) developed *something* in the way of *Existence* knowledge and *Inference* skill if, unlike some other child, a brief program of instruction, behavior shaping, or whatever leads him to display what looks like genuine social inference. In short, what a child can readily learn to do in this area may tell us something useful about what he has already learned.

There are a number of interesting research prospects in the area of percept attribution. With respect to Level 3 phenomena, for example, one possibility would be to try to find out how and when children begin to take projective (retinal) size into account when depicting another's view of an array of objects.[2]

In the domain of Level 2 functioning, there are a number of putative subacquisitions described by Piaget and others that have never really been systematically investigated in themselves. One is the ability to identify or recognize a two-dimensional representation (e.g., a drawing) not of *O*'s, but merely of *S*'s *own* current view of one or more objects. Another is the knowledge that any given *S* or *O* position vis-à-vis an object array defines one and only one view (appearance) of it. Both of these sound like extremely fundamental subcomponents of *Existence* and *Inference* knowledge at Level 2 as contrasted with Level 1, and it would be worth finding out when in development they can first be demonstrated, using very sensitive, low-performance-demands task situations.[3]

[2] I can imagine, for instance, doing a developmental study with an experimental set up of the following kind. *S* and *O* are seated at different points around a very large table upon which are placed two or three identical objects (e.g., balls or blocks). Unlike Piaget's three mountains, the objects are widely dispersed across the table, thereby making for large differences in their relative retinal sizes when viewed from any perspective. *S*'s task is to reproduce their exact appearance as seen by *O* (and also on some trials, by *S* himself) by means of a device that permits him freely to manipulate their apparent sizes as well as their apparent positions and distances with respect to one another. For example, the device might display images of the objects on a screen that can easily be increased or decreased in size, as well as moved around, by means of a set of controls that the child learns to manipulate.

[3] On this latter point, 'live' videotape or moving picture representations of *S*'s or *O*'s visual input would surely constitute more ecologically valid test stimuli for *S* than the customary, 'dead' drawings or still photographs. One could also throw in some camera movement here to simulate *O*'s head movements while looking at the display, and even some movement in the display itself. Some of the child's difficulties in identifying or reproducing perspective representations may stem from the particular kinds of representa-

There is also much to learn at Level 1 and at its interface with Level 2. It would be instructive to know when, for instance, the child first becomes aware of the fact that, although both tiny X and large O are clearly visible to him and although there is no vision-blocking object interposed between the two, O may still not be able to see X because it is simply to far away from him (i.e., O)—thus, a kind of Level 1 counterpart of Level 3 sensitivity to retinal versus real size. Indeed, we really have no systematic research data concerning his growing knowledge about the phenomenon of vision-blocking interposition itself (cf. Piaget and Inhelder, 1956, chap. 7). An object may, in a sense, block O's view of its *own* parts or sub-objects, as when the opacity of a piece of cardboard prevents one from seeing object X depicted on its opposite side (e.g., the Masangkay *et al.* Picture task). I wonder how children of different ages would respond to the repeated question, 'What does O see now?' if such a cardboard were slowly rotated around its vertical axis, so that O first sees X broadside, then in increasingly fore-shortened, slantwise perspective, and then not at all as the cardboard finally moves through its edge-on position. An unambiguously Level 1 child should dichotomize the results of this transformation (at any point in time, O either sees X or he does not), but a child in transition to Level 2 might trichotomize it (e.g., 'good' versus 'bad' seeings of X, in addition to outright nonseeings), or even come to some intimation of the meaning of 'X as seen from a certain point of view' versus just 'X as seen'.[4]

tional media the experimenter has made available to him. As a matter of fact, videotaped representations of viewpoints might make very effective train-ing and task-instruction vehicles in this area, as well as perhaps affording more sensitive measures of S's current Level 2 knowledge. So far as I know, they have not yet been used for any of these purposes.

[4] As for the more typical case where the obscuring object and the obscured object are spatially discontinuous, one can imagine a class of tasks of the following kind. A small object X (the obscured object) is free to move around a circular track, in the center of which stands a rectangular board Y (the obscuring object). O views the board broadside, his head rigidly fixed in position by some kind of movement-restraining device; under these cir-cumstances, the board blocks his view of X over a range of X positions. S is seated at various positions, e.g., broadside to the opposite face of the board (opposite O), or in either of the two side-view positions with respect to it. S's task would be to make the usual Level 1 judgement (i.e. whether O does or

Finally, there are of course perceptual processes other than the visual, and the child must at some point come to impute these to other people. For instance, we presently know nothing at all concerning the developmental acquisition of inferences about O's listening activities and hearing experiences. When does the child first understand the true function of whispering, for instance? Informal observation suggests that very young children may playfully whisper, often in imitation of others, but we do not know if they yet comprehend its effect on others. Is there any meaningful counterpart to our Level 1-Level 2 distinction in the area of audition (or in that of touch, taste, or smell, for that matter): simply hearing or not hearing X, versus hearing it at different loudnesses, as coming from different directions, etc.? I believe that questions and problems like these concerning the ontogenesis of inferences about other people are well worth posing, and also that most of them could probably be answered with the experimental techniques and know how currently at our disposal.

V. *Summary*

This paper describes some recent ideas and research findings on the developmental aspects of social cognition, in particular the child's growing ability and disposition to endow others with thoughts, feelings, motives, percepts, and other inner-psychological properties. The bulk of the paper is given over to the presentation and dis-

does not see X) for given positions of S and X. By complicating this set up only slightly it might even be possible to tape Level 1, Level 2, and transitional-to-Level-2 thinking in one and the same task situation. If X were a meaningful, Fishbein *et al.* (1972) type object, such as a doll, and if it could rotate around its own vertical axis as well as move around the circular track, the child could be asked the following sequences of questions:

(1) Does O see X (a Level 1 question)?

(2) If so, what *part* of X or how *much* of X does he see (e.g., only a 'subobject' such as an outstretched arm—and thus perhaps transitional between Level 1 and Level 2)?

(3) Finally, what *view* of X does he see (e.g., the full-face view—a more clear cut Level 2 problem)?

Potentially fruitful variations on our earlier task IIIE (Flavell *et al.*, 1968, pp. 170–2) can also be imagined.

cussion of two crude, qualitative models of some important phenomena in this area. The first is essentially an information processing,
flow chart type characterization of four general classes of knowledge
or ability that may be brought into play when making inferences
about another individual's inner properties. According to this
characterization, the subject must know that the other individual
might conceivably possess a given property (*Existence*), be aware
that some inferential or other information-gathering activity regarding the existence and nature of that property in the other is called
for by the present situation (*Needs*), be able then actually to carry
out that cognitive activity (*Inference*), and be capable of using the
resulting information about the other as a means to some
situationally-appropriate interpersonal end (*Application*).

The other model is restricted to one specific type of interpersonal-
inference ability, namely, the ability to represent and predict the
visual acts and experiences of another person, based upon whatever
cues are available (e.g., the orientation of various objects with
respect to his line of sight). The model postulates four major levels
of development of this ability: no genuinely symbolic-representational, as contrasted with purely practical or sensory-motor, knowledge of the fact that others have visual experiences (Level 0); the
ability to represent the fact that others do see objects (Level 1); the
ability to represent the added fact that others see these objects in
various perspectives, that is, see particular qualitatively-describable
views of them (Level 2); just a further elaboration of Level 2,
really, the ability to represent with fair quantitative precision
another's retinal, painter's-eye image of a visual display, complete
with attempts to reproduce projective rather than real sizes (Level
3). Developmental studies were cited throughout to illustrate the
various components of the two models, and the paper concludes
with a brief description of some further research possibilities in the
area.

REFERENCES

Baldwin, A. L., Baldwin, C. P., Hilton, I. R. and Lambert, N. W., The measurement of social expectations and their development in children, *Monographs of the Society for Research in Child Development*, 1969, *34* (4), Serial No. 128.

Borke, H., Interpersonal perception of young children, *Developmental Psychology*, 1971, *5*, 263-9.

Brainerd, C. J. and Allen, T. W., Experimental inductions of the conservation of 'first-order' quantitative invariants, *Psychological Bulletin*, 1971, *75*, 128-44.

Cazden, C., Environmental assistance to the child's acquisition of grammar, unpublished doctoral dissertation, Harvard University, 1965.

Cline, V. B., Interpersonal perception. In B. A. Maher (editor), *Progress in experimental personality research*, Vol. 1, Academic Press, New York, 1964, pp. 221-84).

DeVries, R., The development of role-taking as reflected by the behavior of bright, average, and retarded children in a social guessing game, *Child Development*, 1970, *41*, 759-70.

Dodwell, P. C., Children's understanding of spatial concepts, *Canadian Journal of Psychology*, 1963, *17*, 141-61.

Ervin-Tripp, S. M., Sociolinguistics, in L. Berkowitz (editor), *Advances in experimental social psychology*, Vol. 4, Academic Press, New York, 1969, pp. 91-165.

Feffer, M., A developmental analysis of interpersonal behavior, *Psychological Review*, 1970, *77*, 197-214.

Feffer, M. H. and Gourevitch, V., Cognitive aspects of role taking in children, *Journal of Personality*, 1960, *28*, 383-96.

Fillenbaum, S., Psycholinguistics, *Annual Review of Psychology*, 1971, *22*, 251-308.

Fishbein, H. D., Lewis, S. and Keiffer, K., Children's understanding of social relations: co-ordination of perspectives, *Developmental Psychology*, 1972, *7*, 21-33.

Flavell, J. H., *The developmental psychology of Jean Piaget*, Van Nostrand, Princeton, N.J., 1963.

Flavell, J. H., Role-taking and communication skills in children, *Young Children*, 1966, *21*, 164-77.

Flavell, J. H., Concept development. In P. H. Mussen (editor), *Car-*

michael's manual of child psychology, Vol. 1, Wiley, New York, 1970, pp. 983–1059. (a)

Flavell, J. H., Developmental studies of mediated memory. In H. W. Reese and L. P. Lipsitt (editors), *Advances in child development and behavior*, Vol. 5, Academic Press, New York, 1970, pp. 182–211. (b)

Flavell, J. H., An analysis of cognitive-developmental sequences, *Genetic Psychology Monographs*, 1972, 86, 279–350.

Flavell, J. H., Stage-related properties of cognitive development, *Cognitive Psychology*, 1971, 2, 421–453. (a)

Flavell, J. H., Discussant's comments for the 1971 SRCD Symposium: What is memory development the development of? *Human Development*, 1971, 14, 272–8. (b)

Flavell, J. H., Botkin, P. T., Fry, C. L., Wright, J. W. and Jarivis, P. E., *The development of role-taking and communication skills in children*, Wiley, New York, 1968.

Flavell, J. H. and Wohlwill, J. F., Formal and functional aspects of cognitive development. In D. Elkind and J. H. Flavell (editors), *Studies in cognitive development: essays in honor of Jean Piaget*, Oxford University Press, New York, 1969, pp. 67–120.

Fry, C. L., Training children to communicate to listeners, *Child Development*, 1966, 37, 675–85.

Fry, C. L., Training children to communicate with listeners who have varying listener requirements, *Journal of Genetic Psychology*, 1969, 114, 153–66.

Glucksberg, S. and Krauss, R. M., What do people say after they have learned to talk? Studies of the development of referential communication, *Merrill-Palmer Quarterly*, 1967, 13, 309–16.

Hastorf, A. H., Schneider, D. J. and Polefka, J., *Person Perception*, Addison-Wesley, Reading, Mass., 1970.

Hegion, A. G., Role playing and communication: a developmental study. Unpublished doctoral dissertation, University of Minnesota, 1969.

Heider, F., *The psychology of interpersonal relations*, Wiley, New York, 1958.

Hymes, D., On communicative competence, Unpublished paper, University of Pennsyvania, 1970.

Izard, C. E., *The face of emotion*, Appleton-Century-Crofts, New York, 1971.

Jones, E. E. and Davis, K. E., From acts to dispositions: the attribution process in person perception, in L. Berkowitz (editor), *Advances in experimental social psychology*, Vol. 2, Academic Press, New York, pp. 220–66.

Jones, E. E. and Gerard, H. B., *Foundations of social psychology*, Wiley, New York, 1967.

Kelley, H. H., Attribution theory in social psychology, *Nebraska Symposium on Motivation*, 1967, *15*, 192–238.

Kerckhoff, A. C., Early antecedents of role-taking and role-playing ability, *Merril-Palmer Quarterly*, 1969, *15*, 229–47.

Kingsley, P., Relationship between egocentrism and children's communication. Paper read at the Meetings of The Society for Research in Child Development, Minneapolis, April, 1971.

Kohlberg, L., Stage and sequence: the cognitive-developmental approach to socialization. In D. A. Goslin, (editor), *Handbook of socialization theory and research*, Rand McNally, New York, 1969, pp. 347–480.

Krauss, R. M. and Glucksberg, S., The development of communication: competence as a function of age, *Child Development*, 1969, *40*, 255–66.

Laurendeau, M. and Pinard, A. *Development of the concept of space in the child*, International Universities Press, New York, 1970.

Laubengayer, N. C., The effects of training on the spatial egocentrism of preschoolers. Unpublished master's thesis, University of Minnesota, 1965.

Lewis, S. and Fishbein, H. D., Space perception in children: a disconfirmation of Piaget's developmental hypothesis. Paper presented at Psychonomic Society Meetings, St. Louis, November, 1969.

Lovell, K., A follow-up study of some aspects of the work of Piaget and Inhelder on the child's conception of space, *British Journal of Educational Psychology*, 1959, *29*, 104–17.

Marvin, R. S., Attachment- and communicative-behavior in two, three, and four-year-old children. Unpublished doctoral dissertation, University of Chicago, 1971.

Masangkay, Z. S., Feenstra, H. J. and Tayag, A. H., Co-ordination of perspectives among Filipino children. Occasional Paper No. 10, Language Study Center, Philippine Normal College, Manilla, Philippines D–406, 1971.

Masangkay, Z. S., McCluskey, K. A., Sims-Knight, J. and Flavell, J. H., The early development of inferences about the visual percepts of others. Unpublished paper.

Mehrabian, A. and Reed, H., Some determinants of communication accuracy. *Psychological Bulletin*, 1968, *70*, 365–81.

Meyer, A. J., The developmental study of three manifestations of consciousness. Unpublished doctoral dissertation, University of California (Berkeley), 1971.

Miller, P. H., Kessel, F. S. and Flavell, J. H., Thinking about people thinking about people thinking about . . .: a study of social cognitive development, *Child Development*, 1970, *41*, 613–23.

Moore, O. K., Problem solving and the perception of persons. In R. Tagiuri and L. Petrullo (editors), *Person perception and interpersonal behavior*, Stanford University Press, Stanford, 1958, pp. 131–50.

Neale, J. M., Egocentrism in institutionalized and noninstitutionalized children, *Child Development*, 1966, *37*, 97–101.

Peterson, C. L.,, Danner, F. W., and Flavell, J. H., Developmental changes in children's responses to three indications of communicative failure, *Child Development*, 1972, 43, 1463–68.

Piaget, J., *The language and thought of the child*, Harcourt, Brace, New York, 1926.

Piaget, J., *Judgment and reasoning in the child*, Harcourt, Brace, New York, 1928.

Piaget, J., *The construction of reality in the child*, Basic Books, New York, 1954.

Piaget, J. and Inhelder, B., *The child's conception of space*, Routledge and Kegan Paul, London, 1956.

Pick, H. L., Jr. and Pick, A. D., Sensory and perceptual development, in P. H. Mussen (editor), *Carmichael's manual of child psychology*, Vol. 1, Wiley, New York, 1970, pp. 773–847.

Rothenberg, B. B., Children's social sensitivity and the relationship to interpersonal competence, intrapersonal comfort, and intellectual level. *Developmental Psychology*, 1970, *2*, 335–50.

Sarbin, T. R., Taft, R. and Bailey, D. E., *Clinical inference and cognitive theory*, Holt, Rinehart and Winston, New York, 1960.

Savitsky, J. C. and Izard, C. E. Developmental changes in the use of emotion cues in a concept-formation task, *Developmental Psychology*, 1970, *3*, 350–7.

Scarlett, H. H., Press, A. N. and Crockett, W. H., Children's descriptions of peers: a Wernerian developmental analysis, *Child Development*, 1971, *42*, 439–53.

Shantz, C. U. and Watson, J. S., Assessment of spatial egocentrism through expectancy violation, *Psychonomic Science*, 1970, *18*(2), 93–4.

Shantz, C. U. and Watson, J. S., Spatial abilities and spatial egocentrism in the young child, *Child Development*, 1971, *42*, 171–181.

Shantz, C. U. and Wilson, K. E., Training communication skills in young children, *Child Development*, 1972, *43*, 693–8.

Slobin, D. I. (editor), *A field manual for cross-cultural study of the acquisition of communicative competence*, University of California, Berkeley, 1967 (mimeo).

Sullivan, E. V. and Hunt, D. E., Interpersonal and objective decentering as a function of age and social class, *Journal of Genetic Psychology*, 1967, *110*, 199–210.

Tagiuri, R., Person perception, in C. Lindzey and E. Aronson (editors), *The handbook of social psychology*, Vol. 3, Addison-Wesley, Reading, Mass., 1969, pp. 395–449.

The Development and Attribution of Person Concepts

PAUL F. SECORD and
BARBARA HOLLANDS PEEVERS

During recent years a spate of research and theorizing on the attribution to other persons of traits, motives, intentions, and the like has appeared. While the groundwork for this development was begun in Heider's 1944 paper and elaborated at length in his 1958 book, a burst of interest in this phenomenon has appeared only recently. Thus, the many questions raised so far are just beginning to receive initial answers, and much remains to be done before we have extensive conceptual clarity and firm conclusions.

Most of the work on this topic has focused upon attributes connected with a single episode enacted by another person who is a stranger, with special attention to the immediate conditions that influence the form of attribution. Also, most of the research has been conducted on adults. In such research, judgments of strangers (often represented hypothetically) are made without the rich context of knowledge that has accrued for people we know. While this type of research is invaluable for identifying the effects of various conditions on single judgments of the acts of persons, it cannot reveal how our conceptions of other persons are organized, how they fare over time, and how they differ depending upon the developmental level of the observer.

We wish to focus on attribution in a much broader sense. We would like to know how people are conceptualized as individuals. How are they represented verbally? What properties are they given? How does the conception of them relate to the setting in which they are known, and how does it relate to the observer? Attribution research concerned with the judgment or interpretation of specific acts has also occasionally dealt with judgments of oneself. So here, too, it would seem useful to obtain descriptions of oneself as well as of other persons. At least one question that we might ask is whether we attribute the same kinds of characteristics to ourselves that we attribute to other persons, and whether we do it in the same way.

Before raising more questions about attribution, however, we must first ask some more basic ones concerning the nature of the person and the self. What are persons, considered as entities in the world of the individual? For the adult observer, persons are a complex construction of meaning. For the young child, however, his notions of the specific parts of his world are at first fuzzy and vague, and the parts confused with one another. Only gradually does he identify some entities in his world as separate wholes, capable of being considered apart from their surroundings (Werner, 1948).

Objects that move are undoubtedly first to be differentiated. And among the objects that move, those that are alive are likely to receive the lion's share of the child's attention. Live objects not only move, but often make sounds, and sometimes do things to the child. So, in a visual sense at least, human organisms are differentiated very early. They are certainly among the first entities in the child's world to be perceived as discrete. But this is only a first step. Seeing the human organism as a visual entity is a long way from seeing a person. A person fully conceived is a *constructed entity*, having rich meanings for the observer. It is our purpose here to discover some of the basic characteristics of this construction.

We should not assume that the acts of the other person are at first attributed to him or even clearly recognized as acts. Perhaps initially, they are only vaguely associated with the other person and inseparable from the situation as well. Both the attribution of the act to an entity eventually to be characterized as a person, and the separation of the act from the situation are differentiations that are probably only gradually learned by the child. We take an approach here similar to that of Heider (1958). Events are separately identifiable, and the individual constructs his view of the other person. We assume that there is an orderly process by which he does this, a process of which he is mostly unaware. An alternative view is stressed by some phenomenologists, who argue that we have immediate access to other persons's minds. While it may be true that the individual often intuitively grasps the mood or other attributes of a person, and cannot report how he does this, we assume that there is a process to be explained and mechanisms to be identified.

As Heider notes, we are ordinarily interested in the core properties of our environment. We relate primarily to its stable features because they allow us to live in a predictable world. This is true of other persons as well as objects. If what we have said so far is correct, however, the child must only gradually discover or invent the more stable, enduring characteristics of other persons. It follows that the kind of attributes used by children of various ages should be different. At an early age, attributes should be confused with the setting or situation, and less clearly associated with the individual as a person. When older, the child should identify qualities of acts associated with the person alone, independently of the situation, and be able to label those qualities.

Let us continue to think through the process by which the child might eventually arrive at a construction of the concept of a person. One way in which live objects differ from inanimate ones is that they perform actions. And in the child's world, certainly humans are the most active entities. Moreover, many of the actions of the humans closest to the child have important effects or consequences for him. Their actions enable the infant to eat and to get rid of discomforts. Before long, other humans are a source of comfort, satisfaction, and even amusement and enjoyment.

Such actions of others experienced by the young child are the initial source of meanings that persons have for him. In most cases, the mother is undoubtedly the first person in his young life having the richest and most intense meaning. The crying infant stops at the mother's approach, even before she reaches him to relieve his distress. Most babies clearly express happiness and satisfaction during many activities involving the mother. Later, as the young child begins to play and move about, bumps and other painful experiences are quickly soothed by the mother's comforting actions. The mother is the most constant feature of a varying set of experiences and as such is apt to be the most salient feature of the child's world.

The child has quite different experiences with other humans. While some family members might occasionally serve as mother surrogates, and behave in somewhat the same way towards him, other members treat him quite differently. A brother or sister may take his toys away, push him down, scold him. As he grows older, and is able to play in the neighborhood with other children, he learns of new potentialities in other humans.

So far our account has been vastly oversimplified. We have primarily discussed effects or consequences of the performances of other humans for the young child as a source of meaning. But another factor enters in at a very early age. The child soon discovers that he can enrich his experience of his world by investigating it. Just as he pushes, throws, drops and otherwise manipulates objects, he also learns how to modify the effects or consequences that people have on him. Even the infant soon learns that a loud cry will bring his mother to his side, and that sometimes he can obtain things he wants by such techniques. The older child develops a larger repertoire for influencing the actions of other persons. So a part of the child's knowledge of persons comes from active involvement with them.

But this runs ahead of the story somewhat. Before a child can make real progress in influencing other persons, he has to acquire certain basic understandings. Engaging in interaction with another person has certain prerequisites. The child has to be able to anticipate how an act of his will lead to the act of another toward him. He may learn, for example, that if he pushes another child down, he may get pushed back. Or the result may be an uproar from the victim, which in turn arouses the wrath of the victim's mother. So the act of pushing acquires a meaning, woven from the various experiences connected with his act of pushing. In a sense, this meaning is a set of anticipations that pertain to what might follow his act of pushing. And this is a rudimentary kind of knowledge of other persons.

Ultimately, as his experience multiplies, his knowledge of other persons becomes vastly more sophisticated. Perhaps through knowing that he can have a clear goal in mind, such as obtaining a certain toy in the play area, he becomes aware of the intentionality of other persons. Other children often have intentions like his own. Through competition with them, he may be made rudely aware of their intentions. And he learns to discriminate intentional actions from unintentional ones. He learns of the closely related concept of responsibility—the idea that another person may or may not be responsible for a certain act. He learns to see persons as origins of acts (Heider, 1958).

Perhaps most important to his developing idea of a person as a somewhat stable entity in his world is his realization that other persons behave in predictable ways. They can be thought of as following rules. A rule is a specification of a series of actions performed under certain circumstances or in certain situations to achieve a particular act. And ultimately he learns to make discriminations among various situations and to anticipate how persons he knows will behave in those situations. He even learns some generic rules concerning the acts of people in general in certain identifiable situations.

In sum, in a very real sense the child's conception of other persons is constructed from his experience with them. The richer his experience, the more complex his conceptions should be. And the balance of happy versus unhappy experiences should be reflected in the affective quality of his view of other persons: are they to be loved or feared? His conceptions of persons should be roughly commensurate with his age, if we assume that certain sets of experiences are common to children of a similar age. Other vital factors contributing to his knowledge of persons are his family experiences and his social class and ethnic background. Moreover, the style of life characterizing the society in which he lives pervades his view of persons.

Just as the child's concept of a person is construed only gradually, his view of himself emerges gradually from his experiences. Initially this is apt to involve immediate sensations and acts, and is apt to lack continuity. Only with time and much experience does the individual eventually identify at least some properties of a relatively stable nature associated with himself. Both self as object and self as agent are relevant here. Neither of these aspects of self can be clearly developed in infancy. Self as a responsible agent, with intentions, aims, and purposes can only emerge later. We may ask, also, what is the relation between these two aspects of self—usually they are treated as quite independent of each other. Perhaps self descriptions can tell us whether this treatment is warranted or not.

Recent research on attribution to self and other, reviewed by Jones and Nisbett (1971), suggests that individuals attribute their own actions largely to situational conditions, while they attribute the same actions performed by another person to his stable personal dispositions. For example, if an actor is performing a series of tasks, he attributes variations in his performance to differences in task difficulty. But when he sees the same tasks performed by other persons, he attributes the variations to their abilities. Jones and Nisbett point out that the actor has much more information about his emotional state and his intentions than an observer does. Moreover, while he has knowledge of his personal history, the observer may not. This difference in information may partly account for the different attributions of actor and observer. But not only is there a difference in the information they possess. Different bits of information are salient for each of them. The actor is looking outward toward the environment in enacting his performance; the observer is focusing on the actor with the situation as background.

We should emphasize that the research supporting these views rests largely upon experimental situations where the person observed is a stranger, and the sequence of actions covers a very narrow time span. Observer and observed are partners in a scientific experiment having a certain social structure which in turn has effects upon the forms that attribution takes. We can ask whether these ideas about the attributions of an actor observing himself and an observer viewing another person will also hold when the person observed is someone well known to the actor, and when the actor is asked to describe himself as a person. If we are more likely to attribute stable, core dispositions to other persons than to ourselves, then this propensity should be reflected not only in judgments of

We turn now to an analysis of some actual descriptions of discrete actions, but also in the two forms of descriptions.

persons, to see what bearing they might have upon the ideas we have presented.

Descriptions of Persons

In obtaining descriptions of people, we used an interview situation, allowing participants to freely describe other people and themselves in their own terms. The interview was designed with a minimum of structure, to maximize the freedom of an observer in describing another person. Individuals were interviewed privately. After naming three friends and one disliked person, the respondent was asked to tell what each of the named persons was like. Use of the word describe was avoided, because of the tendency of this word occasionally to elicit physical descriptions. When the description of a person appeared to be completed, the interviewer asked, 'Is there anything about him that you don't like?' Also, before going on to the next person, the interviewer asked the respondent if there was anything more that he wished to say about that person. At the end, he was asked to tell about himself. The interviewer remained as noncommital as possible throughout the interview, responding, 'I see', and 'yes' to the participant's remarks.

The descriptions were tape recorded and transcribed. In the basic study, published elsewhere (Peevers and Secord, 1973), we obtained descriptions from 80 individuals, ranging from young children to adults. At each of five grade levels, eight boys and eight girls described three friends, a disliked person, and themselves. The grade levels were kindergarten, third-grade, seventh-grade, eleventh-grade and college.

Having obtained such data, there are a number of approaches to analyzing and interpreting them. Two of these were used here. First a systematic coding system which achieved quantification of the elements of the description was developed. This was analogous to the type of coding used for open-end interviews in survey research. Second, the descriptions were carefully studied to uncover their general qualitative structure and characteristics, and to find qualitative changes that emerged at different ages.

The analysis of the descriptive material by means of a coded content analysis has been reported on in detail elsewhere (Peevers and Secord, 1973). The present paper will briefly present some of this material, and in addition will deal with some qualitative impressions formed from these data, as well as with an analysis of the self concept.

One of the primary ways in which the interview protocols were found to vary with age was in terms of a quality we have called *descriptiveness*. Descriptiveness refers to the amount of information an item yields about a person as a unique individual. Some items are totally unrevealing, such as mention of the house in which a person lives, or the statement that one has known him for a long time. Other items may convey considerable information about an individual, such as 'he's very active in school politics', or 'she is very shy and quiet when she is with boys'. Other items fall in between these two extremes. Essentially descriptiveness is a measure of the extent to which the observer differentiates the observed person from the observer himself or from the situation or setting in which he is known. In line with our previous discussion, we would expect descriptiveness to sharpen with age.

We have identified four classes of descriptive items: undifferentiating, simple differentiating, differentiating, and dispositional. The frequency of occurrence of these four classes of items is shown in Figure 1. Undifferentiating items are the least commonly occurring of the four classes, and they show the least increase from one grade level to another. They include possession and location items (e.g., his house has a basement; she lives up the street); family and friend items (e.g., she is a friend of Sally's; she has a nice mother). Although infrequently occurring as a whole, they occur proportionately more at the youngest age studied, and proportionately less at the college level. Thus, occasionally a child at the kindergarten level was apparently unable either to describe a person at all, or to characterize him only in terms of items that say nothing about him.

Most children at this age, however, have progressed to the point where they differentiate the person as a distinct individual. While they do not use sophisticated concepts in describing him, they often successfully separate him from his possessions or social setting. Commonly they use simple differentiating items. The person is differentiated as an individual, but is described in terms of simple

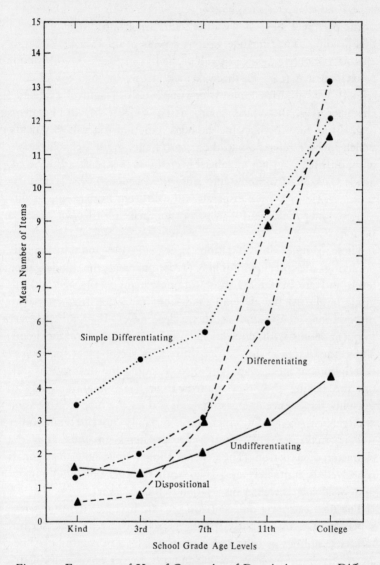

Figure 1. Frequency of Use of Categories of Descriptiveness at Different
Age-Grade Levels

superficial characteristics, global judgments, or his gross relationship to the perceiver. Several classes of items are grouped together under this heading. They include various aspects of appearance or bodily characteristics (e.g., she has red hair, he has a squeaky voice); simple behavioral acts (e.g., he threw a rock at me, she had to stay after school); global dispositions which have only a general evaluative character (e.g., he's nice, good, nasty, weird); like-dislike items (e.g., I like him, he likes me, he bugs me); and role category items, which include references to the person's age, grade, school, nationality, birthplace, group membership, religion (e.g., he's a Boy Scout, he's a Catholic, I've know him since kindergarten). While all these sub-categories are quite disparate, they do seem to share the quality of providing only fairly gross or nominal information about a person.

These simple differentiating items are the most commonly occurring class of items. They predominate at the kindergarten level, and are by far the most common items at the 3rd and 7th grade levels. At the eleventh grade they share top frequency with dispositional items, and at the college level, they remain very frequent along with dispositional items and differentiating items. Thus they appear to be an important component of person descriptions at all age levels studied. Reading the descriptions, one has the feeling that they contribute in some important way to grasping the essence of a person. This is the same type of impression one gets when reading literature; certainly novelists and other writers make use of these kinds of items in presenting the character of a person. These items suggest that how a person is conceived is intimately associated with that person's environment and social role as well as his relation to the observer.

The next category, differentiating items, are those which describe a person in terms of fairly specific personal characteristics, such as interests, abilities or beliefs, or temporary states or conditions. They are relatively informative and distinguish the person as a distinctive individual. They include interests, likes, and activities (e.g., he likes to hunt arrowheads, he smokes, he wants to be a lawyer); ability items (e.g., she's intelligent, he gets straight As, he's not a good athlete); beliefs, values, and experience (e.g., he's a conscientious objector, she has lived a lot, she is liberal politically); and feelings and reactions (e.g., he feels insecure, she's worried about school, she's very unhappy right now).

These differentiating items are less common at the kindergarten, third, and seventh-grade level. Their use increases sharply at the eleventh grade, and at the college level they occur more frequently than any other kind of item. The frequent use of these items provides substance for descriptions of persons, for their prime ingredient is either actions or interest in lines of action. They help to convey an impression that a real person is being described, and this is in large part due to the action component of the descriptions. Action here is less concrete and specific than with young children, and refers to an integrated, focused, complex activity.

The fourth category, dispositional items, describes the person in terms of traits which have implications for his behavior in a wide range of situations. They are apparently the most sophisticated form of description. At the kindergarten and third-grade level, they occur less frequently than any other class of descriptive item. Their use at the seventh-grade level is moderate, but in the eleventh grade and college level they are used about as frequently as differentiating items. In other words, this class of descriptive item shows a greater change from the kindergarten to the college level than any of the other three descriptive categories.

In view of the popularity among psychologists of trait words as descriptive terms, we should note here that in these lay descriptions, other classes of descriptive items are equally favored or more favored than trait words. Below the third grade trait words are little used. On the seventh-grade level, simple differentiating items are almost twice as frequent. At the eleventh-grade level, simple differentiating items are as frequent as trait words, these two classes of items being most favored. At the college level, simple differentiating, differentiating, and dispositional items are used with approximately equal frequency. Thus, it would be a great mistake to assume that dispositional items are the best or most appropriate manner of describing a person. The burden of proving this position rests with the psychologist.

We noted in our introduction that differentiation would be likely to take place in connection with effects on the child that are memorable—events that are dramatic in some way: painful or exhilarating. It appears that early use of dispositional items, our most differentiated concept, is facilitated in just this way. The use of dispositional items appears most clearly in describing *disliked* peers, where dispositional items account for 15 per cent of the items used by kindergarten children, and rise to 31 per cent for third-graders. This contrasts with descriptions of *liked* peers, in which use of dispositional items rises quite slowly with increasing age. This suggests the possibility that children frequently dislike peers because of some specific and striking pattern of behavior, such as 'bullying' or 'acting smart'. Liked peers, on the other hand, do not possess such obvious qualities, and are described in terms of other categories.

Another important aspect of the descriptions of people is *personal involvement*. Personal involvement refers to the frame of reference an individual adopts in describing others: that is, the degree to which he involves himself in the descriptive item. Three classes of involvement have been distinguished, as follows:

1. *Egocentric* items are those in which another person is described in subjective, self-oriented terms. Most descriptions in which 'I' or 'me' are used are of this type.

2. *Mutual* items are those in which another person is described in terms of his relationship to the perceiver. Descriptions of this type are often characterized by the use of 'we' or 'us'.

3. *Other-oriented* descriptions are those in which no personal involvement is expressed.

The concept of personal involvement in the descriptions of other people is suggested in part by the work of Piaget. The age levels chosen for study in this research were selected to represent approximately Piaget's stages. That is, kindergarten pupils are in the intuitive phase of the pre-operational period, in which ego-centricity predominates. Third-graders have entered the stage of concrete operations, in which egocentricity diminishes and reciprocity increases. Seventh-graders are acquiring the stage of formal operations or mature thought processes, and high school and college students represent more advancements in this stage.

Three excerpts from interviews which illustrate use of the categories of personal involvements follow.

1. A kindergarten boy makes predominant use of egocentric items in the following person descriptions.

Well, he kind of scares me—he has a monster act. He's such a silly boy. And his mom teaches me piano lessons. He rides bikes with me, but his bike is bigger than mine. (Interviewer: 'Is there anything about him that you don't like especially?') He talks mean words to me, and sometimes he's mean to me, and that's all.

2. A seventh-grade boy uses a preponderance of mutual items in the following description:

We're both about the same at sports. We both like sports, which really helps getting along, because if I go out and play some sport he can always come along with me and play the same opposite. He's a comedian—I say something, he can go along—same thing about him— he can go back and say something. I think we kinda mix together. I was supposed to go to a track meet with him today and run—we were going to form a relay team.

3. An eleventh-grade girl makes total use of other-oriented items in the following description:

She's quiet and shy and she doesn't like to talk too much. She's really intelligent, especially in languages and English—she catches on really quickly. She's unathletic and likes to read. She's the romantic type who likes all the Victorian novels—you know, sitting in castles and having people row up and play songs under the window. And that's what she is like.

Figure 2 summarizes results for the dimension of personal involvement. Its most dramatic feature is a rise in use of the other-oriented category with increasing age. While this is the most frequently used category at all age levels, it reaches overwhelming proportions of use at the high school and college level. Undoubtedly, this reflects the increasing ability of older boys and girls to adopt an impersonal stance in describing other persons. At the same time, it is worth noting that some egocentric and some mutual items appear at all age levels.

I

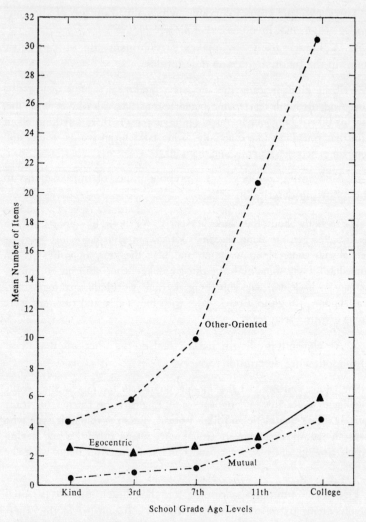

Figure 2. Frequency of Use of Categories of Personal Involvement at
Different Age-Grade Levels

Also apparent from Figure 2 is the fact that the *proportion* of items categorized as egocentric is greatest for kindergarten children, and drops off with increasing age, primarily due to the sharp rise in other-oriented items. Liked peers and disliked peers were also compared. As might be expected, egocentric items were used more frequently in connection with disliked peers than with liked peers, while mutual and other-oriented items were used more in describing liked than disliked peers. This was true for college students as well as for kindergarten pupils.

The high level of egocentricity among kindergarten children and the high frequency of use of simple differentiating items suggests that this kind of cognitive performance may well be a necessary stage in learning to attribute qualities and actions to persons. Very plausible is that what emerges first is the establishment of relations between young children in terms of feelings, feelings that are highly egocentric, and along with these, broad, global impressions and role category knowledge of peers. Only gradually out of these amorphous feelings and impressions do sharper, more differentiated person concepts develop. This sequence of conceptual development would be consistent with the ideas of both Jean Piaget and George Herbert Mead.

Another important aspect of the interview protocols is *depth*. Depth cuts across the descriptiveness categories. Depth involves the degree to which personal characteristics are recognized as conditional upon certain situational, temporal, or internal states. We think of use of the deeper levels as requiring more insightfulness or sophistication in knowing and evaluating other persons.

Depth level 1 includes all of those descriptive items characterized as undifferentiating or simple differentiating. These are items describing a person in terms of his possessions, social setting, superficial characteristics, or global judgments. These items cannot be used at the deeper levels. Depth level 1 also includes simple attributions of an interest, ability, belief, or disposition. In other words, descriptive items of these kinds which are unqualified or unembellished also are categorized as depth level 1. Differentiating or dispositional items, however, can be used in a deeper way.

We have depth level 2 when differentiating or dispositional items involve one or more of the following uses:

1. A discussion of a person's opposing or contradictory characteristics. Examples are: he is sometimes amusing, sometimes annoying; he's opposed to war, yet would join the Reserve.

2. A specification of conditions under which a characteristic is present. Examples are: when he gets drunk he doesn't care about anyone; when he is with older people, he acts very immature.

3. An account of a first impression which was later proved inaccurate. Examples are: until you get to know her, you really don't see these qualities; you think she's tough because of her hard exterior, but when you get to know her you find out that she's very sensitive.

4. Finally: a reference to a persons' trying or not trying to do something. Examples are: he's trying to bring his grades up; it doesn't seem as though she tries at all.

Depth level 3 items are those differentiating and dispositional items in which an *explanation* is offered for a characteristic. The explanation must provide some additional information about the person in the form of a reason for having a characteristic. Examples are: because he is black he is very defensive; she's a snob because she's trying to hide something about herself. Those items require the observer to assume what Jones and Thibaut (1958) have termed a 'casual-genetic' set. The observer is oriented toward explanation rather than, say, evaluation ('I like him.').

The use of depth items is relatively infrequent, but yet is associated with grade level in a rather striking way. Depth levels 2 and 3 do not appear at all at the kindergarten and third-grade levels, and only 2 per cent of the seventh-grade items are depth level 2 items. At the high school and college level 6 and 7 per cent of the items, respectively, are depth level 2. Depth level 3 appears for the *first time* at the high school level, with 2 per cent of the items, and at the college level, 4 per cent. In spite of their relatively infrequent use, this association with age suggests that depth level items require considerable development in the use of person concepts. That the absolute frequency of depth items is low is not of great importance, since it could probably be considerably increased by using an interview structure that encouraged the use of depth items and tested the limits of their use.

Use of Person Concepts to Describe Self

The present section examines the concepts used with a view to discovering their use at various age levels and, in particular, developing a perspective on the nature of the self concept at different ages.

Emergence of a reflective view of self. Even a cursory examination of the protocols indicates that at the lowest age-grade level, kindergarten, a view of self is either absent or of the most rudimentary nature. The question, 'Now tell me what *you* are like', drew a total blank in a few instances. These children stated that they don't know about themselves or cannot tell what they are like —though they have at least said something about what their playmates are like. For them, there appeared to be no reflective process. They did not seem to have developed a perspective from which they can view themselves.

Those kindergarten children who did respond primarily described their play activities, some of them reporting only a few simple forms of play, and then reporting that they were unable to say anything more about themselves. The prominence of play activities in their lives appeared to be mirrored in their rudimentary view of self—they are *merely beings who play*. These self descriptions are relatively parallel to descriptions of peers given at this age, which also consist primarily of play activities. In reporting on self, however, there were more undifferentiating items than there were for peers—items mentioning possessions or family setting. Apparently kindergarten children are more able to differentiate peers from their family and possessions than they are to differentiate self from their own family and possessions: a peer emerges before the self as an individual distinct from the surrounding environment.

For some individuals at all age levels there is some hesitation in talking about themselves. In only a minority of instances does this appear to be a function of embarrassment or unwillingness to report on oneself. Instead, some individuals appear to have a perspective on themselves that is less developed than their perspective on other persons. While they are able to report fully and at length on peers, they seem not to have formulated as complete a view of themselves.

At the next age level, third grade, most of the children had developed a reflective view of themselves. Although their self descriptions predominantly reported play activities and interests—a somewhat broader term for recreational activities that are not exactly play (e.g. reading)—other elements appeared in individual cases. Several children referred to their performance in school—an evaluative perspective on self. One boy showed a future perspective in expressing his aspiration to become a doctor. Another referred to his weird-shaped face, an evaluative term.

Girls at this level mentioned much less their play activities, instead emphasizing their appearance and their relations with friends and family. They commented on whether they were liked by their friends, whether they get angry, and how they behaved toward or felt about members of their family.

Appearance. The use of appearance items in self descriptions represents a rather striking age phenomenon which becomes prominent at the third-grade level, but remains in the background at all of the other grade levels. This is especially dramatic for girls. For girls at the third-grade level, 21 per cent of the items pertained to appearance; at the eleventh-grade level, 2 per cent, with 0 per cent at the remaining levels. For boys at the third-grade level, only 4 per cent of the items pertained to appearance; at the eleventh-grade level, 6 per cent; with 1 per cent or less at remaining levels. Differences in references to appearance are even more striking than these percentages suggest, since they are accounted for by heavy use of appearance items by some children, with others not using them. Thus, it appears that at or about the age of nine years, girls are acutely aware of their appearance and indeed think of it as a prominent part of self in a reflective sense. Later, appearance items almost disappear from the self concept of girls. Boys show a more moderate emphasis on appearance at both the ages of nine and seventeen years, with virtually no attention to it at the other ages studied.

We must suppose that a girl's experiences and activities are such that by the age of nine years, she has been made sharply aware of her appearance by the reactions of other persons—perhaps her parents and other children. In the seventh grade, references to appearance almost disappear from the self descriptions, suggesting that there is less emphasis placed upon appearance at this age. Presumably a similar but less marked phenomenon has taken place for boys, but at two ages, nine and seventeen.

Use of evaluative terms. At the seventh-grade level, evaluative terms and the use of an evaluative context with respect to the self appear with some frequency. For example, evaluative trait terms appear: lazy, selfish, honest, shy. There is also some evaluation of one's activities. One boy said that he was interested in sports—and that sports are important for a boy. Several boys and girls referred to their emotionality in a negative context: saying that they have a temper, get really mad. At the eleventh-grade level, evaluation became still more prominent. Much of the description was occupied with evaluation, evaluation that is less tied to specific activities. Boys spoke of themselves and other persons as having a good personality, as nice guys, as short-tempered. Their self description included direct evaluative discussion, as , for example, of their school perform-ance. Girls similarly emphasized evaluative terms but, except for school performance, focused on different aspects of self from boys. They referred frequently to shyness, not being nice to people, and getting into bad moods. These appeared to reflect the undesirable side of aspects of self that are emphasized in our society as appro-priate for females.

From specific to general. In a number of spheres, the various age levels showed movement from the specific to the general. Kinder-garten children talked about very specific play activities or other behaviors, such as 'I play on my swings' of 'I play with my trucks'. They sometimes mentioned not liking a specific person—their sister or a playmate. With increasing age, attitudes had more general and more abstract subjects. They said, for example, that they liked to be active, to have a lot of things to do. Or that they liked people, or doing things with their hands.

Time perspective. Later ages revealed a distinct broadening of time perspective. While younger children were almost always in the immediate present, older ones referred to the way they were in the past or to how they might be in the future. Besides references to career aspirations, which did appear occasionally at early ages, references to various changes in oneself appeared from the eleventh grade on. We get the impression that individuals are capable of seeing themselves in terms of a life career, extending both backwards and forward, and ever broadening as the individual grows older. Examples are:

And I am shy—I really am. I'm really basically really shy. But I'm starting to get out more and more since my brother came home . . . well, I am 17 but sometimes I like to get out my old paper dolls and try the clothes on the dolls and take out my Barbie doll clothes and look at them. And sometimes I just wish that I could go back, you know— sometimes. But also I think that so many nice things have happened to me since I've gotten older—now I can drive, things like that.

Like even in high school and things like that I was never in the 'in' crowd or anything like that. I was just—I don't know. I had a lot of friends, but . . . Then when I came to the campus, I don't know why, but I just didn't associate with the kids I went to high school with, for almost a year. And in that period my hair grew, and I don't know— I think a lot of the kids I went to high school with were afraid of me. They figure, you know, 'what happened to him? Boy, he took the wrong route'. Then I ran for office and I was elected, which was really strange cause nobody with long hair had ever been—you can imagine the campus—it's a very conservative campus. And so, I was elected, and I just fell in. Like the girls in the sororities who hadn't spoken to me for a year said, 'Hi, Bill, how is it going?' It really shook me up— cause it was just like all of a sudden I was 'in'—I was the thing.

Phenomenal self. By the eleventh grade there were clear and direct references to self in a phenomenal sense—the individual reported himself observing himself in a direct way:

I saw myself back in high school—just like I could sit back and watch myself go to school.

I'm always anticipating—most of the time I'm anticipating good things, but when it comes to other people I find that I tend to—other people or myself—I tend to anticipate bad things. I am afraid of being —I think I am more afraid than most people—of getting involved and getting hurt.

Well, I am trying to be, and therefore I am, if you see what I mean —the fact that I am trying means something. I'm a person who is trying to live life deeply, at the moment, and I want to try to continue this.

I was always so shy with boys—you know, if a boy looked at me, and I saw him looking at me, I thought, it was an insult because I thought he was looking at me—or making fun of me—usually I thought he was making fun of me, you know—look at that funny-looking girl—but after I had some self confidence—when one did look at me I took it as a compliment.

Self-presentation. Also appearing at the eleventh grade was an awareness of presenting oneself to other persons in a particular way. Some examples are:

Like girls interested in clothes—this is something I'm not really the most interested in ... I'd rather go around in a pair of Levis and a sweatshirt—I'm that type of person.
I dress nice, I don't try to look like a crumb.
I don't like people to take me for something I'm not—a lot of times people will take me for being a conservative and it bothers me, but usually I can set them straight before too long.

Moral judgments about self. At the high school and college level, moral judgments about self become common. These are somewhat more specific than the more general category of evaluation, discussed previously. Moral judgments refer to what the individual thinks he *should* do, or they characterize his behaviour as *right* or *wrong*. These occur most often in connection with aspirations for the future, with problems of self control, with achievement of some ideal self. For example:

But I still think that I consider popularity too important—above other things more than I should.

I try to be honest with people, but I don't like to hurt their feelings. And I don't like people who talk about other people behind their backs because its—they wouldn't like it if they were talked about, and I don't think it's right.

Self as agent and self-direction. Perhaps the most striking characteristic of the protocols of high school and college students is the direct glimpse they provide of individuals actively reflecting about themselves, their activities, and their prospects. Many of the descriptions depict agents poised for action. The respondents tell what they are thinking about. Typically, they talk about possible careers, about their achievements or failures in school, about their relation to their girl friends or their parents. They do this in a context of considering alternative forms of action or relations and evaluate the alternatives. There is a kind of projection of activities —self as an agent enacting various scenes, rather than a being with qualities. These lines of action are evaluated, rejected or accepted, perhaps as a goal. They also talk about problems of self-control, for example, of their tempers. There is a very real sense of self direction, as illustrated in the following examples:

I can talk myself into being mad, very easily—if someone has done something to hurt me, or something. And I still—well, like my boy friend, for instance—we went together for quite a while, and then he kind of let me down, and rather than pine away, I talked myself into not liking him. I mean, I like him, you know, but I could never go out with him. And I kind of talked myself into that.

Or:

Like in school if I don't like a subject I won't do anything in the subject—like foreign language—I think that was my lowest grade last year. And I just hated the subject so I didn't do any homework—I never studied for anything—I just went through it with the bare minimum of what I could get through it with. And on the other hand, the subjects I do like—my science and mathematics—I really work and I get fairly—very high grades, as a matter of fact, in science and better than average grades in math. And same in swimming—I'm a perfectionist if I see something wrong with either my own stroke or someone I'm teaching I'll try to correct that. It's just a matter of habit—and pride in what I'm doing—*if* I'm interested in it. If I'm not interested in it than I can forget it just completely.

In connection with self as agent there was much discussion of one's motives. One individual talked, for example, about his self-control, including control of his whims and his temper. Another spoke of work schedules and routines and doing things well, of pushing himself. Another spoke of wanting to do everything—and rattled off a list of several occupations and leisure-time activities. A girl said that the thing she really wants to do is to meet people, but that she's afraid to meet people. Girls often mentioned their efforts to be popular, to be accepted, or to have many friends.

It is commonplace among behavioral scientists to treat the self as an object, often a static one. Self as ego or agent is sharply distinguished from self as object, and separately treated. Selves are reported by means of rating scale profiles or adjective checklists, as if these constituted an accurate representation of a person. This view of self, however, suffers from the fact that the *organization* of the self concept has never been adequately depicted and supported empirically. The present findings suggest that the self as object and self as agent are inextricably entangled. Moreover, when the self is treated as ongoing process, the self as agent appears to be the focal source of organization. What is seen in these protocols is the individual coping with one or more aspects of his life. He reports on his capabilities and other resources for dealing with the problem, and he reports on how well or how poorly he is doing. He also reports on the lines of action he prefers to engage in but which are not problematic. Thus, self-in-process is the most apt term for characterizing these descriptive protocols.

Sex differences. A number of differences appeared between boys and girls in the development of person concepts. Girls in the third grade were more aware than boys of physical aspects of other persons and themselves. They frequently mentioned eye color, hair color, and other aspects of appearance.

At the seventh-grade level, girls emphasized much more than boys trying to behave in particular ways, trying to be a certain kind of person. Mention was made of trying to be friendly, trying to be nice to people, and trying to overcome faults, like a temper or laziness. This appears to be a reflection of the difference in the characteristic socialization of boys and of girls in our society—the tendency to over-socialize girls. At later grade levels, this appeared in the form of a greater concern with self-direction, with aspirations for self, with alternative modes of action and their consequences.

High school and college girls also differed from boys in the greater stress they placed on interpersonal relations. Their descriptions of self and others emphasized being friendly, being liked. There was much discussion of shyness, of having the right emotions with respect to other persons. Their greater sophistication in this respect also appeared in the attention they gave to self presentation. They spoke of putting on an act, telling stories for effect, of being melodramatic, of putting up a front, of trying to be natural, or of brooding—building something up until it became a disaster. Some girls were aware of a protectiveness, of a guarded quality to their relations—they felt that they did not really allow other persons to know them.

These differences between boys and girls and young men and women appear to be a direct reflection of the different life styles of males and females in our society. Older boys and men are oriented toward a lifetime of work and achievement. The women's liberation movement notwithstanding, for girls and women, work is apt to be a temporary or part-time activity, but their interpersonal relations are a prominent part of their life, in such respects as finding a husband and relating to him, and in raising children—in maintaining the interpersonal aspects of family life. These features of life for the two sexes are directly reflected in what they emphasized in their descriptions of themselves and other persons.

Self vs. other persons. If the descriptions are examined over the entire age range, the congruence in the descriptions of self and of other persons given by the same child is readily apparent. The developmental level of the child was reflected both in his description of his peers and of himself. At the same time, this congruence was not just a function of developmental level. Within the same grade level, some children were more advanced than others in the concepts they used, and where this was the case, these concepts were applied both to self and other.

There is, however, a major way in which the orientation to self differs from the orientation to peers. This was reflected in a marked quantitative difference in the use of the four descriptive categories for self and other. Only about one-fifth of the items fell in the dispositional category, and there was little difference in frequency of use in describing *oneself* and describing *peers*, except for college students, who did use appreciably more dispositional items in describing peers. But the use of 'dispositional' in our coding system is restricted primarily to trait terms; in its broader sense, dispositional includes the category we call 'differentiating'.

And we find that in describing *oneself*, approximately half of the descriptive items fell in the category *differentiating*—interests, abilities, beliefs, values. Less than one-quarter of the descriptive items fell in each of the remaining three categories. But in describing *peers*, the most frequent category of item was simple *differentiating*—superficial characteristics, global judgments, gross relations to the observer, or role categories. Only one-quarter of the items describing other persons fell into the differentiating category. Thus, it seems that the findings reported from research on attribution to persons performing specific acts do not hold for more general descriptions of people. Such research reported that in interpreting *specific acts* of their own, actors attribute their behavior to situational circumstances. But in observing specific acts of others, they attribute their behavior to dispositions. In the current research on *describing* oneself and others, however, stable characteristics were attributed to self at least as commonly as to peers—half of the time attributions were of abilities, interests, beliefs, and values. But the most frequently used category for describing peers involved situational material, such as relations to the observer, or role categories. So *description* yields almost a reverse situation from that of interpretation of specific acts.

These differences also appear to reflect different orientations toward describing other persons and describing oneself. Descriptions of self reflected a more subjective, phenomenal attitude. The differentiating items characteristic of self description were predominantly likes and interests, although at the older grade levels, beliefs, values, experience, feelings, and reactions contributed substantially to the frequency of use of the differentiating category. These items had a relatively personal, subjective quality and thus reflected a different orientation toward the description of self as compared with the description of persons. This conclusion is further supported by qualitative findings emphasizing evaluative terms, time perspective, moral judgments, and especially self-direction when describing self but not other persons.

Finally, while it may be true that we *can* have intensive knowledge of the subjective experiences of another person, this research shows that we pay much less attention to such experiences of others, as compared with our own, when we attempt to characterize ourselves and others. This empirical finding appears to argue against the behaviorist view that the self concept is formed by exactly the same process as our concepts of other persons.

REFERENCES

Flavell, John H., *The Developmental Psychology of Jean Piaget*, Van Nostrand, Princeton, N.J., 1963.

Heider, Fritz, Social Perception and phenomenal causality. *Psychological Review*, 1944, 51, 358–374.

Heider, Fritz, *The Psychology of Interpersonal Relations*, Wiley, New York, 1958.

Jones, E. E. and Nisbett, R. E. *The actor and the observer: Divergent perceptions of the causes of behavior*. New York, General Learning Press, 1971.

Jones, Edward E. and Thibaut, John W., Interaction goals as bases of inference in interpersonal perception. In R. Tagiuri and L. Petrullo (editors), *Person Perception and Interpersonal Behavior*, Stanford University Press, Stanford, California, 1958.

Mead, George H., *Mind, Self, and Society*, University of Chicago Press, Chicago, 1934.

Peevers, Barbara Hollands and Secord, Paul F., Developmental changes in attribution of descriptive concepts to persons, *Journal of Personality and Social Psychology*, 1973, 26, No. 3.

Werner, Heinz, *The Comparative Psychology of Mental Development*, Follett, Chicago, 1948.

Some Remarks on 'Rule' as a Scientific Concept

R. HARRÉ

Underlying Theme

The activities of a playwright offer a better model for a social scientist to follow than does the work of physicists (cf. Burke, (1969). At least a playwright has the authenticity of his recreation of social reality checked every night in the theatre by a multitude of people. Intuitively he has profound knowledge of the principles of social behaviour.

The underlying assumption of this paper is that there are no natural forces in men that lead automatically to the formation of a society when two or three hang around together. Human social behavior I believe to be an essentially cultural phenomenon, the intellectual response of an intelligent, self-aware species to the problems of living posed to them by the peculiarities of their biology and of their environment on earth. The method by which human beings manage their affairs, and create society, is by the invention and promulgation of rules, in the following of which social behavior is generated. The substance of this paper will be an account of how social behavior, generated in this way, can be the subject of scientific study.

Or putting the matter another way: if we adopt the concepts of 'rule' and 'rule-following' as our major conceptual tools for the analysis of human social behavior, what sort of picture of social life do we get, what sort of a science of social life would follow their adoption? And what sort of psychological processes and cognitive structures would be required for the genesis of socially meaningful actions?

Clearly the general use of the rule concept for the description and explanation of regularities in people's social behavior needs some justification. Detailed support for the use of the concept will emerge in the course of the paper, but at this point it will be well to anticipate some of the argument in setting out briefly the reasons for the adoption of this way of looking at social life.

It must be conceded that a good deal of social behavior is not produced by deliberately following explicit rules. Many of the regularities in social behavior, such as the rituals of thanks, the control of conversation, the expression of status hierarchy, have more of the character of social habits. This concept is not itself strong enough for scientific purposes since it does not direct one to the processes by which the habit is ingrained, maintained and changed. There are two possible but exclusive conceptual exegeses of the notion of social habit, each directing our attention to a different feature of human life. We could construe social habits as conditioned responses, in which case we move towards such paradigms of the production of action as post-hypnotic suggestion, or we could construe them as the product of deliberate rule-following, in which case we move towards such paradigms as the way someone manages to carry out a ceremony by deliberately doing what it says in the written rules.

Choosing to view social habits as the final product of deliberate rule-following involves at least these matters:

1. The social habit is seen as the final automatization of a process which is originally under conscious control, and which may become so again. Under this construal we are to look for the origins of social habits in such processes as paradigm imitation and the following of precepts, some of the motivation for which may be a rational appreciation by the child of the advantage of playing the game according to the given rules. Thus the *habit* of saying 'Thanks' is to be construed as the end result of deliberate rule-following which may be fostered by the rational appreciation by the child of the advantages of being 'good'.

2. On this model changing a social habit would require not reconditioning, but the making of the person aware of his habit, and getting him to see that there was another rule which could be followed to advantage in the situation. Thus a person may be made

aware of his tendency to talk about himself and his affairs, and may thereafter deliberately choose to follow the maxim that the presentation of an attractive personality requires at the least, the giving of mutual opportunities for egocentric talk.

3. From the conditions required for these applications of the rule notion and its consequences we can derive the possibility of an extremely important class of social actions, which I shall call 'proofs of autonomy'. The fact that a social habit was once the deliberate following of a rule, and may become so again, shows how it is possible for a social action to be monitored, and the process of which it is a part to be abrogated or aborted. This power I believe to be within the capability of anyone, and I can sympathize with the existentialists' feeling that upon it hinge the possibility of all our specifically human powers. It follows that the establishment of one's humanity can be most economically achieved by the aborting of some social habit, say a rule of manners. This accounts well I think for such phenomena as the deliberate cultivation of social brusqueness by Israelis, for the calculated use of obscene language by student revolutionaries and for many of the apparently irrational and perverse refusals of childhood. I would argue that the adoption of the rule following exegesis of the concept of social habit allows us to consider the possibility of a human being going in for a proof of autonomy with respect to *any* social habit. For instance when, after the protracted murder of his rival, Humbert Humbert begins to doubt his freedom to choose and control his course of action, and thus to doubt his essential humanity, he sets about a proof of autonomy by deliberately driving down the wrong side of the road.

4. Finally the choice of a rule-following rather than a conditioned response exegesis of the concept of social regularity opens up the possibility of the construction of a powerful set of analogies for constructing concepts and theories for those social habits whose origin, force and maintenance are, as we might say, enigmatic. A good part of the positive doctrine in this paper concerns the development of concepts and theories by the use of the analogy of the formal episode, the kind of episode in which there is a deliberate, conscious following of rules by the participants.

I shall take for granted that nothing is to be gained by assuming

K

that social behavior is the product of the running together of a complex of pre-social behaviours, and I shall assume throughout that it is a series of phenomena having independent status. Vygotsky's (1962) excellent proposal, that the fundamental element in psychological analysis should be a 'unit' which retains the same kind of meaning for people as that from which it has been analysed, yields, for socio-psychological phenomena, the concept of the 'episode' which is defined around the minimally meaningful social action. In the same spirit I make no use of the notion of a primitive human being. Socially speaking there are none living in the jungle. We owe the elimination of this idea from anthropology to Levi-Strauss (1966). Nor are socially simple beings forced into existence by the tactics of parameter deprivation used by 'experimental' psychologists in their 'laboratories'. I shall assume that all forms of social behaviour have roughly the same level of sophistication, and indeed that human beings are unable to perform in a socially unsophisticated way. Life in the social psychological 'laboratory' is as elaborate a form of life as found anywhere. Social psychologists who think they can succeed in decomposing it into parameters have been tragically deceived and the results of their 'experiments' are largely worthless, except as descriptions of the odd way people carry on in trying to make social sense of the impoverished environments of laboratories.

I propose to show how the concept of 'rule' can be used to form the basis of an explanatory system in micro-sociology and social psychology which is as much entitled to the title 'scientific' as are bacteriology or crystallography. I also intend to indicate, how, in the work of those sociologists and social psychologists who refused to be intimidated by postivism, the paradigm of method of such sciences as bacteriology is already fruitfully exemplified. This is particularly true, as I shall point out from time to time, of the work of Erving Goffman (1969a), which is truly scientific in a sense in which much of the 'laboratory' work of less gifted investigators is merely pseudo-science, based, as it has been, on outmoded positivistic ideas about what science is.

The development of an adequate system of explanatory concepts for human social behavior involves more than just a transition of method from positivist to realist science. It also involves, con-comitantly, the adoption of a conception of the nature of human beings appropriate to the realist methodological scheme. In such a conception the psychological processes 'within' a person by which he monitors and controls his socially meaningful actions must be admitted to a reality at one with that of the social action itself. We shall see that this is achieved by admitting language to its proper status as the indispensable and unique basis of the psychic com-munity of men. Psychology can be polarized around two packages which I shall call the old and the new paradigm. 'Old' and 'new' are used metaphorically in this context, in that the new paradigm is as old as Aristotle, and the old as near contemporary as Skinner.

The Old Paradigm

At the centre of this package is the idea that a human being be treated for scientific purposes as an automaton, responding to environmental contingencies, immediately or mediately. Empirical work has the form of the classical 'experiment', that is it seeks to discover the relations of dependent to independent variables, usually taken in functionally related pairs. The independent variable is identified as that 'controlling' the behavior. The variables are themselves the product of the analysis of the processes into para-meters. It is characteristic of this package that there is no role for conscious awareness in the generation of behavior, and the concept of 'meaning' is replaced throughout by a simplistic notion of cause, usually modelled on the regularity theory of Hume. A human being then is a mere spectator of the flow of causality in processes not amenable to his conscious control, and uninfluenced by his assignments of meaning. The working of this methodo-logical and theoretical package is very well exemplified in a recent study of social facilitation (Zajonc, 1965), the phenomenon in which the presence of another person affects the performance of a task. The one question never raised by the conductor of the study was what social meaning the actor gave to the presence of the other person. The query as to whether the actor perceived the other as

critic or as admiring audience, was not raised, even indirectly. And
of course it is obvious that whether the presence of the other leads to
inept fumbling and a decline in performance, or to the euphoric
efficiency that sometimes goes with showing off, may depend
critically on the exact assessment by the actor of the social meaning
of the presence of his audience.

The New Paradigm

In new paradigm studies a human being is treated as a person,
that is as a plan-making, self-monitoring agent, aware of goals,
and deliberately considering the best ways of achieving them.[1] In
this package empirical work has the form of the classical 'exploration', that is it seeks to identify the existing patterns in phenomena,
and looks for the pattern generators in the nature of the entities
involved. It is like anatomy or chemistry. In anatomy the structure
of living things is explored, and the explanation of the structures
which are revealed by exploration is sought in the genotype of the
species and in the evolutionary history which brought that genotype
into being. According to the new paradigm in psychology conscious
awareness plays an indispensable role in the generation of patterns of
behavior, since it is involved in the monitoring and control of
performance according to a plan, a special case of which is action
according to rule. I have proposed the word 'ethogenic' as a generic
adjective for new paradigm studies in the social field (Harré and
Secord, 1972).

Individual processes of the sort central to new paradigm
psychology are exemplified by the efforts people make to slim by
controlling their eating habits by following a diet chart, or by the
process of giving up smoking by following a certain recommended
regime, or by the learning and reciting of a speech with the help of
mnemonics, and so on. Social processes typical of the new paradigm
would be the deliberate control of one's behavior at a gathering by
reference to a known etiquette in deciding from moment to moment

[1] This idea has already been developed by philosophers, cf. R. S. Peters
(1958).

what to say and do, or the deliberate control of the style and content of one's contribution to a conversation, following some well known principle for making a good impression, such as the maxim that one should never talk about oneself, but encourage others to expand upon their interests.

The important idea of self-monitoring needs a little elaboration. To monitor a process is not only to be aware of that process but to make some sort of record of its various phases, even if it is only in 'note' form. The power of human beings to monitor their actions which forms an essential part of the new paradigm conception of the generation of behavior, is thus to be understood not only as a capability to be aware of the actions one is attempting and of their social meanings, but as the further power to become aware of that awareness. Only if this power exists are we able to keep some sort of record of what we did and how and why we did it, a record which can be referred to when a human actor is called upon to give an account of his actions in a context of justification.

The contrast between old and new paradigm psychology could be taken as a new form of the nature versus nurture controversy in the context of the origin and exercise of those human powers which are involved in the generation of patterns of social behavior. The old paradigm methods assume social behavior to be a complex of simple automatic responses, each individual stimulus-response pair within the complex, having a biological basis, or being the result of simple or operant conditioning. A typical example of the old paradigm at work is the assumption that one can dissect out of the complex process by which one person comes to like another a functional relationship between the frenquency with which an item, not necessarly having anything particularly to do with people, is presented, and the preference shown for that item. The idea that such studies bear any relevance to the generation of emotions, such as liking, must be based upon the further assumption that the complex process involving people will be a complex of such simple processes. The extraordinary hold such an idea can have over otherwise intelligent men can be explained, I believe, only by the fact that a methodological package has been accepted uncritically, whose paradigm of method is derived from the methods appropriate to the study of the mutual variations of parameters in simple physical processes such as the expansion of gases.

The new paradigm encourages the assumption that social interactions, and the emotional responses to people in society are the products of a learned culture, self-consciously self-administered. While the old paradigm embodies the idea that social life consists of the responses of automata, under the new paradigm it is recognized that while the material basis of social interaction may be biological necessities, such as eating, the tendency to which does have something in common with the responses of an automaton, these function in a social context only in so far as they are given social meaning. On this view it will be quite contingent whether a particular biological necessity has this or that social meaning, or indeed any social meaning at all. If it is social meanings, the way they are interrelated and the manner of their understanding, that social science studies, then their material basis is of only passing interest, and as far as the content of the science goes, serves merely as a source of examples.

The concept of 'rule' and the associated idea of 'social meaning' are precisely fitted to be central concepts of ethogenic, new paradigm studies in psychology, both individual and social. The new paradigm emphasizes the role of cognitive processes, such as deliberation, in the genesis of actions, and of conscious self-monitoring and self-control in the individual psychology of the actors involved in a social interaction, while through the mediation of language, it assumes an unbroken continuum between thought and action.

If, as it will turn out, reference to rules forms an essential part of these processes, then the notion bridges the gap between individual and social psychology, since it is involved both in the genesis of social action, in the conscious self-monitored rule-following of individuals, and in the justification of actions so generated by providing others with acceptable accounts in excuse, justification and explanation. Such accounts, from an ethogenic point of view, are to be treated as rudimentary theories to explain the social action, by elucidating the meaning of the action and emphasizing its connection with rule.

Furthermore, the notion of rule functions in the analytic process for the same reason. Using the notion of rule as an analytic concept for the content analysis of social justifications, we can form hypotheses as to the mode of generation of social action by a being who is capable of conscious self-monitoring even when, for one reason or another, the actor is too busy to be aware of his cognitive processes in detail.

This whole approach is in keeping with new methods of investigation in some branches of individual psychology, such as learning, memory and problem-solving, in which the conscious self-monitored cognitive processes such as the use of mnemonics, strategies, imaginative trial and error etc. are studied. In social matters, conscious self-monitoring must refer both to the perceptions of the systematic social expectations of others, and to the accepted code of the primary actors, that is to the rules.

The Genesis of Behavior

How then is human behavior generated, particularly that behavior that can be given meaning as social action? Is it a series of conditioned responses to the state of controlling variables? This idea is both factually false, and methodologically disastrous. We all know that in fact what happens in certain paradigm cases is something like this: people consider various alternative actions and examine their consequences by an imaginative rehearsal of episodes. In the light of this rehearsal and their intuitions about the propriety of each form the episode might take, a particular social action is chosen. The effects of the action are carefully monitored, and rapid modifications of the plan are usually made as the action of the episode unfolds. Gelder's work on the control of the perversions associated with fetishism, is particularly illuminating since the cognitive processes which lead to the commission of perverted actions are long drawn out and may take hours to complete. Gelder (Marks and Gelder, 1967) has shown that it is the process of imaginative rehearsal that is vital to the genesis of the action, since it was only by inhibiting the process at that stage that he was able to prevent perverted actions taking place. This discovery is quite revolutionary in its implications, since it affects our entire view of human action and the nature of the processes by which it is generated.

I shall suppose then that the archetypal or paradigm process by which social action is generated involves the imaginative preplaying of an episode in the course of which various possible patterns are envisaged and checked for their effects and their social propriety, and in the course of which they are related to rules or rule-surrogates such as already established paradigms of common episodes.

The Ethogenic Analysis of a Social Episode

A sequence of socially meaningful actions is to be regarded as a path amongst and through a network of nodal points, at each of which there are various possibilities of action apparently open. In an episode in which the actors are in full control of the actions they perform the alternatives are considered and the appropriate one chosen, or at least that which seems appropriate to the performance of the social acts to which the episode is directed. The action-possibilities being envisaged in the course of the cognitive process by which the actions of the episode are generated, are nearly always much richer than the behavioral sequence being produced, so that a good many possible actions in a situation of a given definition are discarded, and a good many opening moves aborted. For this reason alone, any theory which restricts itself to those behavioral concepts derived from the observation of overt behavior of the action is clearly inadequate, even if the action is properly understood in terms of its social meaning as an act. Only if a theory introduces hypothetical cognitive processes in analogy with the archetypal human way of generating action does it avoid the falsification of the process of action generation. Failure to heed this constraint upon model building is therefore bound to lead to unsatisfactory explanations.

The process by which choices are made at each node is to be regarded as a special case of the archetypal cognitive process by which action is generated.

Systematic sequences of choices may be achieved by reference at each point to a plan, that is to an anticipatory selection of paths at subsequent nodes whose existence social experience enables one to forecast. Pioneering theoretical work in this field has been done by Miller, Galanter and Pribram (1960), but I suspect that the need to proceed by the collection of the reports and accounts of participants in planned action sequences has discouraged the further empirical development of their ideas. Some hopeful signs are evident in some recent studies in learning and problem-solving where people have been asked to report the actual strategies, mnemonics and so on that figured in their imaginative work in finding a solution, etc.[2]

Plans may be particular, having a use for one occasion only, or they may be capable of use on more than one occasion. A plan of the latter sort which contains elements of a normative kind derived from the expectations one has of oneself and others, as it usually does in social interaction, is to be treated as a rule or system of rules, though this is not the only criterion by which rules are to be identified. On this view it is not just generality but having normative force that transforms a plan into a rule, in that the effect of the normative element is to introduce both the possibility that the rule may be broken, and to suggest the existence of something of the nature of a sanction for non-observance, even if it is only the disagreeable experience of private shame. Failure to carry out a plan is not logically connected with an attribution of blame to the deliquent planner.

The cognitive process which is supposed to generate action in accordance with a rule plays a considerable part in the ethogenic account. We claim both that it is amenable to self-monitoring in certain cases, and where it is not, serves as the basis for hypotheses about unobserved cognitive processes, functionally equivalent to whatever processes and mechanisms are actually generating the behavior. Choosing this cognitive process as the source of a model of the unknown generative processes of sequences of action whose planning was not monitored, lends the extra dimension of scientific

---

[2] For medieval studies of remembering, cf. Yates (1966).

plausibility to the imagined model. Without the control of plausibility, there are, in principle, infinitely many functionally equivalent processes.

Most important from the point of view of its empirical application it is capable of public replication in the use of scenarios in exploring the intuitions of social actors, particularly in the study of the methods and criteria of choice amongst alternative possible scenarios on the basis of views as to the propriety of social actions. In this way the cognitive process of the generation of the actions of an episode, the stage for which has been set by a certain definition of the social meanings of the situation, can be explored empirically.

In one application of the scenario method people are asked to give their views on the propriety or impropriety of certain courses of action in defined situations, in short to comment upon the scenario of an episode. This is exactly the process which in imaginative and reflective form an ethogenist would claim to be an essential part of the main generative process in social action. To provide an account is to provide a scenario which is meant to be convincing and to show the propriety of the action which is being accounted for. The method of scenarios is the exact complement of the collection and analysis of accounts and can, I believe, perform the very same scientific function, in giving clues as to the paradigms of correct social action, and the rules according to which various actions and action sequences are decided upon. The method of scenarios has been in unsystematic use for some time, without, I am inclined to suppose, its full significance being understood. It has been greatly illuminated recently by Mixon (1971), who has expressed very succinctly the complementary relationship between the consideration of a scenario and the construction of an account.

As a very simple example of an ethogenic exploration exploiting this technique I would like to describe the method of an as yet unpublished study by Argyle. The subject of study was the proper distance for two people to sit, inclined at 45° to each other. There is an audience whose intuitions of social propriety are to be called upon, in an effort to discover the rule. The social meaning of the situation is first defined. The actors are a man and a woman, and they are described as colleagues in a research project, having no intimate relationships outside the project. The man is the director of the project and the woman one of the assistants. Previous accounts by social actors suggest that knee to knee contact is improper in the situation, and so is separation by twenty feet. Four scenarios are constructed. In the first a professional conversation takes place with knee to knee contact, then the same conversation at two feet separation, then at four, and finally at twelve feet distance. The audience is required to rate the four episodes, acted out in front of them, as to social propriety. This is clearly an 'exploration' and not an 'experiment', as I have defined those terms in discussing the old and new paradigms. The distance apart of the actors is not an independent variable. Rather each new distance is a Vygotskean 'unit', a meaningful social episode, which exists as a whole, and whose propriety as a whole is being considered and judged by the audience.

It will therefore be necessary to go into the structure and phenomenology of the archetypal cognitive process in some detail, since it follows from the above considerations that one of the most important roles knowledge of this process plays is as a source of models for the unknown processes by which action is generated when people are not fully monitoring their reasons for choosing. An understanding of the structure of this process will then play a crucial part in the possibility of applying the classical realist schema of scientific explanation in the study of social phenomena, and of testing one's hypotheses by the scenario method.

The Phenomenology of Action Generation

The following seem to me to be the important elements of the most specific and conscious form of the process, from the preliminary monitoring of my own cognitive processes and from the accounts of others.

1. The first step is the recognition of a situation as falling under a certain definition, that is the reading of its social meaning. This is complicated by the fact that situations do not have social meaning in themselves in the way they have say colour or position, so that

this stage of the process may involve the imposition of a particular social meaning by one or more of the actors, thus defining the social character of the situation by fiat. It has been pointed out that the resolution of disagreement or uncertainty as to what the social situation is may be an essential element in the beginning of social action, and may itself be an episode with a conventional structure of interest to a psychologist. Simmons and McCall (1966) have emphasized how deep this may go since not only is the social meaning to be defined but in defining it the identities of the inter-actors may come up for negotiation, and each kind of social situation demands an appropriate mode of the presentation of self, the production of an appropriate social persona.

2. By the definition of the situation possible actions, with their social meanings, come to be understood as parts of well-defined social episodes.

3. In the most self-conscious form of this process there is an imagined rehearsal of each possible episode together with a rehearsal of the excuses and justifications to be put before a critical audience whose reactions one imagines. It is in the preparation of excuses and justification that rules and rule-surrogates enter the process. I shall call this process 'rehearsal in the Theatre of the Imagination'. For such cognitive processes to be possible there must exist certain cognitive structures. Examination of stages 1, 2 and 3 suggest that there are four kinds of element involved in the cognitive structure. These will be the situational definition (S), the appropriate social identity or 'persona' (P), the idea of the person or persons who will be the chief arbiters of the propriety of socially meaningful actions in the situation (J), and the set of rules, principles and maxims operative therein (R). There will be an ensemble of sets of these elements available to each biological individual. The cognitive structure can be schematized as follows:

$$S_1 - P_1 - J_1 - (R_1)$$
$$S_2 - P_2 - J_2 - (R_2)$$
$$- - - - - - - - - - - -$$
$$S_n - P_n - J_n - (R_n)$$

For a small child one might imagine the matrix beginning with

S_1 = home,	P_1 = home persona,	J_1 = mother,	= (R_1) = family habits
S_2 = school-room,	P_2 = school-room persona,	J_2 = teacher,	(R_2) = school-room rules and customs
S_3 = play,	P_3 = peer group persona, etc.,	J_3 = social arbiter in the peer group	(R_3) = social customs in the peer group

This cognitive structure seems to be very highly formalized and explicit amongst the Japanese, being reflected even in the forms of language, there being different grammar and vocabulary appropriate to each of five well defined social situations.

The origin and development of such cognitive structures is a task for an ethogenically oriented developmental psychologist. There are some hints in Piaget (1932) and Kohlberg (1964), but there is clearly a need for a more structured approach, for instance amongst children the situational differentiation of formulas of request, demand, appreciation, greeting, etc. have not been studied, so far as I know.

It is worth emphasizing that we make no assumptions about overall consistency of the ensemble of sets of elements available to each person. Our moral tradition demands consistency but the example of the Japanese, who make no such demand, suggests that there will, in practice, be considerable falling off from this ideal. 'Cognitive consistency' theories in social psychology seem to us to make an *a priori* assumption of consistency for which there seems to be little empirical warrant. We would suggest that at best consistency is something to be established empirically, and not something that can be assumed *a priori*. In the terminology of Peters' paper (this volume), $P_1 \ldots P_n$ would be 'personalities' and the whole ensemble, 'character'.

4. In the final stage of the process intuitions of social propriety, which in their most explicit and verbal form make reference to the formulated rules that are the substance of excuses and justifications, lead to the rejection of certain episode schemata, and hence of certain action possibilities. The one finally settled upon may with propriety be identified with what philosophers call one's intention.

5. Eventually action follows. Now I am myself very much aware of a peculiar feature of this fifth stage which I admit to be baffling. The passage through Stages 1 to 4 is easily monitored. But I am quite unable to monitor the passage from Stages 1 through 4 to Stage 5. It is this fact, which I believe to be a general feature of human experience, which has led philosophers to crowd in on this transition, swarming about it with a variety of theories about the logical or other relations between decision, intention and action. There are those who maintain that intention and action are logically distinct since they are capable of being separately referred to, while there are those who maintain that they are logically inseparable since a certain behavior can only be identified and properly described as being a certain action by reference to the intention of the actor in performing it.

I do not believe that empirical studies, either introspective or behavioral are likely to cast any further light on the relation between the imaginative preparation for action and action itself. It seems to me naive to maintain that the relation is causal, since it is clear that those are in the right who claim like Miss Anscombe (1957) that actions are only fully identifiable as of a certain kind by reference to how the actor meant them. Perhaps the answer lies in some sophisticated version of the theory that action is in the last analysis a form of thought, in much the way that Vygotsky conceived of speech. This is clearly a part of the province of philosophy, since what is at issue is not a matter of fact but the best choice of concepts under which to subsume the phenomenon.

While our invincible unawareness of the process of transition from Stages 1 through 4 to Stage 5 requires the services of philosophy, the fact that we are often unaware of some or all of Stages 1 to 4 calls for scientific remedy. It is just the situation in which to apply the full realist paradigm of scientific explanation.

Incompleteness of awareness can be got around in much the same way as the limits of resolution of the microscope are circumvented, namely by using what we already know of the things, structures and processes in the field to construct models of that which we cannot examine. In this case the phenomenology of the specific form of the archetypal cognitive process serves as a source of models of the cognitive processes of actors too involved in the action to be fully self-aware. The most powerful form of such a model is none other than the use of scenarios to simulate the imaginative rehearsal of episodes and to bring out intuitions of social propriety in the justificatory accounts that one can ask from the participators under each imagined choice of path.

The investigative process begins with the collection of accounts, or in the case of young children, with the monitoring of what Piaget called 'egocentric speech', more correctly identified by Vygotsky with commentary upon imaginative action rehearsal and the making of plans together with trials of simulated courses of action to test their outcome. When accounts are analyzed they can be made to yield the material for the construction of scenarios, which are then, as in one of the methods suggested by Mixon, checked in various ways against real intuitions of social propriety. The interaction between account analysis and model building is clearly a two-way process since accounts contain items whose presence and significance is only to be explained by reference to the models of cognitive processes which the actors have not individually monitored. I am inclined to think that one of the ways of understanding Freud would be to see him as engaged in this process of the construction of scenarios from accounts and the feedback from those scenarios to accounts again. As far as I have been able to determine by some rough and ready investigations full self-monitoring and awareness of the archetypal cognitive process involved in social action occurs only when there is some doubt about how to proceed, sometimes through uncertainty as to the definition of the situation, sometimes through uncertainty as to the rules for proceeding in a situation whose definition has been understood. It will obviously be more common among the young, the socially inept, and the very socially sophisticated, than amongst most folk.

For instance I have investigated several cases of hesitant or inappropriate hand-shaking. The situation may be problematic in one of both the above ways. Sometimes the person wonders why the hand of the inter-actor has been put forward. Is it the opening move in a greeting ritual? Is it the beginning of a request for something? Are we about to wrestle? Such a situation I have called a 'node'. Choice of definition calls forth a certain set of rules and the appropriate episode develops. Sometimes the person realizes that a hand has been put forward as the opening of some greeting ceremony but does not know what to do with it, that is the beginning of a greeting ritual has been identified, but the rule for proceeding is unclear. Are they Anglo-Saxons, expecting a firm grip? Are they Orientals expecting a limp touch? Are they Royalty expecting a kiss? And so on. The next stage of this study will involve the construction of scenarios and the acting out of various action-possibilities, and the collection of further accounts from the actors, which in turn will lead to refinements of the scenarios. The scenarios and accounts at each stage constitute a more refined theory of that class of social action.

In investigating such cases one soon comes to see that Stages 1 to 4 of the cognitive process are logically interlocked. I shall return to this point in discussing the results of rule analysis in the next section.

One final point about the importance of taking the investigation of cognitive processes seriously and their phenomenology as a starting point: the process I have called 'archetypal' can be given a system theory analysis. From that analysis one can generate hypotheses about neural structure. We need to be cautious at this point not to slip into the reductive fallacy committed by so many devoted cyberneticians. Physiological hypotheses generated from system analyses are not hypotheses about the performances or powers of the entities involved but are hypotheses about the natures of those entities which, in virtue of having this or that structure could have the given powers. Discovering that the decisions of social actors are made by means of physiological mechanisms has no implications whatever as to the analysis of the decisions made and tasks performed by those actors. No doubt social competences are the powers of physiological mechanisms, but since social competence is competence in social tasks, there need be no physiological or even biological element in the analysis of social competences. We will see that the biological basis of life provides material to be given social meaning, but has no social meaning in itself.

There is one further and very important consequence of supposing that social phenomena are cultural rather than biological in origin. On the ethogenic view the methods by which relative status is fixed between individuals, the way people control who shall speak next in a conversation, the means to be adopted to win friends, and so on, are all to be treated as part of a culture. And a consequence of that is that they must be supposed to be learned by precept and by imitation. For this to be possible a culture must be replete with the materials for social explanations and have resources for the formation of theories about the social actions of its members. Gossip, as anyone who has studied it much will agree, consists largely of theorizing about the social behaviour of one's acquaintances. All this is possible only if the language of the culture is equipped with the conceptual resources for this kind of intellectual activity. There is no reason to suppose that gossips are inept at social theorising, rather the contrary. This suggests that in analyzing accounts and constructing scenarios we should exploit the terminological and conceptual resources of our culture, and that of course is to turn our attention to the possibilities of ordinary language. So far as I can see there is no reason whatever for thinking that some artificial set of terms is better, or even as good as the highly refined and sophisticated language of the actual culture.

The Results of a 'Rule' Analysis of the Genesis of Social Action

So much for the preliminaries. Let us now look at what has actually emerged from the work of those who have knowingly or otherwise, used the new paradigm, ethogenic methodology.

The first thing to come out is that there is apparently a hierarchy of rule systems. The resolution of the envisaged possibilities at each node in a sequence of actions involves, in principle, reference to three orders of rules, principles or maxims.

L

First order rules fall into ensembles constituting the 'etiquettes' for each well defined social situation. An etiquette will tell one for example how to resolve the possibilities represented by an out-stretched hand; identified as the first move in a greeting ritual. The problem is whether to kiss, to shake, lightly or firmly, to touch or to ignore. The identification of the exact social meaning of the out-stretched hand as, e.g. the opening move of a wrestling match, enables one to choose the appropriate ensemble of first order rules or etiquette one should refer to in resolving the problems of specific choice of action, e.g. an etiquette for greeting, or for giving and taking, or for judo etc. Choice of etiquette equips one with a ready made reference system for providing a justificatory account, when required, or for constructing an account in advance of the action, to justify the specific actions one performed. E.g., 'I thought he was going for his gun, so I hit him'.

Situational definitions determine the choice among etiquettes. The situations themselves may be of a variety of general forms. There are those that could be spoken of metaphorically as *games*, that is rule-bound competitive episodes with conventional upshots. At the other extreme there are *rituals*, that is rule-bound cooperative episodes with conventional upshot, or some combination and blend of cooperative and competitive elements, such as occurs in pro-fessional wrestling or Malayan marriage ceremonies. This ordering of etiquettes between games and rituals expresses our general conception of the nature of human social life as the amelioration by *conventional* devices of the tension between the cooperative and competitive demands of human conditions of life. Lévi-Strauss has seen the origin of competitive situations in the perennial shortages of necessities, such as food and women, around the treatment of which rules have accumulated in all societies. There may be other sources for this basic tension. Goffman (1969b) has drawn attention to something similar in the conditions for the satisfaction of the needs of 'action', the highly rule-bound and conventional life within a gambling saloon, for instance, being the product of the necessity for people to cooperate in the essentially competitive business of gambling.

The rituals and ritual-like action sequences of social life serve to construct social relations and to confirm them into some kind of system or structure, maintaining certain invariants, such as status hierarchy. For instance there are ritualistic sequences by which victory in a status competition is marked and defeat conceded, and there are proper styles in which these rituals must be performed. This is shown, for instance, at the end of a greeting ritual by which a stranger is incorporated into a microsociety. If the incumbent maintains status advantage over the stranger one hears the incumbent say 'Glad you could join us' and the stranger respond with 'Nice of you to have me', while if the stranger has won the immediately preceding status game he says 'Glad I could be with you' and the incumbent responds with 'Nice of you to come'. In practice this may be modified sometimes by a pseudo-status accorded to the stranger merely as visitor.

At this level of analysis a very important distinction begins to emerge. It is that between the specific forms that a certain kind of social episode takes in a specific micro-culture, and its general form as that kind of episode. For example a greeting ceremony involves, amongst other things, an exchange of names, physical contact and a determination of relative status. The general structure and meanings of the rituals may be found universally, but its specific forms may be very various. Amongst Europeans the appropriate physical contact is hand-shaking, amongst Polynesians nose rubbing, among Pathan 'pressing of hearts', and so on. Amongst Europeans exchange of names is by simple statement, amongst Polynesians by an elaborate guessing ritual which avoids the denigrating admission by one or the other of those being introduced that he has not heard of the other person.

At the specific or etiquette level, and the general or social meaning level there are *constitutive* rules which define what is appropriate to the particular 'game' or 'ritual'; and in the case of competitive episodes or 'games', say such an episode as that in which a status hierarchy is established, there are *strategic* rules, the following of which assists a participant in winning within the rules which are constitutive of the practice. I propose to distinguish both constitutive and strategic rules at the social meaning level as the *principles* of 'rituals' and 'games'.

This is not the end of the matter. There is a higher order of rule yet. Performance in games and rituals demands the presentation of the self to and among others. Success at this vital part of the performance is ultimately referrable to the dramaturgical maxims involved in the presentation of the self to others and the preservation of that image in the perception of the other. These constitute the third order of rules for social action. It is by knowingly employing and exploiting these maxims that Goffmanesque man, the most self-aware and well controlled of human beings, masters *fortuna* by the exercise of *virtu* in a world of ultimately meaningless contingencies, imposing if he can the meanings that he wills upon them. In being able to control the persona he presents he has an immense advantage over those who are dominated by social habits, and he can that much more easily, impose his meanings upon situations.

But few human beings can aspire to that exalted condition and most stumble on in parts, the scripts for which they have no conscious hand in. Hypotheses as to the cognitive processes of such humble wretches must be derived from models of the processes by which the most self-aware order and control their performances. And this requires yet another application of the realist paradigm of scientific explanation.

A person presents himself as a type through the style and manner of the social tasks which he performs. Stylistic qualifications appear as adverbial modifications of the verbs for the performing of tasks and actions. 'He gave it', we say, 'grudgingly'. 'He made the introductions nervously (confidently, brusquely, carelessly, meticulously. . . .)' In each qualifying adverb part of a person presentation is being built up, since it is part of the logic of our social reasoning to sum up a consistent set of such qualifiers in the attribution of a certain nature to the human being who performs in a certain consistent manner and style. A person thus gains a permanent niche in our taxonomy of human types on the basis of ephemeral and situation relative impressions of the style and manner in which he performs the social tasks which come his way. The deliberate control of the manner and style of social action is thus the highest order performance that a human being can undertake. Goffman, as we all know, has begun the investigation of the principles and rules of human control of action at this level, but I believe that his pioneering work can be pushed a good deal further with a systematic study of the maxims involved.

It is worth noticing that control of style for dramaturgical purposes is the exact opposite of the psychological process involved in the Stanislavsky 'method'. There the actor is advised to think himself into the performance at the lower levels of social action so that his performance is controlled by instinct and intuition. Goffmanesque man, suspecting his intuitions and the propriety of his immediate reactions in sustaining an image, seeks to control the manner of his performance in accordance with certain maxims, in the direction of some socially recognized image of self that he wants to create.

It is in the stylistic qualifications of actions too that the emotional tone of an episode becomes manifest publicly. It cannot appear in an etiquette, nor in the set forms of a 'game' and 'ritual'. But it can and does appear in the style in which the etiquette is followed and the social tasks performed. Thus its social manifestation is removed from the underlying level at which it is operative in the genesis of behaviour, which is in the self-monitoring which does not appear in public. Hence at the dramaturgical level there are great possibilities for the simulation of emotion, or for the presentation of meretricious emotions by the adoption of the appropriate styles. And these too may add to the piling up of minutiae the totality of which determine the way one's social selves appear to the others with whom one interacts from time to time.

Though etiquettes may be learned by rote and their rules followed blindly, their detailed recommendations ought in principle to be justifiable by reference to the game-ritual level and ultimately to the dramaturgical maxims which generally control the style of the actions generated by the following of the lower order rules and principles. For example there is a rule at the etiquette level which enjoins that one should never say 'I know a lot about that' when a subject is introduced in conversation, but rather something like 'That is a very interesting thing, and fascinating to read about'. Why this particular rule? In explanation one can refer to the general dramaturgical maxim that one should provide the material from which one's virtues and talents can be inferred, rather than state them outright.

Goffman has pointed out the importance of seeing the stylistic element in social interaction as the work of cooperation between more than one person, the group he has called a team. The commonest easily observable example of a dramaturgical team is a husband and wife, who usually cooperate rather well in the presentation of their joint and several selves. Observation of the behavior of marital pairs can also readily provide cases of the ways stylistic efforts can break down. There may, for instance, be disparities between the images of their marriage projected by each member of the couple, or there may be a more fundamental break down in the performance because different principles are being drawn upon to control the presentation of the same image.

Behavior at all levels of the paradigm is set within a larger framework provided by the possibilities of the formulation and expression of excuses and justifications for what is done. Testing out possible action sequences is partly by reference to trial justifications or excuses tried out in the imagination against possible interlocutors or inquisitors. This need not, and often does not come after an action, though a very clear form of this form of rehearsal is commonly prompted by a guilty conscience.

It was pointed out long ago by C. Wright Mills (1940) in an unjustly neglected passage that we often do what we have excuses and justifications prepared for, and that the justificatory resources of a person may be related fairly directly to his linguistic resources and hence indirectly his linguistic resources limit the possibility of action, for him. It has also been pointed out to me by Dr. N. Scott-Brown that the function of the general medical practitioner in our society is often best seen as the provider of very powerful justifications and excuses for courses of action, otherwise beyond the linguistic and intellectual power of their performers. This feature of human life is yet another manifestation of the fact that the psychic community of human beings is created by their linguistic powers.

The most important scientific consequence of adopting a generally ethogenic point of view is that the change from the old paradigm can be given systematic expression as a shift in the sources for models for the generative mechanisms of the action of participants in social interaction episodes.

It is easy to identify the purely biological episodes in which several people take part, in which each stage is causally related to the previous stages by biological mechanisms. A typical example of such an episode is that in the course of which two people become parents.

It is easy to identify purely formal episodes in which each stage is related by convention and meaning to the previous stages by explicit and stated rules and in the course of which a change in the social order is brought about. A characteristic example of such an episode would be that in the course of which two people become married.

Most social episodes are *enigmatic*, with respect to either of these paradigms. Usually there are no obvious biological mechanisms at work, nor are there any explicitly stated rules. The traditional, old paradigm move, in social psychology has been to draw upon biological episodes for models of the processes involved in the generation of enigmatic social happenings. For instance the biological concept of 'response competition' has been drawn upon in an attempt to explain the alleged increase of liking with greater familiarity.

In new paradigm studies the genesis of formal episodes serves as a model for the understanding of the enigmatic. This will involve the postulation of hypothetical rules on the model of those known to be referred to in controlling one's behaviour in corresponding formal episodes. The postulation of the hypothetical rules will be associated with the postulation of hypothetical cognitive processes of rule-consultation, imaginative rehearsal and so on, modelled on those known to be involved in self-aware episodes. Thus the change to the ethogenic point of view opens up new sociological perspectives through the study of the rule hypotheses, their origins etc. and new psychological fields through the study of the mechanisms of self-monitored control, and the cognitive structures necessary to their exercise, both as to their function in the adult and their origin and development in the child.

The range of hypotheses as to the structure of enigmatic episodes will be identical with the range of known structures amongst formal episodes. This leads by another route to the game-ritual dichotomy to which I have had occasion to refer, in discussing the hierarchy of rules that seem actually to be referred to in social matters. Formal episodes having a social upshot in which people engage, seem to be capable of classification as one or the other, or some subtle combination and interweaving of the two. It is necessary to recognize two categories of formal episodes without social meaning: routines which bring about physical changes (e.g. servicing a car), and pastimes, whose upshot is mere entertainment. As Berne (1966) has pointed out, pastimes may not be fun.

With respect to the etiquette-game/ritual-dramaturgical hierarchy, as I have already pointed out, the upper two tiers are usually not explicitly referred to, and must be filled in by an analogous process of hypothesizing as is involved in filling in the ethogeny of a wholly enigmatic episode. Again, in accordance with the classical schema of explanation in natural science, the set of rules assumed in the model will be justified for plausibility by the fact that there are some cases where the whole process is under full self-control, and is explicitly monitored throughout, so that an account of that episode will contain items which refer to all levels of the hierarchy.

Thus the classical schema of natural science[3] is capable of being applied in the study of social behaviour in several dimensions, and at several levels in the system of rules. Only with its help can the complex inter-relations of the hypotheses involved in new paradigm explanations of social action and interaction be disentangled.

I have shown how the notion of rule can function constructively in the application of the classical schema of explanation to provide hypotheses as to the nature of some of the psychic mechanisms and processes involved in the generation of social behaviour. It has also become clear that since the psychic *community* is constituted by the community of users of a common language the accounts, particularly those produced in justificatory contexts, whether in advance of action, along with it or after it has been carried out, become the most important empirical material upon which an ethogenist will

---

[3] For a detailed discussion, see Harré (1970), esp. Ch. 2.

work. In the analysis of accounts the concept of 'rule' necessarily plays a complementary role to that which it plays in the origin of theories about the generation of behavior, since, in a certain sense, an account *is* a theory about a certain action within the structure of an episode in the actions of which some socially meaningful act is performed.

In ordinary language permissions usually appear in an account along with a statement of a want or need, the function of which is to explain the act of choice. This is an essential part of the account since all that the statement of a permission can do is to indicate what possibilities are open. It leaves the choice which was actually made or was expressed in action, unexplained. The usual verbal formula which completes the explanation involves reference to a want or a need. In contrast, in ordinary language an explanation is reckoned to be complete in the case of mandatory rules, prohibitions or obligations by reference to the rule alone, without any account of the psychological conditions of its application. If to the query 'Why don't you go through under there?' the explanation 'You're not supposed to' is given, there seems to be nothing further to be done to complete an explanation. This turns out on examination to be one of the points at which social psychology connects on to both sociology and developmental psychology. In accepting the citation of a mandatory rule as a complete explanation of an action or for a refraining from action adherence to the rule is presupposed. The reason why *each* case of following a mandatory rule can be explained by reference to the rule alone is that the acceptance of the rule is general, and the one act of acceptance is thus sufficient for all its applications. Science advances on the usual demands of ordinary language at this point since it is clear that two further questions can be asked:

Why do these, and not some other rules exist as the accepted system of the person or micro-society involved?

How did it come about that these people in fact accepted these rules? That is by what process are they learned and acquire thereafter mandatory force?

The search for answers to the first of these questions takes us back to the hierarchy we have already remarked, since the game-ritual continuum and dramaturgical maxims are supposed to account for the general form of the etiquettes revealed in the rules extracted from accounts, while their particular content is to be explained through the historical contingencies that have beset these people and their ancestral mentors. Thus *a man* walks on the outside of the pavement or sidewalk in order to protect the woman he is with from offence, thus showing himself as a cavalier, but that he presents himself favourably by doing *just* that is a tribute to the state of the roads and the sanitary services of medieval Europe.

That *I* know and follow the rule about where to walk when accompanying a lady in a town, and someone else does not, is to be explained of course by the fact that I was taught to do that by my father, and the teaching reinforced at school, while my bucolic contemporary possessed neither of those dubious advantages.

Limitations on the applicability of the 'rule' concepts

A.   There is an obvious distinction between the action of an episode and the background against which the action develops. One can distinguish those rules which are involved in the creation of the background from the means by which it is maintained. Typical of background creating episodes are ceremonies of status passage and/or confirmation. The rules for the correct performance of such ceremonies can be regarded as the rules for creating a stable background. When it is established by ceremony which of two people has the higher status, then they can proceed to further social action against the background of that fixed relationship. If we are to speak at all of rules for the maintenance of background we would find them to be prohibitions of a very general character. This seems to me to have been shown by the results of the technique of 'garfinkeling', which involves deliberately wild and expectation denying behavior, from people's reactions to which their assumptions of stability can be discovered. If someone is not disconcerted by a particular garfinkel, then the behavior of which the garfinkel consists is not ruled out as part of the background (cf. Garfinkel, 1967).

But it is not at all clear that the notion of 'rule' is exactly what is required to express the background. The point can be illustrated by an actual case. Ceremonial kissing of people is usually part of a greeting or parting ceremony, at least among Europeans. At a recent dinner party a social psychologist, under the momentary spell of the garfinkel idea, ceremoniously kissed the hostess in the middle of dinner. It would have been perfectly proper, and indeed customary in that social circle to have kissed the hostess ceremoniously either on arrival or when leaving the house or both. Analysis of accounts subsequently showed that the effect of the garfinkel was not to draw attention to the rule, presumably a negative conjunct of the kissing rules, which had been violated, but to call in question the entire background in all its aspects. The people involved reported having kept, from the moment of the garfinkel on, a rather wary eye on the garfinkeler, with something of the feeling, 'Whatever will happen next?' In short one disturbance in the background called the whole background into question. It seems odd then to maintain that the maintenance of the background is a matter of rule. Once the situation has been defined then that definition allows certain positive developments of the action only, and thus *a fortiori* rules out all others. Hence, since these are effectively unlimited in number, no specific set of rules could express the background. Children find it easy to learn what behavior is wrong, but only discover what is right by running up against the boundaries of prohibited action. Goffman has recently opened up the subject of background in his *Relations in Public* (1970), and it is clear that considerable theoretical and empirical attention needs to be paid to this aspect of the study of social action.

It seems clear then that a great deal yet remains to be done in the exploration of the types of definable situations and the means, both ceremonial and otherwise by which they are defined. For example some of Berne's domestic 'games' can be looked on as ceremonial reaffirmations of the family status-hierarchy since they seem to be preordained in outcome and involve the ritual degradation of the one party and the triumph of the other. We may then perhaps preserve the rule taxonomy, at least formally, by means of a notional or formal rule which forbids any conduct likely to deny a situation which has been defined. At this point one might begin to make some use of a concept used rather generally by both

Shwayder (1965) and Sherif (1936), namely that of expectation. Once a situation has been defined then the actors who share in the definition are entitled to share in certain expectations one of the other, and disruptive behavior (as against for instance, merely irrelevant or decorative behavior) could be defined as that likely to be taken as violating those expectations.

For the further classification by content of the rules which advance the action we return to the system of etiquettes, the game-ritual spectrum, and the dramaturgical maxims of a society. In this way particular rules for advancing the action can be classified 'horizontally' by reference to the etiquettes of which they form a part, and 'hierarchically' by reference to whether they are involved in the immediate generation of particular actions, or are of higher order tactical or strategic significance, or are those the following of which enables one to present a particular personal style.

B.   In some cases social regularities cannot be explained by reference to conscious rule-following, nor does what little is known about their origins make the rule-following model plausible, e.g., the conventions by which linguistic interactions are controlled are known not to be consciously monitored. In other cases social regularities may be automatic responses, with an evolutionary basis, e.g., the warm social feeling produced by smiling. Both, of course, may be exploited by educated Machiavellians by being formulated as a rule and used in the control of their behavior. But it would be inappropriate and misleading to describe either of these kinds of regularity as social habits, since this clearly suggests a rule-following theory of their origin.

C.   1. Garfinkel and others have emphasized that each social episode involves an indefinitely large ensemble of different rule-systems, interacting (cf. Cicourel, 1967). The social scientist can never hope to identify all the interacting rules. This may be true of any one episode, but presumably our knowledge of the rules will emerge from sustained study of many episodes, each yielding an aspect of the total system.

2. As has been pointed out, the rule-following model demands attention to the perception of the social meaning of particular situations. This is itself

a. rule-controlled

b. fraught with contingency. The full follow-through of this thought is to be found in Lyman and Scott (1970), Machiavelli, etc., in which the actual meaninglessness of episodes is emphasized and the attention turned to the process by which they are, *sub specie aeternitas*, arbitrarily given meaning.

D.   In writing up social perceptions in a social way, a further set of rules and conventions supervenes, e.g., the rules of rhetoric for getting articles published, such as the need for statistics, graphs and numerical tables, etc. These determine in their turn the way meaning is given to the social episodes analyzed. Thus the rule model, though inevitable, is both circular at its base, and involves an infinite regress at its apex.

The concept of rule appears both in a literal and in a metaphorical use in the theory of social action so far outlined. In higher order self-monitored formal episodes there are quite literally rules which people follow, while the concept is used metaphorically as the basis of hypotheses about cognitive functioning in the explanation of actions in those episodes I have called enigmatic. All this can be expressed schematically, and related to the hierarchy of rules suggested in Toulmin's paper in this volume. It will be seen (Fig. 1, p. 174) that there is a remarkably good fit between the two systems.

Rules and Social Universals

A perennial issue in the theory of social science has been that of the limits of the universality of any principles and patterns discovered. It has been discussed in recent years in the context of historicism, that is of the question as to whether there are any universal laws discernible in the history of societies. This has proved, in the end to be a rather uninteresting form in which to discuss the problem of universality, since the issue has been seen to hinge on the arbitrary degree of limitations of the openness of the *ceteris paribus* clauses attached to alleged universal laws. The rule theory of social behavior I believe offers a more promising context, in that it emphasizes the problem of social universals as well as drawing

Psychological Process	Type of Episode	Degree of Awareness	Toulmin Rule
2nd Order	FORMAL	Necessarily Conscious	Toulmin
Self Monitoring		Possibly	Rules 5-7
	ENIGMATIC	Conscious	
1st Order			Toulmin Rules 2-4
		Rarely, if	
Self Monitoring	BIOLOGICAL	ever conscious	Toulmin Rule 1. Biological Episodes satisfy *only* Sense 1.

Figure 1. Summary of Theory, and Comparison with Toulmin Rule Hierarchy

attention to new ideas in anthropology and gives due weight to the particularity of cultural norms and the idiosyncrasy of private performance.

Considered at the most superficial level of analysis social forms show very great variety. In the ethogenic theory this will be reflected in a corresponding variety of etiquettes. I would guess that it is true to say that even the most widespread rule of etiquette is somewhere contradicted in the social practices of a culture. For instance in a great variety of cultures greeting involves some kind of bodily contact. One might be tempted to discern a universal element in that feature of greeting ceremonies, seeing the Polynesian nose-rubbing, European kissing and hand-shaking, merely as specific forms. Yet Indians doing 'namasthai' do not touch each other, and hand-shaking is dying out very rapidly in some circles in England, being replaced as a greeting ceremonial by a curious oblique nodding movement by which the gaze is swept in an arc down across the face of the other, from left to right, passing just below the eyes, without actual eye contact being made rising again to a high oblique angle. At the same time a vague circular motion is made with the right hand, in which each interactor contrives to be holding something. I believe this social form to have had its origin in an apologetic, 'I'm sorry I can't shake hands. I can't find any-where to put down this glass (book, handkerchief etc).' The English abroad, on the other hand, kiss and shake hands with enthusiasm. Marriage ceremonies, even in Europe, have ranged from the ring-giving and oath-taking of the conventional church marriage, to the custom that bride and groom urinate in the same receptacle, a practice until recently current among the gypsies of northern Europe. The analysis of etiquettes is not likely, I believe, to yield anything much in the way of universals.

But, of course, at the game-ritual level the social meanings of the practices generated by the following of etiquettes are involved. Once a certain practice is recognized as a ritual, say a greeting ceremony, then the intelligibility of the practice as a ritual depends upon understanding its social meaning. At this level one might be tempted to say 'Every culture must have "rituals" by which mating pairs are formed, by which strangers are incorporated in the group, and must have "games" by which status is determined among individuals, and so on'. The problem now becomes the explanation of these apparent universals. For instance why do human beings universally (if they do) form mating pairs? Why do they incorporate strangers into a group? Why do they have relatively stable and fairly enduring status hierarchies? And so on through the list of all the items that might have some claim to be universal, such, for instance, as the institution of some modicum of private property.

It has become increasingly common to seek a biological basis for these supposed universal traits of society. I want to examine this tendency in some detail since I believe it to be a fundamentally confused idea, and to foster some very misleading assumptions about human life and its range of possible forms. The first point to notice is that there are in fact two quite distinct uses to which biology can be put in attempting to explain the alleged universality of the social meanings of certain rituals and games. It may be claimed that human beings have just the same needs and drives as do certain animals, that is that there is a biological identity between men and animals. Or the claim may be the rather different one that the rituals and games of human social life can be understood on the analogy of certain features in the lives of animals. This turnabout is common to both the identity and the analogy theory. While we reject the idea that animals 'marry' as anthropomorphic, we are recommended by certain authors to treat the more or less permanent union of the sexes found in many human cultures either as literally an instance of pair-bonding, or as analogous to that features of the life of some animals and birds.

Both the identity and the analogy theories come in two levels of sophistication. There is a pre- and post-Lorenzian form of each (cf. Tinbergen, 1969). In the pre-Lorenzian form the biological necessities are limited to the need for air, water and food, mating, and perhaps certain environmental requirements like adequate warmth or shelter. Each has been related to a semi-mythical 'drive', anthropomorphically identified as hunger, thirst, sex and so on. Post-Lorenzian ideas are exploited by the popular writers, Ardrey and Morris, who draw upon such ethological concepts as territoriality to explain certain very general features of human life. This may even go so far as Morris's identification of pathological states of overcrowding in animal communities with the leading features of social life in some cities. Both Ardrey (1967) and Morris (1969) seem to me to offer a confused melange of the identity and analogy versions of the post-Lorenzian form of the theory that sees human social forms as explicable in terms of the social forms of animal communities. This is not the place to undertake any detailed critique of their theories. I want to concentrate the discussion upon an underlying theoretical idea that informs all such theories, professional or journalistic, in either the identity or the analogy form.

The clue to this underlying theoretical idea can be found in the way the pre-Lorenzian version of the theory has been developed. To relate the needs to the appropriate behavior the theoretical concept of a *drive* has been introduced, and plays a well-known part in general psychology. The post-Lorenzian form of the theory that human society is directly related to a biological basis simply consists in an extension of the list of 'drives', connecting a specific form of behavior, such as the acquisition of private property, with the need, territory, through the theoretical notion of a territorial drive. In some recent writers this theory has reached a high state of elaboration. Argyle (1969) is prepared to consider such drives as 'aggression', 'dependency', 'affiliation', 'dominance' and 'self-esteem'. The theory goes like this: a human being is observed to act so as to try to get others of his species to admire him. What is the explanation of this behavior? Answer: it is the effect of the 'self-esteem' drive. And so on. Clearly an explanation which utterly fails to explain! The connection of genuine ethology with evolutionary theory through the hypothesis of the evolution and selection of valuable behavioral routines is supposed, I imagine, to reflect a rosy glow of 'scientificality' upon the drive theory.

Even if some drives are acknowledged to have some kind of existence, does the theory serve as an adequate general account of social practices in such a way as to serve as the progenitor of hypotheses of social universals? To answer this question let us compare the social functions of eating and drinking with their biological functions. Does the biological need for nourishment explain eating and drinking as social phenomena, or are eating and drinking incidental to the social meaning and purpose of the acts and actions of food and drink taking episodes among people? In short, how often is the actual form and meaning that eating takes as a social practice explicable by reference to hunger alone?

The old paradigm schema of the genesis of eating behaviour would be something like this:

Drive state —(1)→ practice —(2)→ for biological end, (1) being a physiological and (2) a suitably demythologized teleological causal relation. For example in the case under discussion the specific form of the schema would be:

M

Hunger ——(1)——→ eating, ——(2)——→ for nourishment, and ultimately for the survival of the individual, and through him, or her, the species. Thus the ultimate explanation of the existence of the practice would finally rest on evolutionary biology. There are several objections to this as a schematic account of the social practices of eating.

i. Eating performances in society are not always biologically based, e.g. a banquet, which is a ceremonial eating performance, may be arranged to resolve a problem of status uncertainty by illustrating and ceremonially confirming certain status relations. The banquet is eaten towards a social end, and there is demonstrably on occasion no immediate biological need being answered. Notice how much of social eating, whether it be banquet or humble supper, is unrelated to hunger, to the end of nourishment and so on. One should be aware however that while post-Lorenzian ethology would quite properly seek an evolutionary origin for the social practices of which eating may form an incidental part there would be no place for the intermediate causal hypothesis of the specific *social eating drive*. The 'drive' which would lead to status-confirmation performances would be more general. Thus the drive theory could never explain why in certain cultures eating is used to confirm status.

ii. Performances, even when demonstrably biologically triggered, often have a superimposed social role. Differences in the eating patterns of families can often be seen to be more or less directly related to the social structure of the family, and can be plausibly construed as affirmations of it, even in those cases where the family is eating because they are demonstrably hungry.

In fact one is inclined to say that biological needs and their satisfactions are made use of for social purposes, rather than that society arises as a special way of ensuring their satisfaction. That is since they are a regular and repetitive source of actions they provide a natural sequence of overt behaviours which can be invested with social meaning and so have a role in the creation and maintenance of society. Almost any regular biological phenomenon can be used for social purposes, witness the bizarre practice in America of the host accompanying male guests, and the hostess the ladies to the 'rest rooms', a habit clearly intended to increase *gemütlichkeit* but disconcerting in the extreme to a foreigner.

iii. Even in general psychology the drives theory now seems pretty suspect. There seems to be no way to eliminate semantic considerations, even from such apparently direct and unproblematic cases as the practice of eating when hungry. Meaning intrudes between arousal and performance in humans, even in those cases most evidently biological, that is even when there seems to be a tight-linked physiological chain through blood sugar, stomach contractions, pangs of hunger and so on to eating. It seems that the recognition of a felt state as, say, hunger, involves an ineliminable semantic component as Schachter, and others have shown.

Consider also the mating urge: of all 'drives' this has taken the lushest bouquet of bizarre practices and social forms, for a large class of which one must surely seek cultural explanations. Notice too how inappropriate the independent/dependent variable model appears in this context. Since that methodological model is an essential part of the drives theory, being a direct consequence of the generally Old Paradigm style of that theory, doubts about its applicability cast doubt upon the theory itself. The abrogation of normal sexual routines by self 'discipline' consequent upon certain social and cultural factors, such as beliefs in a limited store of 'vitality', or adherence to a particular moral system, is a crucial feature of human sexual behavior. Self discipline of this sort involves a high degree of second-order monitoring of the state of the self and of current action, and a correspondingly high degree of self control with respect to certain remoter ends. This sort of monitoring and conscious control was very clearly exemplified in the behavior of girls following the old morality, according to which 'heavy petting' was the limit of licenced sexual activity among the unmarried.

It is clear from all this that neither the traditional biological 'drives' nor their post-Lorenzian successors are suitable candidates for social universals. They are no more than *bricolage*, which by being given a social meaning can be utilized for social purposes. It is very important to realize that there is no necessary connection between the behavior which fulfills a biological need and the social meaning with which it has been endowed in a particular culture. It follows, *a fortiori*, that one must look elsewhere for social universals, if indeed there are any at all. Even from this very brief critique it seems to follow that social universals must exist, if they exist at all, in the realm of social meanings.

The ethogenic analysis can lead to the identification of several different possible universals. Hypotheses concerning them can be reached by noticing certain features inherent in the hierarchy of rule systems. The theory identifies the following three levels:

i. Etiquettes: these, it will be remembered, are systems of rules to which explicit referral is made by an actor in the generation and/or justification of action and which specify the details of social action. They are always of such a nature that they can be followed with awareness. We have already remarked that there is no reason for expecting any social universals to emerge from analysis and cultural comparison at this level, since etiquettes seem to be culturally idiosyncratic.

ii. The Game-Ritual Continuum: explicit reference to the principles in force at this level is unusual but certainly not impossible, and tends to occur in situations of uncertainty. Perception that the general form of an interaction lies somewhere along the continuum between convention controlled cooperative and competitive episodes leads to choice of a particular etiquette to control the interaction. The control of competitive and cooperative social performances by rule provides the possibility of the stabilization of an inherently unstable situation. Such would be the way a conventional specification of the criteria of victory in some game-like episode, say a case of sexual rivalry, allows the episode to be closed in a stable way, the loser acknowledging the triumph of the victor. 'Ritual', says Lévi-Strauss (1966, p. 30), 'is like a favoured instance of a game, remembered from among possible ones because it is the only one which results in a particulary type of equilibrium between the two sides.'

From this level a very weak universal can be isolated. It may be supposed that potentially competitive situations exist in all society. There may be a biological basis for this, or it may be derived, as anthropologists are prone to think from the universal existence of shortages, particularly of food and desirable women. For society to exist there must be an amelioration of this tension through some measure of cooperation, to reduce the competitiveness to reasonable proportions and by ritual to maintain whatever equilibria are favoured by a society. Thus the human solution is to *bind behavior by rules*. A simple example would be the very detailed and precise rules for the division and distribution of the meat of each specific animal species, in force among the inland tribes of New Guinea. This mode of solution to a universal problem is possible for, and natural to an organism specifically capable of second-order self-monitoring, and hence of the deliberate control of first order performance. It follows that from the ethogenic point of view the universality at this level lies only in the general form of the method by which the universal 'paradox of society' is solved.

iii. The fact of the high degree of control of performance that is possible at the lower levels allows control of the kind of self presented through the manner of the performance of lowel level tasks. This leads to dramaturgical constraints on performance which can be taken as maxims of style for the control of the impression produced by one's performance in games and rituals and in the everyday manner of carrying out the injunctions of local etiquettes. Knowledge of these maxims affects both capability at games, for example in the successful management of dissimulation, and the binding force of ritual, whose acceptances by others depends in part on proper presentation of ceremonial roles. There is no doubt that dramaturgical maxims, such as those perceived by Goffman to be at work in our society, exist practically universally as a matter of fact.

Reflection on this level of the control of social performance prompts two obvious queries:

Are there, in fact, any universally recognized social *types*?

If there are, does it follow that there are universally recognized conventions for the portrayal of the types? And would these conventions be used by educated machiavellians in the social portrayal of the selves they favored?

I know of no systematic research having been done on this topic. It would also involve the integration into this of anthropologists' reports on the life-styles aimed at in various places and times, and the means by which these styles are projected to others. The Italian notion of *bella figura* and the Spanish conception of *machismo* have often been commented upon but phenomena such as these need a new kind of study in the context of ethogenic social psychology, in which the conventions by which they are portrayed are closely studied.

The correctness of hypotheses derived from such studies could be checked by specific applications of the scenario method, to see to what extent the recognition of social types and the understanding of the meaning of their conventions of presentation has any interesting degree of universality. There would still remain the question of the explanation of the universality of certain social types and presentational styles.

It is worth noticing that the ethogenic system draws upon putative social universals which would lead to its being characterized as a 'structuralist' theory in Piaget's (1971) sense. The social universals we have glanced at would be treated from the structuralist point of view as internal equilibrating principles, and would constitute a set of rules and operators for transforming the system into itself. Thus by following the rules, and by presenting socially authentic selves, people succeed in transforming one social set-up into another set-up, which is still social. Failure to adhere to the rules, or to the principles by which stable and coherent selves are presented, would lead out of the system, that is they would transform a social set-up into a non-social anarchy.

REFERENCES

Anscombe, G. E. M., *Intention*, Blackwell, Oxford, 1957.
Ardrey, R., *Territoriality*, Collins, London, 1967.
Argyle, M., *Social Interaction*, Methuen, London, 1969.
Berne, E., *Games People Play*, Andre Deutsch, London, 1966.
Burke, K., *A Grammar of Motives*, University of California Press, Berkeley and Los Angeles, 1969.
Cicourel, A. V., *Method and Measurement in Sociology*, Free Press. New York, 1967.

Garfinkel, H., *Studies in Ethnomethodology*, Prentice Hall, Englewood Cliffs, New Jersey, 1967.

Goffman, E., *The Presentation of Self in Everyday Life*, Allen Lane The Penguin Press, London, 1969a.

Goffman, E., *Where the Action Is*, Allen Lane The Penguin Press, London, 1969b.

Goffman, E., *Relations in Public*, Allen Lane The Penguin Press, London, 1971.

Harré, R., *The Principles of Scientific Thinking*, University of Chicago Press, Chicago, 1970.

Harré, R. and Secord, P., *The Explanation of Social Behaviour*, Blackwell, Oxford, 1972.

Kohlberg, L., 'Development of Moral Character and Ideology', *Review of Child Development Research*, Vol. 1, Russell Sage Foundation, New York, 1964.

Lévi-Strauss, C., *The Savage Mind*, Weidenfeld and Nicolson, London, 1966.

Lyman, S. M. and Scott, M.B., *A Sociology of the Absurd*, Appleton-Century-Croft, New York, 1970.

Marks, I. M. and Gelder, M. G., 'Transvestism and Fetishism', *British Journal of Psychiatry*, *113*, 1967, pp. 711–29.

Miller, G. A., Galanter, E. and Pribram, K. H., *Plans and the Structure of Behavior*, Holt, New York, 1960.

Mills, C. Wright, 'Situated Actions and Vocabularies of Motives', *American Sociological Review*, V, 1940, pp. 904–13.

Mixon, D., 'Behavior Analysis treating subjects as Actors rather than Organisms', *Journal for the Theory of Social Behavior*, *1*, 1971, pp. 19–32.

Morris, D., *The Human Zoo*, Jonathan Cape, London, 1969.

Peters, R. S., *The Concept of Motivation*, Routledge and Kegan Paul, London, 1958.

Piaget, J., *The Moral Judgment of the Child*, Routledge and Kegan Paul, London, 1932.

Piaget, J., *Structuralism*, translated Chaninah Maschler, Routledge and Kegan Paul, London, 1971.

Sherif, M., *The Psychology of Social Norms*, Harper, New York, 1936.

Shwayder, D. S., *The Stratification of Behaviour*, Routledge and Kegan Paul, London, 1965.

Simmons, J. L. and McCall, G. J., *Identities and Interactions*, Free Press, New York, 1966.

Tinbergen, N., 'Ethology', in R. Harré (editor), *Scientific Thought*, (*1900–1960*) Clarendon Press, Oxford, 1969, Ch. 12.

Vygotsky, L. S., *Thought and Language*, trans. E. Haufmann and G. Vakar, MIT Press, Cambridge, Mass., 1962.

Yates, Frances A., *The Art of Memory*, Routledge and Kegan Paul, London, 1966.

Zajonc, R. B., 'Social Facilitation', *Science*, *149*, 1965, pp. 269–74.

Rules and their Relevance for Understanding Human Behavior

STEPHEN TOULMIN

I

Introduction

In the preceding essays, the main concentration has been on the notion of a person, and on the part which this notion plays in accounts of human behavior. From these essays it is evident, at least, that *person-talk* does indeed have some special features, which differentiate it from accounts of the phenomena in which inorganic objects are characteristically involved (*thing-talk*); and, furthermore, that this distinction also throws light on the differences between 'actions' and simple 'movements' (Taylor, 1964), and, so on what remains for our own generation of the Mind/Matter dichotomy. And, finally, Rom Harré has taken the additional step, of relating these special features of 'person-explanations' to the associated concepts of *rules* and *roles*.

This additional step immediately calls to mind a whole series of episodes in the development of philosophy and psychology over the last three centuries. For while such analyses as those given by Harré and Goffman enable us to recognize a richness and inner complexity in 'explanations' of human conduct which earlier philosophers failed to appreciate, their more general thesis that human conduct conforms to 'rules', which differ essentially from the scientist's 'Laws of Nature', is a much older one. In this respect, Harré's argument takes its place in a long and respected tradition (Mischel, 1969). Indeed, the very starting-point of the debate about Cartesianism, which has dominated psychology and mental philosophy since A.D. 1630, lay precisely in Descartes' recognition of an incongruity between the categories of 'causality', 'mechanism' and 'law-governedness', which lay at the heart of seventeenth-century physics, and the categories of 'rationality', 'thought' and 'rule-conformity', involved in all understanding of higher intellectual function in Man (Toulmin, 1967).

So, at this point, we may step back and consider the relevance of 'rules' and 'roles' to the notion of 'persons' against a broader backdrop, in the hope of circumventing the obstacles to earlier attacks on this problem. By distinguishing sharply between 'persons' and 'things', 'actions' and 'movements', 'rules' and 'laws' (let us ask) are we merely committing ourselves to yet one more rigid dichotomy, and treating the differences between human conduct and natural phenomena as not merely *authentic* but *absolute*? Or can we now find a way of doing justice to those authentic differences, while at the same time showing how the distinctive features of 'person' and 'thing' explanations are *related* to one another? This is the question towards which the central argument of the present paper will be directed.

It is a topic whose contemporary implications go far beyond the limits of the present discussion. Questions about 'rules', and their role in human conduct, arise repeatedly nowadays in methodological discussions of mental philosophy, cognitive psychology and psycholinguistics alike. Yet the term 'rules' itself—like the associated term, 'concept'—remains one of the great *unanalyzed analysanda* of cognitive theory. Thus, the well-known disagreement between Skinner (1957) and Chomsky (1959) over linguistic behavior turned on the question, whether it was possible to account for the development of our capacity to follow linguistic 'rules' by appeal to the 'laws' of operant conditioning alone. So one might have expected psycholinguists to attack, quite directly, the consequent analytical problems about the nature and function of rules'. Yet by now, a dozen years later, they have done scarcely anything to demonstrate the special features of 'rule-governed' and 'rule-following' behavior, and so to establish the significance of rules for theoretical psychology. Even George Miller, despite his earlier attention to this problem (Miller and Isard, 1963), is still able to do little more than emphasize the significance of the problem itself

(Miller, 1970). As a result the basic disagreement—between those philosophers and psychologists who regard *behavioral rules* as a sub-species of *natural laws*, and those who do not—remains as unresolved as ever.

In principle, however, it should not be beyond the wit of man to disentangle the crucial likenesses and differences between laws and rules, and put them in a clear perspective. Of all the traditional puzzles about 'rationality' and 'causality', indeed, the problem of 'rules' appears the least abstract and the most manageable. By comparison, the overall validity of the Mind/Matter dichotomy, and the general nature of Consciousness, are essentially theoretical issues, to be debated on a high (even stratospheric) level of abstraction: the notions of 'Mind' and 'Consciousness' are not so much *found in* human cognitive performances as *introduced by philosophers to account for* the special features of those performances. Meanwhile, on a directly empirical level, the existence in human conduct of sequential procedures conforming to rules, and the part played by such rules in structuring intelligent behavior, are familiar circumstances of everyday experience which should lend themselves to direct investigation and analysis. If we can hope to break into the conceptual shell surrounding the traditional Cartesian impasse, and open it up to empirical criticism, it should accordingly be at that point.

The central thesis of this paper can be summarized as follows. The debate about *rationality* (rules/rule-conformity) and *causality* (laws/law-governedness) is too often pursued in a way that fails to allow for the complexity and diversity of the points at issue: as a result, philosophers and psychologists too often end in cross-purposes. If the only question were simply whether 'rules' are or are not a sub-species of 'laws', we might hope to decide it by demonstrating or refuting, in quite general terms, the existence of some single, straightforward set of differentiae. Yet the very first thing to recognize—as will be argued here—is that 'rule-explanations' and 'law-explanations' are *not* to be related and/or distinguished by any such clear and straightforward set of differentiae, in all contexts and for all purposes: rather, they are linked and/or differentiated, in one context or another, by a whole spectrum of likenesses and differences. Within different inquiries—psychological or linguistic, philosophical or neurophysiological—different combinations of features may be of crucial, or 'essential', significance; and picking on some *one* characteristic of Mind, Consciousness, mentality, rationality as being its 'essence', i.e. as having an overriding significance regardless of context, merely precipitates a needless intellectual deadlock.

The central part of the present paper is a critical comparison of some six or seven varieties of description of explanation in which *rules* are invoked as accounting for human conduct. At one extreme, there are pure cases of natural (e.g. physiological) phenomena which happen) 'as a rule': at the other, high-grade intellectual performances involving the self-critical application and testing of 'rules' of (e.g) computation or inference. This analysis leads to a 'taxonomy' of rules ordered on different principles from those discussed in Harré's paper, and suggests that the phenomena, actions, utterances, thoughts, intellectual performances, etc., found in human conduct fall not—as the traditional dichotomies all suggest—into *one* or *two* clearly distinct kinds, but into at least *seven* different types, with correspondingly different orders of complexity.

If that conclusion holds water, many of the standard arguments about things and persons. Matter and Mind, brain and behavior, movements and actions, performances and thoughts (as well as *laws* and *rules*) are irredeemably over-simplified. For instance, the current debate in philosophical psychology over the so-called 'identity thesis' (Borst, 1970) takes it for granted that brain-processes and mental experiences must be regarded either as *one* class of events or as *two*: the question then is, are they fundamentally the *same*, or are they essentially *different*? Yet the very assumption, that the relationship between brain-processes and mental experiences can be as simple and easily stated as this, is itself a prime source of confusion. Certainly, this relationship is neither one of fundamental identity, nor one of absolute unrelatedness. And the same can be said about all the other pairs of terms that have been used to dichotomize human conduct: in each case, the empirical subject-matter to which our cognitive theories must finally be referred back for criticism has a richness and complexity that defies such over-simplification. By studying the variety of ways in which 'rules' are used to account for human conduct (in short) we shall come to see that any adequate theory of higher mental functions, or personal relations, must be based, not on any kind of a *dichotomy*—whether of substances or anything else—but, at the very least, on a *heptachotomy*.

II

The Varieties of Rule-Relevance

In his well-known essay, 'A Plea for Excuses', the late J. L. Austin pointedly refused to attack traditional philosophical problems about the Will head-on, but launched instead into an elaborate and detailed piece of analysis, which demonstrated the great *variety* of distinct linguistic devises that men employ to disclaim, qualify or mitigate full responsibility—on behalf of themselves or others— either for actions or for the consequences of actions. Austin's method was consciously designed to change our way of *viewing* the problem of 'voluntary' conduct. Instead of assuming that the 'gearing-in' of the Will to the production of actual behavior demands some single, crucial feature (he implied) we should start by setting aside all simplistic notions about responsibility, and face the multiplicity of dimensions that this issue involves in actual practice (Austin, 1956).

Our method here is similar. The first step will be to set aside any lingering assumption that the relation between rules and laws can be finally clarified by some single, straightforward step: e.g., by showing *either* that rules are, after all, a simple sub-species of laws, *or else* that some one crucial feature differentiates absolutely between rules and laws. We are in fact accustomed to invoking 'rules' as relevant to human behavior in so wide a range of different situations that we cannot hope to make progress unless we first consider a sufficiently broad and representative set of examples. In this section, I shall assemble a first collection of examples, so as to hint at the complexities that any full taxonomy of rules will have to accommodate. The notion of 'rules' (as we shall see) is not automatically linked to those of 'rationality' and 'consciousness'. At one extreme, we explain the things that befall human beings in terms of 'rules', without implying that the generation of those events involved any element of rationality or consciousness. At the other extreme, by contrast, the notion of 'rules' is linked quite rigorously to the 'conscious' employment of 'rational' procedures. In intermediate cases, our readiness to regard 'rule-conforming' human conduct as rational or conscious is—in one respect or another—weakened, qualified or conditional. Just as the complexity and variety of rebuttals, excuses and pleas of mitigation was, for Austin, the primary datum in any adequate analysis of 'responsibility' and the 'Will', so too for us, the primary datum in any adequate understanding of the links between 'rules', 'rationality' and 'consciousness' will be the *complexity and variety of these cases*:

(1) We may begin at the non-rational extreme, where the term 'rule' has a familiar application to natural phenomena and human conduct equally, in the context of the phrase 'as a rule'. We say, for instance, 'After a passage of a cold front, the cloud layer *as a rule* (i.e., generally) breaks up, producing a clear sky.' In the same way, we can say, 'After an evening of heavy drinking, a man *as a rule* (i.e., generally) wakes up the next morning with a headache and an upset stomach', or alternatively, 'After the fever subsides, an influenza patient *as a rule* (i.e., generally) begins to perspire freely and demands fluids'. The type of regularity involved in these cases has nothing directly to do—either way—with rationality or consciousness. In one sense, no doubt, a headache or a desire for fluids is, by its nature, something 'conscious'; but we cannot describe the regular meteorological or physiological relationships involved in such phenomena as having anything specifically 'rational' about them. The clouds do not 'have a reason' for breaking. Nor do such regularities rule out all kinds of rational considerations either. A particular influenza patient may refrain from asking for fluids, and so be an exception to the general rule, because an earlier vow of abstinence gives him a 'reason' for tolerating even extreme thirst. It is in this sense of the term 'rule' that scientists commonly speak about natural phenomena as exhibiting 'regularities', without any

implication that these phenomena 'follow' or 'act in conformity to' the rules which *we* frame in order to characterize them.

(2) Moving away from plain physiological phenomena to actions, considered on a gross, functional level, we find human conduct displaying somewhat similar 'regularities', even where much more is involved than a simple physiological syndrome. A devout believer goes to church regularly; a thrifty householder regularly saves money to keep his house in repair; an epileptic exposed to external social demands is regularly afflicted with *petit mal*; an emotionally-disturbed student regularly loses the paper on which he has jotted down his class-assignments. Where the conduct in question is a product of experience and/or enculturation, there is correspondingly more room to speak of the agent as having 'reasons' for acting as he does: still, the reasons relevant in such cases will normally be very broad and unspecific. The devout man will 'have his reasons' for going to church as unfailingly as he does; but the more regularly he in fact attends, the less likely he is to call those reasons to mind. In this type of case, far from the *rationality* of the conduct in question being tightly linked to its *regularity*, they are unrelated. The things that a man does 'regularly' may be done *for reasons*, but then again they may not. The regularity itself is a matter of observation: how far it is to be explained in 'rational' terms is another matter.

(3) In the course of enculturation, human conduct acquires certain internal patterns, or sequential structures, which are the first step towards the modes of behaviour discussed by Goffman and Harré. At this point, we find a further type of regularity, and a fresh application of the term 'rule'. These inner patterns or structures are of several kinds: they may have functional, problem-solving aims, or they may alternatively be merely ritual: they may include arbitrary linguistic elements, or be purely behavioral and non-linguistic. Either way, they will have an 'emic' significance, in Pike's generalized sense (Pike, 1967): being 'seen as' meaningful, in some respect or other that goes beyond all straightforward physical or 'etic' (e.g. phonetic) characteristics. It is to structures and patterns of this particular kind that the term 'behavior' refers, in colloquial usage. The mother says to the child, 'You must learn

to behave yourself'; with the implication that the child must come
to act in ways governed by the rules 'appropriate' to situations of
this particular type. This kind of learned regularity, or 'rule-
governed' sequential structuring, can already be found in the
conduct of children who have not yet learned to talk, and some
linguists (e.g., Bateson, 1970) actually regard the development of
such rule-governed patterns as continuous with, and paving the way
for, the acquisition of language. As one instance among many: the
games that mothers play with children, such as Peek-a-Boo,
comprise standardized series of distinctive actions performed in
sequence, not just 'as a rule' or 'regularly', but also in a 'rule-
governed' pattern. In due course, much of the behavior which is
'rule-governed' in this sense becomes second nature, and forms the
foundation for more complex skills. So learning (e.g.) to march up
stairs deliberately, one step at a time, serves as a preliminary to
learning to *count* (Cf.: Geach, 1957).

(4) Consider, next, those structural elements within 'rule-
governed' behavior that have an arbitrary and conventional significance (or 'emicity') varying from culture to culture. Certain of
these conventional elements will form recognized *systems* of
utterances or signs, which may be substituted ('symbolically') for
other structural elements within the characteristic behavior-patterns
of a particular culture; and the elements in question thereby display
a further kind of arbitrariness or conventionality. The collectively-
recognized system of 'rules' to which this symbolic substitution
conforms give the elements not merely a general, cultural 'significance', but also a specifically *linguistic* 'meaning', which can be
spoken of, less as 'rule-governed', than as 'rule-conforming'.

Thus, 'rules' are relevant to sequential behavior in two different
kinds of ways, and the performance within a given culture of some
standard sequence of behavior can accordingly be judged 'correct'
or 'incorrect' in either of two respects. It may be normal or
eccentric, conformist or unconventional; and so (perhaps) open to
criticism as a solecism, i.e. as falling outside the accepted range of
requirement in some significant respect. Alternatively, it may be
either good English or ungrammatical, clear or unintelligible, lucid
or misunderstood; and so open to criticism for failing to conform

to the systematic rules of syntax, phonology and /or logical grammar. By comparison with the rule-governedness of the 'emic' structures within non-linguistic behavior, which lacks the systematic exactitude of language and is commonly a matter of degree, the conformity or non-conformity of our utterances to linguistic rules is an all-or-nothing, right-or-wrong affair. While there may be some situations in which non-linguistic sequences have to be performed (as we say) with 'liturgical' exactitude, more typically there is greater room for flexibility, and a substantial range of somewhat differing elements can all be equally acceptable at a given point ('slot') in a behavioral sequence.

A side-comment may be included at this point, which applies both to rule-governed, and to rule-conforming behavior. The 'regularities' manifested in these cases once again have nothing essentially to do with 'rationality'. The ability to behave in a rule-governed, or to speak in a rule-conforming way, does not—by itself—constitute a manifestation of a man's rationality. More precisely: the specific ways in which *rules* are relevant to such rule-governed or rule-conforming conduct has no direct bearing on its rationality or irrationality. A man who salutes with the wrong hand, changes his car gear faultily, speaks ungrammatically or mispronounces particular words, contravenes the recognized sequences of technique, culture or language, but none of his actions constitutes—in itself—a failure of 'reasonableness' or 'rationality', or a defective use of the 'reason'. (So much for recent attempts to equate Cartesian rationality and the human language capacity.) Nor do such examples throw any useful light on consciousness, either. While such mistakes may be the results of inattention—and, in this sense, 'failures of consciousness'—they may alternatively be the products of defective education or training: i.e., instances of inappropriate behavior correctly performed. Even where the rule-governed or rule-conforming character of our behavior is not in doubt, therefore, the question commonly remains open how far, and in what respects, we acted as we did 'rationally', 'reasonably', 'for reasons' or 'with conscious attention'.

That last question raises issues on other levels, to which we may now turn.

N

(5) To start with, let us narrow down our attention to *problem-solving* behavior. We can then recognize a further, distinct sense in which 'rules' are relevant to human conduct, and one that begins to have some direct connection with rationality. In practical and intellectual life alike—in carpentry and cooking, physics and chess —we learn problem-solving procedures, whose sequences of steps are decided in the light, not of cultural convention, but of their functional efficacy. To blend a mayonnaise, to make a mortice-and-tenon joint, to solve an eigen-equation, or to play an Indian Defense: each of these procedures applies a particular type of structured behavioral sequence as a means of bringing about a certain end-result. The rules constitutive of such a procedure ('First break your eggs, and separate the yolks and the whites; next, blend the yolks and add olive oil one drop at a time, until the yolks become creamy . . .') are not just *conformed to* but *applied*, the steps being followed systematically and in order, until they yield the desired result.

To begin with, such procedures are learned by rote, without any understanding of how each successive step contributes to the efficacy of the entire procedure. (You can mix a perfect mayonnaise without knowing just why it is so important to blend in the olive oil one drop at a time.) On the other hand, what makes such a sequence of steps a 'rule-applying procedure' rather than a mere 'rule-governed ritual' is—precisely—its externally-directed goal. To mark this distinction here, we may conveniently contrast the *internal consistency* of conventional and/or systematic behavior (which is 'rule-governed' or 'rule-conforming') with the *external efficacy* of problem-directed procedures which are 'rule-applying'.

(6) While procedures of manufacture and problem-solving (whether manual or intellectual) are initially learned in the public domain, by imitation, instruction or example, many of them are quickly committed to memory ('internalized') so that we can go through them 'without having to think' or 'in our heads'. To the extent that practical procedures do become matters of routine, in this way, it may cease to be evident from our actual performances what exact procedure (and so 'rules') we are in fact applying; and, likewise, once intellectual procedures have become thoroughly

mastered, so that we do not need to work them through explicit on paper, it may again cease to be manifest on any particular occasion what exact procedure we are applying. Yet, despite the elimination of many overt steps from such a sequence of behavior, there is a clear respect in which we 'follow' the same procedures when whipping up a sauce unthinkingly, or doing a sum in the head, that we originally learned to 'apply' explicitly, when we still had to follow the instructions in the recipe book step-by-step, or lay out the full calculations openly on paper. In this respect, the same rules that account for our entirely overt 'rule-applying' behavior are equally relevant in the case of subsequent, less overt behavior, where the rules are 'followed' rather than 'applied'. (This is the point the Würzburg psychologists were apparently concerned with when they spoke of a man's 'awareness of a rule', or *Regelsbewusstsein*, as the 'determining tendency' responsible for bringing about the rule-following behavior in question.)

(7) Problem-solving procedures, however, are not always learned by rote and followed out unthinkingly, as matters of routine. Alternatively, they may be devised deliberately, and employed in an attentive, critical manner. Supposing (for instance) that we go through the steps of such a procedure, monitoring their effectiveness —and the consequences of varying them—in succession as we go, we shall in this way bring the entire procedure, together with all its constituent 'rules', under critical review. Instead of applying Snell's procedure for tracing a light-ray through a glass prism unquestioningly, we may (e.g.) subject this very procedure to critical comparison against the observed behavior of actual light-rays in an experimental apparatus.

In such a situation, it is clearly inadequate to think of the 'rules' applied in that procedure merely as 'determining tendencies', having some quasi-causal power over our behavior. For those rules themselves have now become the *objects of our intellectual activity*, and not merely *elements in its production*. Where rules of procedure are applied (as we say) with 'conscious, critical attention', they thus acquire a new, and yet more complex relevance to the human conduct in which they figure. And, once we reach this particular stage in our analysis, we are clearly face-to-face with 'rules' whose

relation to 'conscious, rational behavior' is beyond question. For
Descartes, as for all succeeding philosophers, this self-critical
application of intellectual procedures is the *prototype* of 'consciousness' and 'rationality'.

III

The Levels of Complexity of Cognitive Functions

Given this first sample set of 'rule-relevant' modes of conduct, let
us now ask what is the theoretical significance of the differences
between these various kinds of 'rules', and what light those
differences throw on our understanding of human conduct. Five
points can usefully be made here.

(A) The different samples discussed in the preceding section were
not, of course, set out in a random order. Rather, we have passed,
step by step, from physiological situations in which the term 'rule'
figures in a causal or quasi-causal sense, to intellectual activities in
which the 'rules of procedure' themselves become the objects of
conscious, critical, and so rational, attention and application. And
the first point to be made about these examples is simply the fact
that one *can* order them in such a spectrum: adding new complexities in succession, and so moving bit-by-bit from clearly 'causal'
to clearly 'rational' cases. At one extreme, the experience of extreme
thirst following a fever is something that just *happens* to a patient,
as a straightforward 'effect' of physiological 'causes': evidently, it
makes no sense to regard this thirst as an 'action', as a linguistic
'expression' or as a 'thought'—least of all, as exemplifying the
conscious, critical application of a sequential procedure. At the other
extreme, the critical testing-out of a procedure is the kind of 'rational'
activity which Descartes wished to exempt from all 'causal' explanation: however completely we may unravel (say) the cortical mechanisms called into play in such activities, their significance as rational
performances is intelligible only when they are seen in the context
of the larger pattern of externally-directed problem-solving activities
(e.g., the science of optics) within which they belong.

Viewed descriptively, therefore, the examples at opposite ends of our spectrum are as profoundly contrasted as any Cartesian could demand. At the same time, no single transition-point can be picked out, as we move from example to example between these extremes, as the uniquely significant cleavage-line, separating mere causality from true rationality, brain from thought, automatism from spontaneity, conditioning from freedom, laws of nature from rules of conduct, and also phenomena from actions, all at the same time—in short, as the line separating Matter from Mind. Viewing the full variety of 'rule-relevant' conduct *theoretically*, we find ourselves facing at least *six* transitions, each of which introduces some particular new element of complexity, which may well be the one that especially needs emphasizing, in this-or-that philosophical, linguistic or psychological discussion.

> *Question:* What is the *essential* difference between 'rational conduct' and 'causal phenomena': between the highest mental activities and the simplest physiological symptoms?
>
> *Answer:* No *single* difference exists which it is 'essential' to emphasize in all conceivable contexts.

In one context, the significant feature to emphasize will be the goal-directedness or functionality of actions; in another, the conventional structuredness of behavior; in another, the systematic generativity of language; in another, the external directedness of problem-solving; in yet another, the inwardness of silent thought; in yet another, again, the critical awareness of the man who monitors his procedures in the process of employing them. Within one or another *specialized* inquiry, any one of these features (or some collection of them) may throw special light on the specific problems of that inquiry: a *comprehensive* account of human mental functioning, by contrast, must mention them all, yet without equating them.

(B) An adequate theory of 'mentality', in other words, cannot be built around a fundamental *dichotomy*: it calls at the very least for a *heptachotomy*. And the appeal to 'rules' will have a different kind of relevance, depending upon where the piece of human conduct in question lies along our spectrum. How we assess its significance, whether we ask 'causal' or 'rational' questions about it, what 'regularities' we find in it, and so on, and so on: all of these reflect the *order of complexity* of the relationships within which the conduct in question is an element.

The conscious, critical checking-out of a procedure (7) against the results of experiment (in, say, geometrical optics) is an activity at least *one degree more complex* than the application of the same procedure (5) on trust. The application of mathematical formulae in the solution of externally-directed problems (in, say, physics) similarly involves a complexity absent when those same formulae are discussed for their own mathematical sake alone. To go further: the correlation of some conventional system of linguistic expressions (e.g., the numerals) with standard sequences of non-linguistic actions (e.g., the placing of successive objects on a scale) can give rise to entire 'language games' (e.g., that of 'counting') whose order of complexity is greater than that of the two constituent activities, taken individually. And, even near the opposite extreme, the performance of structured sequences of individual action (3) in an 'emic' manner has a complexity and 'significance' greater than that of any single constituent action (2), taken in isolation.

(C) How are the 'explanations' that we give of these different modes of conduct related to one anther? What bearing do alternative accounts of the same sequence of human actions, when viewed as having different orders of complexity, have upon one another? Over this question, we can learn from nineteenth-century arguments about physiological 'explanation', notably from Claude Bernard (1867).

The phenomena of respiration, for example, may be studied from several standpoints. We can investigate the manner in which oxygen from the air penetrates the semi-permeable membranes of the lung, and becomes loosely bound to the haemoglobin molecules of the blood-corpuscles: in doing so, we relate these biophysical and biochemical *processes* to general principles of physics and chemistry. Alternatively, we can investigate respiration as a physiological *function*, considering how it contributes to the life of the organism, and how different pathological states manifest themselves in corresponding 'diseases' or 'disablements'. More widely again, we can study respiration as a specific *adaptation*, i.e. from the standpoint of organic evolution: regarding the physiological function itself as a biological variable having a long-term evolutionary significance for the mode of life of the species. We then explain the different ways in which respiration is effected in different species, orders and phyla as 'adaptations', by appealing to causal factors and historical events long antedating the origin of the particular species under discussion.

Now: in the sense we are using here, explanations of physiological function have a greater 'order of complexity' than explanations of biophysical and biochemical process. They show how the occurrence of such physio-chemical processes within an organism contributes to the life of the entire creature in a way that requires to be described in more complex physiological terms. In consequence (Bernard argued) physiological explanations are not *in conflict with* physical and chemical ones: rather (as he put it) the physiologist studies the functional significance that physico-chemical processes acquire, when carried out 'in the special field of life' (Goodfield, 1960). Similarly, for the transition from physiological to evolutionary explanation: if we ask why a particular type of respiration is 'adaptive' for a given species, we thereby 'embed' questions about the *current* physiological functions of respiration within a *historical* context, involving the evolutionary ancestry of species concerned, and the modes of life of their precursors. Much of the deadlocked controversy over (e.g.) respiration between those 'mechanists' who insisted that all biological explanation must be purely physico-chemical, and those 'vitalists' who retorted that 'vitality' was an agency quite distinct from anything in inorganic physics or chemistry, was therefore (Bernard argued) the result of a cross-purpose. Biological questions, hypotheses and explanations having different orders of complexity are not, as such, in direct competition. Nor does the 'vital' significance of physiological functions entail that biophysical and biochemical processes violate the general principles of physics and chemistry. What principles are relevant to our understanding in any particular case, what terms are at home in our explanations, depend on the context and purposes of our discussions, and so on the complexity of the relationships we have in mind.

The relationships between biological questions of different kinds are, however, limited in one direction. Considerations on one order of complexity can be meaningfully embedded in questions of higher order of complexity, but not the other way about. When we discuss the *function* of respiration, for instance, we may ask what exact physico-chemical processes it calls into play; and the physiological significance of the function may be fully explicable, only when we bring to light these biophysical and biochemical details. Yet we may (on the other hand) scrutinize the biophysical and biochemical processes involved in respiration, and analyze them on physico-chemical principles as much as we please, without having any occasion to introduce physiological (or 'vital') factors into consideration. The immediate effect of focusing in on these processes *qua* physico-chemical processes (indeed) is to abstract them from their larger, 'functional' context; and, in doing so, to eliminate all direct occasion for talking about physiological considerations and categories.

Psychological explanations having different orders of complexity are related in a similar way. To start with, they are not in direct competition with one another, still less in conflict. A biophysical process or biochemical reaction may serve (or be involved in) a physiological function; and a bodily movement or an electro-physiological brain-process may similarly be called into play in a cognitive function or purposive action. But to discover the brain-process or describe the movement is not to say anything either way about its function or purpose, still less about its *lack of* function or purpose; nor does the functional characterization of an action directly entail, or rule out, anything about the specific movements and processes it calls into play. Likewise, on other levels of complexity, the formal character of (e.g.) a methematical procedure is one thing, the problem-solving character of its externally-directed application in (say) physics is something quite else, and we can discuss the same procedure from either standpoint without entailing anything specific on the other level.

The different orders of psychological explanation, too, are subject to certain one-way relationships. The critical testing (level 7) of a rule-applying procedure, for instance, is an activity which embodies the application of the relevant rules (level 5) as one constituent sub-element within it: in order to understand it fully, we must consider *both* what is involved in applying these rules, *and* how their effectiveness is monitored. Understanding the straightforward use of rule-applying procedures, by contrast, does not necessitate asking whether their effectiveness is being taken on trust, or monitored: in order to explain what is involved in 'rule-applying', we do not have to take into account the success, failure and/or experimental foundations of these procedures. Understanding in full what 'counting' is, likewise, requires knowing (a) what is involved on level (4), in the way of reciting the sequence of numerals, (b) what is involved on level (3) in the way of handling or marking off sequences of objects in succession, and also (c) how these linguistic and non-linguistic modes of behavior are put into correlation. Taken separately, by contrast, the linguistic and non-linguistic behaviors can each be analyzed without bringing in the more complex level (5) activity, viz. 'counting', of which they may in due course become constituent sub-elements.

This last example can be generalized, so as to throw light on the whole one-way relation between syntax and semantics. Discussions of linguistic 'meaning' always require us to embed grammatical forms and relations (level 4) into broader patterns of behavioral relationships (level 5) whose semantic order of complexity is greater than that of syntax itself. The general form of the semantic question then is: How are such-and-such syntactically-defined forms of expression put to such-and-such standard uses, so as to acquire a specific 'meaning'? (That is why the hope of mapping semantics entirely on to syntax was always a vain one.) Abstracted from the behavioral contexts of 'language games', questions of grammar and syntax can be discussed only in formal terms; and these will either ignore their semantic significance, or else take it for granted.

Similar relations hold good in other cases. If we consider 'thoughts' (level 6) as re-applying in 'internalized' form procedures which were originally learned as overt performances (level 5), we can fully understand what they involve only by making explicit the rules followed in the thinking, whose manifest structure is suppressed by internalization. As both Wittgenstein and Vygotsky recognized from their different standpoints, the implicit criteria for judging the 'correctness' of tacit or inner thoughts are the same as were explicitly relevant to the original, public procedures. By contrast, the rules embodied in a procedure can be specified fully, without raising any questions about whether it will be 'applied' explicitly and overtly, or 'followed' implicitly and inwardly. The general process of internalization can be studied, equally, without reference to the *particular* rules of procedure being memorized and followed. (Notice, in passing, that—at this particular point in our sequence of 'levels'—there is not a single unambiguous order to be found. A case can be made, in fact, for regarding levels 5 and 6 as *parallel*. Each level is more complex than level 4, but in different ways.)

(D) In one way or another, then, all our examples of rule-relevant conduct, other than those on level 1, represent more-or-less complex cognitive *functions* and/or *adaptations*. This fact has one further consequence. As we saw, physiological statements about the 'functional' or 'adaptive' aspects of respiration (say) go beyond the descriptive reporting of processes, reactions and occurrences, and involve judgments about the 'success' of these events, as contributing *either* to the current life of the individual organism *or* to the evolutionary development of the entire species. So here, too, psychological statements—about the character of 'purposive' actions, 'structured' behavior, 'problem-solving' activities, 'thoughts', and other related mental functions—involve implicit or explicit judgments about the 'success' of the conduct in question. The description of a bodily movement is never the description of an 'action', as such: a movement can qualify, count, and/or be regarded, as an 'action', only if it belongs to a general type that fulfills a recognizable function or purpose. A structured sequence of bodily movements or actions, similarly, does not constitute a specific piece of 'behavior' as such: it can qualify, count, and/or be regarded as 'behavior', only if it confirms to a standard, rule-governed pattern having some established 'emic' significance. In each case, the fulfilment of the function, or the conformity to the significant pattern, represents—in the required sense—a 'success' rather than mere 'happening'.

When we ascribe a function, a cultural significance, a linguistic meaning, a problem-solving character, or whatever, to a piece of human conduct—that is to say—we imply that this conduct has 'brought something off': it is in the nature of the case, as a result, that such psychological ascriptions make use of 'achievement words'. Physical processes, chemical reactions, bodily movements, and other natural phenomena, may vary indefinitely in different directions, and in doing so are in no way 'correct' or 'incorrect'. By contrast, functions, adaptations, actions, utterances, thoughts, problem-solutions, and the like, are judged with an eye to their *sense* (significance, intentionality), and spoken of either as successes, attempts, or failures. To 'act' is not-to-fail, to 'behave' is not-to-misbehave, to 'say' is to succeed in expressing something (note the French use of *vouloir dire*—'wish to say'— for 'mean'), to 'think out' a problem is to solve-it-inwardly, and so on. In each case, the status of psychological terms as 'achievement words' reflects the implicit or explicit judgments of success/attempt/failure that distinguish the language we use for characterizing action and language, thought and problem-solving, from the language we use to report functionally neutral events, processes and happenings.

(E) Finally, we may touch on the connections between the present analysis of 'levels' of cognitive function, and Harré's discussion of 'ethogeny'. The taxonomy of rules developed in this paper is primarily designed to *classify* the different ways in which 'rules' are used to explain human conduct. But the fact that we *do* use the term in all these different ways is not, of course, a matter of arbitrary choice on our part. Far from it: we do so because we *can* do so—i.e., because human conduct, in its full richness and complexity, *lends itself* to explanation on all these different levels. This said, we can at once go on to add a further significant comment. For not all these different levels of characterization and modes of rule-explanation are relevant to the conduct of human beings at all ages, and stages of life, equally. To cite the extreme case: two-week-old infants are not equipped to check out the scope, adequacy and reliability of formal problem-solving procedures in physics. But more generally, too, there is a rough correspondence between the 'orders of complexity' of the rule-explanations applicable to the conduct of an individual, and the 'stages' of cognitive development through which he passes on the road to full consciousness and rationality. (The correspondence is rough, rather than exact, because of the ambiguities over e.g. the order of level 5 and level 6.) At any particular stage, the child or adolescent is equipped to achieve functional successes up to, but only up to a certain 'complexity'. He will be able, e.g., to coordinate hand and eye, to imitate a set sequence of actions, to talk, to do simply money-sums, and/or to solve abstract problems in geometry; and rule-explanations will be relevant to our characterization of his conduct up to, but only up to, the corresponding level of complexity.

Our taxonomy can, accordingly, be seen as having a significance for developmental psychology. On the face of it, speaking of a bodily movement 'qualifying as' an action on certain conditions, or a procedure 'qualifying as' a piece of conscious, rational criticism on certain conditions, involves us in speaking *explicitly* only about the (timeless) relations between modes of explanation with different orders of complexity, and the concepts appropriate to each. However, what we say in such cases *implicitly* has consequences also for our (temporal) understanding of mental and intellectual growth. For, in each case, the 'conditions' in question are ones that can be fulfilled, only *at or after* some particular stage in human life. So the taxonomic question, 'On what conditions does conduct on level n qualify for characterization on level $n + 1$ also?' leads on at once, to the *ethogenetic* question, 'In what circumstances, and through what kind of learning, does conduct on level n come to qualify (i.e. begin to, or acquire the additional functional complexity required in order to qualify) for characterization on level $n + 1$ also?'

In this respect, the successive levels of complexity exemplified in our sequence of examples (1) to (7), can be read as having also *temporal* implications. The analysis in this way throws light on the successive stages by which, during the child's enculturation and education, his conduct acquires a progressively richer structure, is embedded in behavioral and contextual relationships of greater complexity, and so becomes more 'rational'. Whatever the newborn infant may or may not possess by way of 'native capacities', or 'potentialities', the actual behavior of the neonate during his early weeks of life can be exhaustively described in the terms appropriate

—at most—to our first three classes of examples alone. Initially, even the elements of sequential structure (level 3) are present only in a highly schematic form; while the more complex skills of language, problem-solving, internalized thought and critical self-monitoring are developed only subsequently, and in rough succession. And it should be clear enough from the results of our analysis just *why* this particular sequence of steps is, in certain respects, a 'necessary' one. The capacity to subject a rule-applying procedure to empirical test, for instance, presupposes and builds upon the capacity to employ that procedure strightforwardly: a man can hardly learn to *criticize* a rule, unless he already knows how to *apply* it. The ability to count, similarly, presupposes and builds upon prior abilities to recite the numerals, and to handle or mark off objects in sequence: we could hardly agree to describe a child as 'counting', unless it were clear that he already had a grasp of these other, simpler skills.

In the life of the infant as much as the college student, therefore, progressively higher cognitive functions can be developed only by following through a standard, and largely inescapable, sequence of 'prerequisites'. The task of understanding what it is that makes a man 'rational'—the central problem of philosophical psychology from the time of Descartes on—accordingly requires us to demonstrate how he *becomes* rational: i.e. what sequence of stages the individual needs to pass through, on the way to becoming a fully 'rational' thinker and agent, capable of manifesting his potentially 'rational' status in fully 'rational' actual performances.

IV

Rules, Roles and Personal Relations

At the beginning of this paper, we remarked on the connection that Harré and Goffman emphasize, between the notions of *rules and roles*, one the one hand, and the concept of *persons* on the other. Now, in conclusion, we may return and reconsider this connection, asking:

Does the distinction between social 'roles' and natural physical movements, or that between 'rules' of conduct and laws of nature, throw any
helpful light on the differences between *persons* and *things*? Is there
some single, sharply-definable sense in which personal interactions
involve the playing-out of 'roles' and conformity to 'rules'? Or do the
characteristic features of person-talk, person-perception and personal
interactions have as great a variety—i.e. include features on as many
levels of complexity—as we have already found in the case of 'rules'
more generally?

In particular: on which of our taxonomic levels of complexity are
we to locate the *rules* that are most typically and directly involved
in 'personal' relations? And does the connection between the
concepts of *persons* and *roles* justify us—any more than the other
dichotomies we have considered— in drawing a sharp line demarcat-
ing *person*-explanations from *thing*-explanations?

As a first clue, let us remark on one feature of Harré and
Goffman's so-called 'dramaturgical' model that easily gives rise to
misunderstandings. This has to do with the seemingly *manipulative*
tone of this account. The use of the model to explain interpersonal
behavior generally can give the impression that human beings deal
with each other at all times by consciously and deliberately adopting
—even, by simulating—attitudes, feelings and patterns of conduct
that have no authentic roots in their personalities or long-term
intentions. Indeed, the inexperienced reader may even end by
wondering whether—for the dramaturgical theorist—it even makes
sense to talk of our having 'long-term intentions' towards one
another at all; for are we not all simply actors caught up in a social
drama over whose script we have no control?

If we can begin by tracing the sources of this impression, we shall
at once be led to see that 'rules' and 'roles' are relevant to interpersonal transactions—as they are to the conduct of individuals—on
several different levels and in several different ways. For the root
of the misunderstanding is this. The behavior of the actor who
'takes a part' in a drama, and the behavior of the individual whose
conduct the actor simulates, have something very definite in
common: viz. that sequential structure which the actor has to
reproduce, in all its socially and psychologically significant respects,

if the audience is in fact to recognize and understand the 'part' he is playing. On the other hand, what distinguishes the original conduct from that part is, precisely, the fact that the actor is deliberately *simulating* sequentially-structured behavior of kinds that the normal agent performs *naturally and unthinkingly*. (That after all is the difference, in normal parlance, between an 'actor' and an 'agent'.)

For the social psychologist who employs the dramaturgical model in analysing and explaining *normal* human conduct, the important thing just is the common structure linking the actor's performance and the agent's conduct. The theorist's aim is to throw light on the internal structuring of social or 'interpersonal' transactions, and for this purpose the common sequences in 'role' and 'conduct' are alone of direct significance. Just because this model is *only* an explanatory model, however, the differences between the normal agent's natural, unthinking conduct and the actor's deliberately simulated performance can, for the purposes of this particular style of analysis, be neglected. Hence the unguarded reader's impression that the dramaturgical theorist is *equating* everyday conduct with play-acting—motives and all.

This observation helps to throw light on the limits of the drama-turgical approach, as well as its strengths. Just because any theatrical role, simply *qua* role, involves donning a deliberate 'mask', nothing can safely be inferred from it about the 'real' feelings and person-ality of the actor. The very terminology of 'roles', as a result, tends to import into our thought about normal everyday conduct hints of deliberation, design, even deceit, that attach essentially only to play-acting. To adapt a remark of Jeremy Bentham: 'The best way of influencing people is to seem to love them; and the best way of seeming to love them is to love them indeed.' Quite aside from analyzing the common structures and sequences shared by everyday conduct and theatrical roles, therefore, we shall also need to explain what *differentiates* these two things: i.e. how it is that the highly complex and structured things which an actor does in the theatre designedly and deliberately may be done by agents in everyday life, from childhood on, quite unthinkingly—even, by 'second nature'.

In some practical situations, it is true, we may have occasion to work out deliberate *techniques* for dealing with people: typically, people in positions of power or authority. The members of a university department, for instance, may discuss just what tactics the Chairman should use in negotiating the departmental budget with the administration. ('How is Ted to square the Dean?') In such special situations as these, Harré's terminology seem particularly apt: there, it can be appropriate to speak *quite literally* of the Chairman's approaching the Dean with a 'plan', governed by 'ground-rules', and all the rest. The relation of those 'rules' to our understanding of the Chairman's subsequent transactions will then be precisely what we have already seen in the case of individual conduct on levels 5, 6 and 7: viz., conscious, rational and/or deliberate conduct. In such cases, we may even perform 'experiments' in order to 'monitor' the effectiveness of our 'ground-rules', and so discover (e.g.) what kind of approach works best with a newly-appointed Dean; and these experiments will have the same status relative to the 'plans' and 'tactics' of interpersonal behavior that physical experiments have for our behavior towards (say) prisms and lenses. It is of the essence, by contrast, that most everyday conduct does *not*, in any literal sense, involve the conscious and deliberate adoption—*ad hoc*—of behavioral 'tactics' and ground-plans'. Indeed, the ways in which people deal with one another *qua* people, in the ordinary course of life, and the 'personalities' they manifest in those dealings, are philosophically perplexing—not least—because they *lack* the elements of conscious design that so often mark (say) negotiations with superior authority; and it is a weakness of the dramaturgical model that it tends to obscure that difference. Given their common behavioral structure, we must accordingly ask, how and why do the 'quasi-roles' of unthinking everyday interactions differ from the consciously-adopted 'roles' of the actor, the negotiator or the official spokesman?

At this point, our taxonomy of rules can again be of help: especially, if we take it in its developmental (or 'ethogenetic') interpretation. For the modes of conduct that we label as 'second nature' become stabilized very early in our basic upbringings; and these modes comprise many features of our 'personalities', as revealed in the ways in which we habitually deal with our fellow-men. Typically, the young child who learns 'how to behave' is entirely unaware that there is any 'rule' with which his personal conduct is being compared and brought into line. In these respects, his conduct does not 'apply' or 'follow' rules of procedure or technique, still less employ such rules 'critically' or 'consciously' (levels 5, 6 and 7): at most, the child learns to conduct his personal relations in a 'rule-governed' or 'rule-conforming' manner (levels 3 and 4). As a representative example, we may here take the game of Pat-a-Cake, in which—unlike in Peek-a-Boo—the child is required to produce a sequence of actions coordinated in time and space with the actions of an adult. In the early stages of the child's upbringing, therefore, it is at most the *mentor* who has a 'rule' or 'role' in mind, and who corrects the child's behavior in such a way as to consolidate the required patterns in his conduct. (Does this imply that the child is being taught to 'play a role', when he doesn't even know there is a 'play'? This way of putting the point only has the effect of obscuring once again the distinction between 'play-acting' and 'behaving normally'!)

More significantly, one may argue, the infant's activities will often acquire a recognizable structure without *either* the infant *or* the mentor being explicitly aware that there are 'rules' and/or 'roles' embodied in that structure. The temporal patterns of the mother-and-child's pre-verbal interactions, for instance, carry over into their play-chatter, and so merge continuously into those of their later linguistic colloquy (Bateson, 1970). Similarly, habits of order and punctuality in the everyday life and/or liturgy of a culture may apparently serve as a foundation for the later historical development of intellectual and practical exactitude in the culture (Mumford, 1934). In short: there is much to suggest that the transmission of a specific 'culture' from one generation to the next takes place primarily through a kind of behavioral 'infection'. The elders transmit to their young intuitive standards of correctness and/or deviance of which neither party is explicitly thinking, or even aware. Far from either party acknowledging and applying 'rules' or 'roles' (level 5), we must therefore see the elders—as much as their young—as entering into their transactions, at most, in a 'rule-conforming' (level 4) and/or 'rule-governed' (level 3) manner.

At this point, uncritical use of the dramaturgical model generates its deepest irony. The idea of a simulated 'dramatic role' (like the concept of an 'hallucination') was first introduced precisely *in contrast to* that of 'real life' (or a 'real thing') with its authentic motivation (or physical character). Now, however, we seem compelled to obliterate this contrast. An entire culture is made to appear a kind of elaborate network of unwitting play-acting, into which elders and children are swept up without anyone concerned being aware of what is going on; and all our apparently authentic 'motives' are, as a result, made to seem factitious—not just in fact, but in principle. Yet what is this consequence of the model but the same 'phenomenalist redescription' of the facts that John Wisdom analyzed long ago when he pointed out that, if carried through to the point of utter consistency, a 'mass hallucination' would become —Borges-like—phenomenologically indistinguishable from a 'real thing'? And why should we allow the practical distinction between the sincerely-motivated actions of a normal agent, and the simulations of the play-actor, any less importance than it actually has? It is just the 'joint patterns of behavior' that constitute familiar, unthinking everyday life that actors *presuppose*, and have to *simulate*, if they are to 'play a role' at all. The attempt to characterize the nature of lower-level interpersonal transactions by invoking such higher-level notions as that of 'play-acting'—as though we could explain what 'playing golf' is, by saying, 'Well, you know what *pretending* to play golf is: *playing* golf is the same as that, but for real'—thus throws light on nothing but the common structure shared by normal conduct and its simulation, and if pressed further only drives us into an ironic reversal.

Meanwhile, we need to know much more than we do about the interactions by which mentor and child explore, and exploit, one another's responses; and so collaboratively build up the *joint* patterns of behavior characteristic

    (i) of normal development in the human species,

    (ii) of personal relations in a specific culture, and

    (iii) of dealings between individuals having particular personalities.

For this purpose, we require a much more exact and detailed picture of the manner in which stable behavior-patterns are developed in the early years of life, during which *all* conduct is learned and performed on the lower levels (2 to 4): the nature of consciously manipulative behavior and literal 'role-playing' (levels 5 to 7) is something we can understand and explain subsequently, as activities secondary to—and parasitic on—the familiar everyday modes of behavior that they presuppose and simulate. And, in the course of the resulting account, we must expect to find all the same complexities, and levels of complexity, reappearing in the relations between different 'persons' that we recognized in the central sections of this paper in the conduct of individuals.

This being so, there is no reason to suppose that the contrast between 'persons' and 'things' will serve us—any better than that between 'actions' and 'movements', that between 'rules' and 'laws', or any of the other familiar philosophical dichotomies—as a means of distinguishing sharply and finally between the World of Mind/Volition/Consciousness/Reason and that of Matter/Necessity/Blindness/Causality. Rather, we should be prepared to recognize a spectrum, or sequence, of functions in the world of 'personal' and 'interpersonal' conduct, and in the development of individual 'personality', as irreducible to any simple dichotomy as before. In the world of personal relations, as in our relations with material things, we travel during our lives a long and complex journey, from the simple reflexes and regularities of the cradle, by way of the rule-governed and rule-conforming structures and sequences of childhood, to the critical, rule-applying adult capacity for fully conscious, rational and deliberately monitored self-command.

V

The Individuality of Personal Relations

Yet, even after all this is said and done, one further, more radical objection still needs to be brought against the dramaturgical model, and against all attempts to tie personal relations strictly to the adoptions of *roles* and *rules*. This final objection has to do, not with the manipulative appearance of the model, but rather with another of its seeming implications: viz. the suggestion that human beings respond to, and deal with, one another always in abstract, stereotyped patterns—as instances of general types, to which corresponding rules and roles are appropriate—never as genuine individuals, having their own particular histories, characteristics and tastes. And the thrust of this counter-argument can be hinted at by recalling the classic protest of the individual human being against the 'imperssonality' of, e.g., bureaucrats and bigots:

Don't treat me as a type-cast student (black/foreigner/cipher/anonymous statistic): for God's sake, treat me as a *person*.

To indicate the underlying basis of this objection: recall, first, what we said about the relationship between the notions of 'rules' and 'consciousness' in the case of an individual dealing with systems or situations in the non-human world—e.g. the flowers in his garden, or the apparatus in a physical experiment. Such actions may, or alternatively may not, involve him in applying, following and/or critically monitoring rules or procedures. In cases where rules or procedures *are* involved, the question of 'consciousness', like the question of 'rationality', then arises in particular where the efficacy and relevance of the procedures are being critically or 'consciously' monitored. (By contrast, the uncritical, rote or routine application of rules or procedures can be carried through in an unthinking manner, lacking the conscious attention characteristic of their rational, critical employment.)

To say this much, however, tells us only what makes those *particular* kinds of conduct which are rule-applying or rule-following 'conscious' and/or 'rational': it does nothing whatever to give us a general account of the criteria that mark off 'consciously' or 'rationally' performed conduct *as such*. Quite the contrary: many of the actions that an individual performs, rationally and/or consciously, in his dealings with the non-human world *do not* involve him in employing specifiable 'rules' or 'procedures', in any straightforward sense of those terms. At most, if we are to use the terms in extended senses, they will involve him in three kinds of

judgment that go beyond the simple application of specific procedures: viz. (a) employing several different procedures, either
simultaneously or in complex succession, (b) recognizing how, when
and at what points, each of those procedures is appropriate, and
(c) monitoring the joint functional outcome of all the procedures, as
so employed. The 'consciousness' and/or 'rationality' of the actions
in question will then depend, not on the *general* rules that the
agent applies, but on his being sensitive to all the *special* elements
in the particular situation or system which are relevant in any way
to judgments (a), (b), and (c). His conduct is, thus, rational to the
extent—and only to the extent—that he is conscious in sufficient
detail of the *realities* of the particular situation; and this will require
him to do much more than merely classify the situation abstractly,
as belonging to a particular general type for which an explicit,
established rule or procedure is already available. His way of dealing with the resulting problems may have to be that much the more
'intuitive'—a matter of 'art' rather than 'science'—but it will be
none the less rational or conscious for all that. If anything, such
judgments call for a *higher* degree of awareness or conscious sensitivity to the detailed and specific actualities of the particular case.

With this relationship between 'rules' and 'consciousness' in
mind, we can throw light on the parallel relationship, between
'roles' and 'rules', on the one hand, and 'persons', 'personality'
and 'personal relations' on the other. To some extent—but only to
some extent—personal interactions may require the parties concerned to adopt roles and/or employ rules. (That much, the work
of Goffman and Harré puts beyond doubt.) The characteristic
behavior of a father towards his children, of a host to his guests, a
judge to a defendant: all such types of conduct respond well to
analysis in dramaturgical terms, and it is Goffman's great virtue
to have seen that this kind of pattern can be carried much further,
and applied to familiar everyday conduct in more detail, than had
earlier been recognized.

Once again, however, all that such an analysis demonstrates is
that *a great deal* of interpersonal behavior can be explained in terms
of 'roles' or 'quasi-roles': it does nothing whatever to give us a
general account of the criteria that mark off 'personal' relations

and interactions *as such*. Quite the contrary: there is some kind of polar opposition between the idea of dealing with people in accordance with specifiable, generalized roles, and the idea of dealing with them in a fully individual or 'personal' way. During most of a criminal trial, for instance, it is a judge's business to avoid seeing the defendant as a particular human being with a complex history and an individual personality, and to view him instead as, say, a man charged with fraud. (Meanwhile, the attitude of one subway-rider to another may be even less individual and discriminating: he may simply view the other man as a physical obstacle.) By contrast, we act towards one another as 'persons', in a strictly 'personal' manner, and/or with due allowance for the claims of individual 'personality', only at the point where we leave aside or go beyond such generalized 'role-patterned' modes of conduct, and deal with one another in ways that are sensitive to *all* the relevant individual features of the other's background, temperament, past history and present inclinations.

The resulting interactions will be fully *personal* to the extent—and only to the extent—that the agents involved are conscious, in sufficient detail, of the realities of one another's actual situations and states of mind; and this kind of awareness can be achieved only to a limited degree, if they perceive each other as belonging to generalized types towards which one can act in accordance with explicit, established 'roles'. For the rest: to the extent that human interactions set aside, or go beyond, all playing of specific roles, they will once again have to be that much the more intuitive—a matter of 'having a feeling for' the other's individual experiences and point of view, rather than of seeing him 'as a type'—but they will be only the more 'personal' as a result. It is (in short) the human interactions in which all the parties concerned display the highest degree of conscious sensitivity to the detailed and specific actualities of one another's positions and feelings—and, by so doing, go beyond all specific 'role-playing'—that most fully and characteristically represent interactions between *persons*: i.e. interactions involving the entire 'personalities' of the individual human beings who are the parties to them.

REFERENCES

Austin, J. L., 'A Plea for Excuses', *Proceedings of the Aristotelian Society*, Vol. 57 (1956–7), pp. 1ff.

Bateson, M. C., 'The Interpersonal Context of Infant Vocalization (in press).

Bernard, C., *Introduction to the Study of Experimental Medicine* (Paris, 1867), trans. by Henry C. Green, The Macmillan Co., New York, 1961.

Borst, C. F. (editor), *The Mind/Brain Identity Theory*, St Martin's Press, Inc., New York, 1970.

Chomsky, N., Review of B. F. Skinner's *Verbal Behavior*, in *Language*, Vol. 35 (1959), pp. 26–58.

Geach, P. T., *Mental Acts*, Routledge and Kegan Paul, Ltd., London, 1957.

Goodfield, G. J., *The Growth of Scientfiic Physiology*, Hutchinson and Co., Ltd., London, 1960.

Miller, G., 'Four Philosophical Problems of Psycholinguistics', *Philosophy of Science*, Vol. 37, (1970), pp. 183–99.

Miller, G. and S. Isard, 'Some Perceptual Consequences of Linguistic Rules', *Journal of Verbal Learning and Verbal Behavior*, Vol. 2, (1963), pp. 217–28.

Mischel, T., 'Scientific and Philosophical Psychology', in T. Mischel (editor), *Human Action*, Academic Press, New York and London, 1969.

Mumford, L., 'The Monastery and the Clock', in *Technics and Civilization*, Harcourt Brace Jovanovich, Inc., New York, 1934.

Pike, K. L., *Language in Relation to a Unified Theory of the Structure of Human Behavior*, 2nd edition, Mouton, The Hague, 1967.

Skinner, B. F., *Verbal Behavior*, Appleton-Century-Croft, New York, 1957.

Taylor, C., *The Explanation of Behavior*, Humanities Press, New York and London, 1964.

Toulmin, S. E., 'Neuroscience and Human Understanding', in *Neurosciences*, G. C. Quarton, T. Melnechuk and F. O. Schmitt (editors), Rockefeller University Press, New York, 1967.

Understanding Neurotic Behavior: from 'Mechanism' to 'Intentionality'

THEODORE MISCHEL

I

'Our understanding reaches as far as our anthropomorphism'. It is, in a way, surprising to find that Freud said this at a meeting of the Vienna Psychoanalytic Society in 1907 (Nunberg and Federn (editors), 1962, I, p. 136). For while there is much in Freud's clinical writings that suggests, as does this dictum, that psychoanalytic understanding depends on the framework of intentionalistic, purposive concepts ordinarily used in talking about persons, there is also much, particularly in the metapsychology, that suggests an attempt to conceptualize neurosis in terms of models drawn from the physical sciences. Moreover, such concepts as ego, id, and super-ego, have sometimes been criticized by psychoanalysts for being 'dramatic in an anthropomorphic sense'; they argue that while such concepts may provide metaphorical descriptions of clinical facts, 'Freud used physiology as his model' and his use of 'metaphors should not obscure the nature of the concepts and their function in psychoanalysis as a science' (Hartmann, Kris and Loewenstein, 1946, pp. 15–17).

Some philosophers have taken a similar line in commenting on psychoanalytic theory, but tend to appear as critics rather than defenders of its scientific status (e.g., Nagel, 1959). Others, more influenced by Wittgenstein, take a different tack. Thus MacIntyre distinguishes sharply between the descriptive and explanatory use of 'unconscious' and argues that 'Freud's achievement lies not in his explanations of abnormal behavior but in his redescriptions of such behavior' (1958, p. 61). Of course, Freud meant to explain the derivation of psychoneurotic symptoms from childhood experiences in terms of the unconscious, and the related notion of repression. But if these concepts are to explain anything, they must be theoretical constructs whose 'explanatory role' is specified by the theory, on analogy to the way scientific theories in physics or physiology specify their theoretical constructs. Since Freud failed to do this, MacIntyre concludes that

... in so far as Freud uses the concept of the unconscious as an explanatory concept, he fails, if not to justify it, at least to make clear its justification. He gives us causal explanations, certainly; but these can and apparently must stand or fall on their own feet without reference to it. He has a legitimate concept of unconscious mental activity, certainly; but this he uses to describe behavior, not to explain it (ibid., p. 72).

That is, causal correlations between infantile events and adult traits or disorders can be formulated without reference to the unconscious. And while Freud 'describes' behavior in terms of unconscious purposes, this does not justify the unconscious as 'a theoretical and unobservable entity introduced to explain and relate a number of otherwise inexplicable phenomena' (ibid., p. 71)—its explanatory role has not been specified.

Where Hartmann, Kris and Loewenstein see Freud's 'anthropomorphic', i.e., intentionalistic, descriptions as merely dramatic metaphors, MacIntyre sees the whole value of Freud's work in illuminating 'redescriptions' which enable us to see an unconscious purpose or intention in behavior which seemed to lack all purpose or intention. Where they think that Freud's theory can easily be de-anthropomorphized—e.g., they suggest that when Freud speaks of the super-ego's 'approval' or 'disapproval' of the ego, it would be 'more rigorous' to speak of diminution or increase of 'tension between the two psychic organizations' (1946, p. 16)—MacIntyre would, presumably, argue that the proposed translation trades on an anthropomorphic sense of 'tension' (e.g., as something experienced in self-hate) and so is nothing like the use of 'tension' as a theoretical construct in physics. But, and this is the crucial point, both sides agree that if Freud explains the derivation of neurotic symptoms from childhood incidents in terms of repression and the unconscious, then the logical form of his explanations cannot differ from explanations in the natural sciences.

It is easy to find passages in which Freud does seem to conceptualize the etiology of neurosis in terms of a biological model in which repression is something like a theoretical construct. Since the academic psychology of his time was dominated by Wundt, who held that the unconscious can have no place in psychology because the mental is identical with that of which we are immediately conscious (cf. Mischel, 1970), it was hardly suited to the expression of Freud's insights. Besides, a physician who studied neurology under Brücke, a leading figure in the stridently anti-vitalistic Helmholtz school of physiology (cf. Amacher, 1965), and whose practice in nervous diseases was devoted to treating patients who clearly suffered from something, could hardly avoid biology in thinking about the 'diseases' to which his 'patients' has succumbed. Freud's intellectual background and medical training did not provide him with much by way of conceptual grounds for distinguishing between the form which our understanding of persons, be they normal or neurotic, may take and the form which our understanding of physical or biological processes takes.

Not only philosophers, like MacIntyre, but also neo-Skinnerian proponents of behavior modification (e.g., Ullman and Krasner, 1969) and some psychiatrists (e.g., Szasz, 1962), have focused on this 'medical model' in their criticisms of Freud. But a sympathetic reading of Freud provides good reasons for not putting too much emphasis on that model. After all, psychoanalysis began with the recognition that 'hysteria behaves as though anatomy did not exist or as though it had no knowledge of it' (1893, I, p. 169);[1] that is, a hysterical paralysis corresponds to popular conceptions of anatomy, 'it takes the organs in the ordinary, popular sense of the names they bear' (ibid.) without regard to the anatomy of the nervous system. Since hysterical symptoms are thus rooted, at least in part, in the hysteric's conceptions, hysteria is very different from a physical illness.

Freud later expressed this point in terms of the 'sense' of neurotic

[1] Unless otherwise indicated, references are to the Standard Edition of Freud's works, with Roman numerals used to indicate the volume.

symptoms. He writes: 'It was discovered one day that the path-ological symptoms of certain neurotic patients have a sense. On this discovery the psychoanalytic method of treatment was founded' (1916, XV, p. 83). But if neurotic symptoms have a sense, our conception of such symptoms cannot be like our conception of physical symptoms. This becomes clear when Freud argues that his explanation of errors as 'psychical acts' that arise 'from mutual interference between two intentions' (ibid., p. 60) has

... won for psychology phenomena which were not reckoned earlier as belonging to it.

Let us pause a moment longer over the assertion that parapraxes are 'psychical acts'. Does this imply more than what we have said already—that they have a sense? I think not ... Anything that is observable in mental life may occasionally be described as a mental phenomenon. The question will then be whether the particular mental phenomenon has arisen immediately from somatic, organic and material influences—in which case its investigation will not be part of psychology —or whether it is derived in the first instance from other mental processes, somewhere behind which the series of organic influences begins. It is this latter situation that we have in view when we describe a phenomenon as a mental process, and for that reason it is more expedient to clothe our assertion in the form: 'the phenomenon has a sense'. By 'sense' we understand 'meaning', 'intention', 'purpose' and 'position in a continuous psychical context' (ibid., pp. 60–1).

An error might be due to the fact that someone was tired, and we could say that the error 'means' (i.e., is a sign, or indication) that he was tired; but such an error would be meaningless in the above sense. A Freudian error, on the other hand, has meaning in the sense that the person himself meant, or intended something when he made the error. Not, of course, that he intended to make the error—an error made on purpose is not really an error—but rather that the error arises from the 'mutual interference between two intentions'. When the Assistant Lecturer asks his audience to hiccough (*aufstossen*), instead of drink (*anstossen*), to the health of the Chief of the Department (ibid., p. 49) we can (if he really felt contempt for him, etc.) understand his error in terms of other 'psychical acts' which have 'meaning, significance, intention'; it is thus capable of psychological explanation, quite apart from the underlying neurophysiological processes. To recognize something as a Freudian error thus involves reconceptualizing it; we can no longer see it as something that just happened to the person, since it arose out of his own intentions. Similarly, to say that neurotic symptoms have meaning is to say that we can understand them in terms of what the person himself intends or means, and this requires a reconceptualization of the nature of such symptoms.

To illustrate, consider one of the compulsions from which Paul Lorenz (the 'Rat Man') suffered. While vacationing, it suddenly seemed to Lorenz that he was too fat (German *'dick'*) and that 'he must make himself slimmer'; he then felt compelled to embark on an almost suicidal regime of exercising and dieting, but could think of no explanation for this 'senseless obsessional behavior' until it occurred to him, in his analysis, that his girl had been there in the company of an English cousin of whom he was jealous. 'This cousin's name was Richard and . . . he was known as *Dick*. Our patient, then, had wanted to kill this Dick; he had been far more jealous of him and enraged with him than he could admit to himself, and that was why he had imposed on himself this course of slimming by way of a punishment' (Freud, 1909, X, pp. 188–9). Had one asked Lorenz, at the time, why he was dashing up a mountain in the heat of August he would, of course, have said that he was slimming—he (consciously) intended to get rid of fat (*dick*). His murderous rage against his rival has been forced out of consciousness and replaced by an obsessive need for slimming, whose self-punitive character is equally unconscious. But to understand his obsessive behavior we must understand, so Freud claims, that Lorenz unconsciously intended both to get rid of Dick and to punish himself.

Obviously, slimming could not really get rid of Dick. But to argue that Freud cannot be giving an intentionalistic explanation because the behavior in question could not achieve what was intended (cf., Alexander, 1962) is to forget, among other things, that a symptom is a 'compromise formation'. Like certain kinds of errors, symptoms are an expression of mutually interferring intentions (cf. IV, below). We could not say, without qualification, that the Lecturer intended to make the error, or that Lorenz intended to get rid of Dick. But getting rid of fat (*dick*) is, so Freud contends, a compromise between these further unconscious intentions—this is why neurotic symptoms, unlike physical symptoms, have 'sense' and can be explained psychologically in terms of their place in a 'continuous, psychical context'. Nor will it do to argue that such behavior cannot be an expression, in the ordinary sense, of the corresponding desire because the connection between desire and behavior rests on 'far-fetched psychoanalytic connections' (Shope, 1967, p. 432). For the connection between desire and action is always *via* belief, so that whether or not something can be an expression of a certain desire must depend on what the person believes. Lorenz's association of '*dick*' with 'Dick' indicated that slimming had this (unconscious) meaning for him and so could be construed as, in part, an expression of his desire to get rid of Dick. Freud also mentions the case of a French patient with a brother named Richard; here the association was with '*richard*' (French for 'rich man'), and obsessive brooding about how to get rid of his fortune had a meaning analogous to the meaning of slimming for Lorenz (1909, X, p. 189).

In this connection Freud speaks of the way neurotics use names and words 'for the purpose of establishing a connection between unconscious thoughts (whether they are impulses or phantasies) and symptoms' (ibid., p. 189). The point is important because it brings out the way symptoms depend on the thoughts under which they are subsumed by the neurotic. Lorenz's slimming is a neurotic symptom that has 'sense' because doing this has another significance for him, as a result of its connection with an (unconscious) thought, so that in doing this he unconsciously intends something more. He could not have this symptom apart from (unconscious) thoughts in virtue of which his obsessive slimming can be construed as a behavioral expression of his (unconscious) desires. But to see that neurotic symptoms mean something in this way is to conceptualize them in terms of our ordinary, intentionalistic framework.

One might put this in terms of Harré's 'ethogenic' approach (cf. pp. 143–84, this volume) by saying that neurotic symptoms are social behaviors whose generation involves cognitive processes, even if these processes are (dynamically) unconscious. And this in turn suggests that the medical model is, indeed, inappropriate for understanding the etiology of neuroses. How then should we conceptualize neurosis? Surely it is wrong to say, as Szasz does, that, e.g., hysteria is a game 'characterized by the goal of dominance and interpersonal control. The typical strategies employed in pursuing this goal are coercion by disability and illness. Deceitful gambits of various types, especially lies, also play a significant part in this game' (1962, pp. 278–9). For this makes it sound as if neurotic behavior were a self-conscious put on, slurs over the difference between deception and self-deception, and fails to account for the fact that neurotic behavior is typically rigid, self-defeating and not in the person's control. If the neurotic 'plays a game' he does not know it and, indeed, cannot come to know it without special help; in a sense, he is the victim of a self-defeating 'game' which he cannot help playing. And this is one of the things Freud was trying to explain in terms of the unconscious.

An adequate model would have to do justice both to the dynamically unconscious and driven character of neurotic behavior, and to the social and cognitive, rather than merely biological, nature of neurotic symptoms. The important difference between neurotic and normal social behavior is, of course, that the neurotic can neither account for, nor control, his own behavior. So if we are to succeed in construing Freud along Harré's 'ethogenic' lines, we shall need to explain why in the case of neurotic behavior, unlike what is the case in other 'enigmatic' episodes, the person cannot (rather than simply does not) consciously self-monitor and control what he does. Much of what Freud said about 'defense mechanisms' and the unconscious was intended to explain this, and it was in this context that Freud tended to move from the use of intentionalistic, purposive concepts, which characterize his clinical writings, to the quasi-physical concepts involved in the 'economic' and 'topographical' points of view.

Is it possible to construe the psychoanalytic account of defense, repression and the unconscious, as an *explanation* of these clinical facts in terms of intentionalistic, purposive concepts which belong to the same family as those involved in the 'redescription' of neurotic behavior as unconsciously motivated? Can we construe repression and the unconscious, not by analogy to theoretical constructs in physics, but as concepts whose 'explanatory role' depends on the framework of concepts ordinarily applied to persons, the framework in which neurotic symptoms have 'meaning'? In what follows I want to examine the Freudian account of conflict and defense with a view to answering these questions.

II

Reflecting on the development of his theories, Freud said that 'the transition to psycho-analysis' came when he, in contrast to Breuer, recognized that 'an idea became pathogenic if its content was in opposition to the predominant trend of the subject's mental life so that it provoked him into "defence"' (1923b, XVIII, p. 237). Initially, Freud used 'defense' to designate an intentional act of suppression whose motive is to avoid a conflict that seems insoluble. The subject, we are told, 'decided to forget about it [an incompatible idea] because he had no confidence in his power to resolve the contradiction', and Freud speaks of the patients' 'efforts at defence, their intention of "pushing the thing away", of not thinking of it, of suppressing it [*unterdrücken*] (1894, III, p. 47). Two years later it had become clear that there may be no conscious intention to suppress, and Freud now says that 'symptoms arose through the psychical mechanism of (unconscious) *defence*—that is, in an attempt to repress [*verdrängen*] an incompatible idea' (1896, III, p. 162).[2] But while Freud no longer thought that the person is aware of repressing, he still thought of repression as the active and defensively motivated suppression of a memory— since it is not a conscious suppression we get the technical term 'repression' (*Verdrängung*), borrowed from Herbart's 'mechanics of ideas', probably via Freud's teacher Meynert (cf. Dorer, 1932; Ed.'s Intro., 1893–5, II, p. xxii). And Freud now offers the following account of the etiology of 'defence neurosis': when guilt or

---

[2] See S. Freud, *Gesammelte Werke* (1892–9), vol. I, p. 62 and p. 379, for the corresponding German texts.

shame attaches to the memory of a sexual event that occurred early
in childhood, the person defends by repressing the memory and we
get a 'period of apparent health, but actually, of successful defence';
the onset of illness is characterized by the *return of the repressed
memories*—that is, therefore, by the failure of the defence'; but the
failure is only partial since symptoms 'take the place of the
pathogenic memories' in the form of a '*compromise* between the
repressed ideas and the repressing ones' (1896, III, pp. 169–70).
The psychoneuroses thus derive from a traumatic event (e.g.,
sexual seduction) in childhood, and Freud regarded 'defence as the
nuclear point in the psychical mechanism of the neuroses' (ibid., p.
162).

Though Freud, following Herbart, speaks of a 'psychical
mechanism', it is clear that the concept of repression, or defense, was
first introduced in an explicitly intentionalistic context to designate
an (unconscious) attempt to defend against ('fend off') a memory
that conflicts with the mature personality. At this stage in Freud's
thinking, the meaning of the concept of (unconscious) repression
derived from the meaning of (conscious) suppression; one could
understand why a person represses certain ideas in the way one
understands why he suppresses (intentionally refuses to think about)
a conflict when he lacks 'confidence in his power to resolve it'.

This account of repression began to change in 1897 when Freud
abandoned the 'childhood seduction theory' (Freud, 1887–1902,
Letter 69) and replaced it with the notion of normal infantile
sexuality (ibid., Letters 71, 75). The fact that many neurotics had
not actually been seduced in childhood seemed to show that the
vicissitudes of the child's interpersonal relations lack theoretical
importance; and Freud's interest turned instead to instinctual drives
and their development. He now proceeded to sketch a model of
sexual development in which repression is no longer an abnormal
result of interpersonal experiences in childhood, but is instead something that happens in normal instinctual development towards
sexual maturity. The new account of repression runs as follows:

In consequence of the belated appearance of the secondary processes,
the core of our being, consisting of unconscious wishful impulses,

remains inaccessible to the understanding and inhibition of the pre-conscious. ... These unconscious wishes exercise a compelling force upon all later mental trends. ... Among these wishful impulses derived from infancy, which can neither be destroyed nor inhibited, there are some whose fulfilment would be a contradiction of the purposive ideas of secondary thinking. The fulfilment of these wishes would no longer generate an affect of pleasure but of unpleasure; and *it is precisely this transformation of affect which constitutes the essence of what we term 'repression'*. ... They [infantile wishes and memories] are left to themselves—'repressed'—and thus it is that the presence of a store of infantile memories, which has from the first been held back from the *Pcs.*, becomes a *sine qua non* of repression (1900, V, pp. 603-4).

Repression no longer seems to be a defensive act, but seems instead something that just happens to everyone in the course of develop-ment. Infantile 'wishful impulses' (instinctual components) are left behind in the course of normal sexual development, their satisfaction at a later stage of development would no longer be pleasant, and this is now 'the essence' of repression. Repression, as such, is not pathological, but 'excessive' repression is—'neuroses can be traced back to an excessive repression of libidinal trends' (1906, VII, p. 277).

A similar construal of repression is apparent in the metapsy-chological papers, where Freud distinguishes between *'primal repression*, a first phase of repression ... [in which] a *fixation* is established' (i.e., an instinct component is left behind and so excluded from consciousness and further development) and the 'after pressure' exerted in 'the second stage of repression, *repression proper*, [which] affects mental derivatives of the repressed representative' (1915, XIV, p. 148). Repression operates on ideas which are 'psychical representatives' of an instinct that has been 'fixated' at an infantile stage, and if the repressed subsequently returns there will be a 'transformation of affect' and symptom formation. The concept of instinct is itself introduced by an explicit analogy to 'the concept of a "stimulus" and the pattern of the reflex arc' (1915b, XIV, p. 118). Instincts are stimuli arising within the organism, so that they cannot be avoided by a flight reflex, but the function of the nervous system is to get rid of them, or to reduce

P

them to a minimum (ibid., pp. 118–20). Freud's conception of instinct is, at this point, clearly biological rather than psychological; he is thinking of instincts as forces or energies within the organism that are not essentially directed towards objects: 'the object . . . is what is most variable about an instinct and is not originally connected with it' (ibid., p. 122). Similarly, anxiety is regarded as a transformation of libidinal energy that results from its 'damming up' in repression (1915, XIV, p. 155), affects are energy charges attached to the 'idea that represents the instinct' and Freud traces the 'vicissitudes' of such ideas and of the 'quota of affect' belonging to them (1915, XIV, p. 153, 1915b, 1915c, *passim*).

In this metapsychology Freud tried to express what he had learned clinically about repression in different neuroses in the terminology of 'cathexes' and 'anticathexes' (i.e., investments or withdrawals of energy) suffered by ideas 'on the border between the systems *Ucs* and *Pcs* (*Cs*)' (cf. 1915, XIV, p. 154 ff.; 1915c, XIV, p. 180 ff.). The story about defenses has been replaced by a story about the 'vicissitudes' of instincts; ideas no longer seem to have meaning, but have become entities—'psychical representatives' of somatic instincts 'cathected with a definite quota of psychical energy . . . coming from an instinct' (1915, XIV, p. 152)—that get pushed from one region ('system') of the topography to another by these exchanges of energy.

Freud had abandoned his early, unpublished attempt at speculative neurophysiology (1895), and he now says that 'our psychical topography has *for the present* nothing to do with anatomy' (1915c, XIV, p. 175). But, with repression embedded in a theory about the development of instincts and neurosis tied to 'excessive repression' of libido, Freud was now trying to conceptualize repression on analogy to biological processes. Instincts have somatic sources—it is 'the somatic processes in which the essential nature of sexuality is to be looked for' (1906, VII, p. 277)—and, correspondingly, Freud now thought that 'the essence of these illnesses lies in disturbances of the sexual processes . . . in the psychoneuroses [we can recognize] the *psychical* effects of those disturbances' of the sexual metabolism (ibid., pp. 278–9).

Commentators have noted that now ' "defense" was dropped

from Freud's usage, and "repression" became virtually his only term to refer to . . . the various defense mechanisms' (Madison, 1961, p. 29). Surely the reason for this is that defense, a psychological concept correlative with danger or conflict—in 1894, Freud wrote 'Conflict coincides with my concept of defence (or fending off)' (1887–1902, p. 85)—no longer fits. In this biological model of sexual development, infantile repression is not something the child does from a motive (either conscious or unconscious), but something that happens to the child; infantile component instincts undergo repression by being 'left to themselves' as the organism develops toward genital maturity and they constitute 'the repressed' (cf. Brenner, 1957, pp. 26–8). Nor is there a motive for later repression since it is simply an 'after-pressure' attracted by whatever is associatively connected with the primally repressed (1915c, XIV, p. 180 ff.). While defense is something a person does, even if he is not doing it consciously, in response to some danger or conflict, repression is now the working of a quasi-biological mechanism. The notion that neurosis is rooted in a psychological response to a hopeless conflict involving other persons seems to have given way to the idea that it is the 'psychical effect' of excessive repression, a disturbance of the sexual metabolism. Freud himself described the change in his conception of the etiology of the psychoneuroses by saying that

accidental influences have been replaced by constitutional factors and 'defence' in the purely psychological sense has been replaced by organic 'sexual repression' (1906, VII, p. 278).

Could this model fit the clinical facts? Such plausibility as it had derived from the fact that the practical concern of psychoanalysis was focused on uncovering the infantile impulses that had been repressed, rather than on the ego that does the repressing. And these impulses not only seemed totally alien to the mature person, they also interfered with his purposive, rational behavior in ways that he could neither control nor understand through introspection, or the like. Consider another of Paul Lorenz's symptoms, the compulsion, when he was studying late at night, to interrupt his work in order to open the front door and expose himself. Freud says:

This crazy conduct becomes intelligible if we suppose that he was acting as though he expected a visit from his father at the hour when ghosts are abroad ... he was to be delighted at finding his son hard at work. But it was impossible that his father should be delighted at the other part of his behavior; in this therefore he must be defying him. Thus, in a single unintelligible obsessional act, he gave expression to the two sides of his relation with his father (1909, X, p. 204).

This sounds as if we could understand this ritual as an expression of his desire to both please and defy his father—except that his father had been dead for nine years, and the ritual could not express that desire unless Lorenz believed that his father could witness it! In fact, Lorenz was unable to admit his father's death for eighteen months, and when he finally did he became uncharacteristically superstitious and 'extended the structure of his obsessional thoughts so as to include the next world' (ibid., pp. 174–5). Freud interprets this as a 'compensation for these death-wishes which he had felt against his father . . . it was designed . . . to undo the fact of his father's death' (ibid., pp. 235–6). In going through his ritual Lorenz was thus 'proving' that his father was still, in some way, alive—how else could he be doing this to please and/or defy him? And he had to hang on to that 'belief' because as a child he had desperately wanted him dead. The irrationality of Lorenz's thought and behavior, the alien character of these childish impulses, and the neurotic's inability to understand and control his own behavior, all make it very different from cognitively mediated social behavior that can be understood in purposive, intentionalistic terms; so perhaps it is just the 'psychical effect of disturbances of the sexual metabolism'.

But surely this won't do. How does Freud arrive at a hypothesis that explains Lorenz's symptoms? He analyzes what Lorenz says about his life, listens to his free associations, and looks for a hypothesis that could explain some aspect of his present behavior in terms of what he may have felt or believed as a child. For example, early in his analysis Lorenz says that when he was six years old he wished to see girls naked 'but in wishing this I had an uncanny feeling . . . for instance, *that my father might die*' (ibid., p. 162). Freud asked himself 'What can have been the meaning of the child's idea?' (ibid., p. 164) and suggested that 'when he was a child of under six he had been guilty of some sexual misdemeanor connected with masturbation and had been soundly castigated for it by his father' (ibid., p. 205). In this way Freud reconstructs, on the basis of what Lorenz *says* (and sometimes fails to say) about his relations with his father, childhood attitudes, fears and beliefs, that might constitute the repressed conflict that is 'returning' in his symptoms. And this 'scenario' is confirmed when Lorenz comes to see this account, not as an explanation derived from Freud's theory, but as the account he himself is now disposed to give for his behavior. (Cf. Harré, this volume, on the method of scenarios and accounts.)

Freud's clinical method thus depends on construing the 'sense' of symptoms in terms of love, hate, guilt and other motives involved in the relation, between persons. But such intentionalistic concepts can find no foothold in an essentially biological model of the development of instincts that are identified in terms of their somatic sources—i.e., in terms of 'erotogenic zones' rather than intentional objects—and whose vicissitudes are concepualized in terms of energy exchanges. Freud never lost sight of the fact that neurotic symptoms have a 'sense', and this means that they cannot be mere 'psychical effects' of disturbances in the sexual metabolism, that they must have a psychological explanation. The tension in Freud's thinking is apparent in the way he talks about both 'forces' and 'purposeful intentions' in the same breath, e.g., psychological phenomena are to be understood 'as signs of an interplay of forces in the mind, as a manifestation of purposeful intentions working concurrently or in mutual opposition' (1916, XV, p. 67). During this period, Freud's concept of repression straddled two different models—'Repression may, without doubt, be correctly described as the intermediate stage between a defensive reflex and a condemning judgement' (1905, VIII, p. 175)—and it is simply not clear how we are to understand it. (Cf. Peters, 1958, pp. 92–4.)

But this was not Freud's last word on the subject. When the 'topographic' account (*Cs.*, *Pcs.*, *Ucs.*) gave way to the 'structural' account (ego, id, super-ego) in 1923, Freud also proceeded to change his conception of repression and anxiety. The new account

was set forth in *Inhibitions, Symptoms and Anxiety* (1926) and
Freud later pointed out that, with respect to anxiety,

we have learnt two new things: first, that anxiety makes repression and
not, as we used to think, the other way round, and [secondly] that the
instinctual situation which is feared goes back ultimately to an external
situation of danger (1933, XXII, p. 89).

Previously, Freud had thought of neurotic anxiety as a transformation of libido and had, therefore, distinguished it sharply from
'realistic anxiety, which is invariably a reaction to danger' (1917,
XVI, p. 401 ff.). But now the two forms of anxiety are closely
linked because the neurotic's anxiety about his own instinctive
impulses goes back to a real situation of danger. For example, the
'Little Hans' (1909b, X) case is now reinterpreted and his neurotic
fear of being bitten by a horse is traced back to 'a realistic fear, a
fear of a danger which was actually impending or was judged to be
a real one' (1926, XX, p. 108); that is, the child believed (falsely,
of course) that he was in danger of being castrated for his impulses
and this is why they were construed as dangers and repressed (ibid.,
p. 145; 1933, XXII, p. 86 ff.).

On this account, 'the anxiety felt in animal phobias . . . differs in
no respect from the realistic anxiety . . . except that its content
remains unconscious and only becomes conscious in the form of a
distortion' (1926, XX, p. 126). Where Freud previously said 'I
think "*Angst*" [anxiety] relates to the state and disregards the
object' (1917, XVI, p. 395), he now says 'anxiety [*Angst*] has an
unmistakeable relation to *expectation*; it is anxiety *about* something' (1926, XX, pp. 164–5). Anxiety thus has an intentional
object, even though the person is either unable to say what he is
afraid of, or says that he is afraid, e.g., of a horse when he is really
afraid of something else. Since anxiety is now essentially directed
to objects in the child's social world, and since Freud now recognizes
that 'anxiety makes repression', it has becomes the motive for
'fending off' impulses whose expression would be (or so the child
believes) dangerous in his circumstances. In effect, Freud has
returned to his earlier 'purely psychological' view of repression and
defense. The social realities of the child's situation are again of

central theoretical importance since they are the real, external ground of the anxiety that leads to repression. Instincts still play a key role, but they do so in relation to the child's social situation: the conflict that led to Little Hans' neurosis was not with an incompatible memory, but an conflict between the demands of his developing instincts (love for mother) and his construal of the interpersonal situation in which they could find satisfaction (fear of father, whom he also loved).

No wonder Freud says that 'in the course of discussing the problem of anxiety I have revived a concept . . . of which I made exclusive use thirty years ago . . . but which I later abandoned. I refer to the term "defensive process" ' (1926, XX, p. 163). The structural point of view, in which the ego is no longer equated with consciousness but may have defenses of which it is (dynamically) unconscious, has brought Freud's attention back from repressed instincts to the ego that does the repressing, and the passive account of 'organic sexual repression' is now dropped. In its place we get the notion that the ego actively initiates defensive processes in response to anxiety which is a signal of danger. As soon as the infant has 'found out by experience' that if its mother is absent it will be helplessly overwhelmed by instinctual tensions (e.g., hunger), the danger it fears becomes absence of the mother and this 'represents a transition from the automatic and involuntary fresh appearance of anxiety to the intentional reproduction of anxiety as a signal of danger' (ibid., pp. 137–8). Anxiety is now a signal that alerts the ego to an expected danger against which it must defend itself (ibid., pp. 161–2, 166–7). Different dangers characterize different stages of development, so that anxiety later signals danger from the father (castration fear) and then danger from the super-ego (ibid., pp. 135–42).

Though signal anxiety is always the basis of 'later repressions', Freud said that 'the first and original repressions arise directly from traumatic moments', so that there is 'a twofold origin of anxiety'— it can be an automatic response to excessive stimulation or a signal of danger (1933, XXII, p. 94). In order to unify this account, Freud suggested that automatic anxiety is always 'on the model of birth' (ibid.), it 'corresponds to' (signals?) the trauma of birth (cf. 1926, XX, p. 141). Psychoanalysts still differ on whether there is any need for retaining 'automatic anxiety', a matter that depends, in part, on how the 'traumatic' neuroses (i.e., those with a contemporary etiology) are to be construed (cf. Rangell, 1955). But for our purpose it is sufficient that, whatever may be involved in the etiology of the traumatic neuroses, Freud held that signal anxiety is 'typical for that of the psychoneuroses' (1926, XX, p. 141); and he also maintained that even the 'repressions [that] take place in early childhood . . . are primitive defensive measures taken by the immature, feeble ego' (1937, XXIII, p. 227). Freud's final view thus seems to be that primal as well as later repression is an (unconscious) activity of the ego; 'the old concept of "defence" . . . [is] a general designation for all the techniques which the ego makes use of in conflicts which may lead to neurosis', repression being one 'special method of defence' (1926, XX, p. 163).

III

If defenses are techniques used to 'fend off' consciousness of instinctual urges which produce anxiety because their expression would (or so the person believes) lead to a dangerous conflict, then there should be no difficulty in understanding their 'explanatory role'. Why did 'Little Hans', being in love with his mother, displace his fear of father to horses? Because he also loved his father and the displacement 'enables a conflict due to ambivalence to be resolved' (1926, XX, p. 103). Moreover, as in the case of the agoraphobic who displaces fear of sexual temptation into fear of being in the street, 'what he gains by this is obviously that he thinks he will be able to protect himself better in that way' (1933, XXII, p. 84). 'Little Hans' could hardly avoid his father, but he could avoid horses by staying in the house (cf. 1926, XX, p. 126).

Just as the understanding of neurotic anxiety now depends on our understanding of realistic anxiety in a situation of danger, so the understanding of neurotic defense now depends on our understanding of techniques that could be used for self-protection. We are not appealing to theoretical constructs when we explain what someone is doing by making clear his aim and the technique he is using to achieve it, nor are we postulating a 'mechanism' that produces the behavior independent of him. But we can certainly understand what brought about certain behaviors when we can link them into a pattern of intentional activities directed to some goal.

It will, of course, be objected that I am talking about the neurotic's defenses as if they were conscious deployments of more or less intelligent techniques. But 'Little Hans' did not consciously displace his fear, indeed, he was not (consciously) doing anything; he just found himself afraid of horses. No doubt, the neurotic is neither conscious of using defenses nor able to become conscious of this through introspection, or the like. But the thing to notice is that Freud himself now appeals to normal psychological processes in order to elucidate the operation of neurotic 'techniques' of defense. In the new account of repression in response to signal anxiety 'the ego notices' that satisfaction of an instinctual demand would lead to danger, so that it must be 'somehow suppressed, stopped, made powerless', and then 'helps itself by a technique which is at bottom identical with normal thinking' (1933, XXII, p. 89). Freud adds:

I must admit that I have tried to translate into the language of our normal thinking what must in fact be a process that is neither conscious nor preconscious, taking place between quotas of energy in some unimaginable substratum. But that is not a strong objection, for it cannot be done in any other way (ibid., p. 90).

Freud's point may be that, while we don't know what goes on in the 'unimaginable substratum', neurotics are persons rather than creatures totally alien to us, so that we can exploit analogies with normal psychological processes in trying to understand the abnormal. The neurotic's behavior is not rational, but it is organized at a level complex enough for it to have 'sense', and this makes the concepts used to understand normal, purposive and intentional behavior *relevant* for understanding neurotic behavior[3] (cf.

[3] Though Freud never abandoned energetic considerations, he did say that his new 'conception of anxiety as a signal . . . does away with the necessity

Toulmin, this volume, on 'internal consistency' vs. 'external efficacy' of behavior).

To see this, consider the technique of 'isolation', a 'defense mechanism' characteristic of obsessional neurosis. Paul Lorenz has not forgotten the 'uncanny feeling' about father's death when he wanted to see girls naked, nor, when he was older, the thought that a girl would be kinder to him if his father were to die, etc., but he sees these as irrelevant thoughts that just happened to occur to him (cf. 1909, X, pp. 178, 221 ff.). The disturbing thought is thus 'deprived of its affect, and its associative connections are suppressed or interrupted so that it remains as though isolated' (1926, XX, p. 120). To explain how this comes about, Freud points out that 'the normal phenomenon of concentration provides a pretext for this kind of neurotic procedure' (ibid., p. 121). That is, all directed thinking involves focusing one's attention and excluding irrelevancies, so that 'in the normal course of things, the ego has a great deal of isolating work to do' (ibid.). Now as far as Lorenz is concerned, he merely concentrates his attention on what he sees as relevant; but this concentration is a 'pretext' for intentionally excluding awareness of connections that he does not want to see, and thereby blocking the anxiety that would overwhelm him if he were to realize consciously that he hates his father. In this way Lorenz brings it about that his 'aggressiveness appears to the ego not to be an impulsion but ... merely a "thought" which awakens no feeling' (ibid., p. 117). But Lorenz is not conscious of intentionally isolating so as to protect himself from his conflict, and so he would not say that he is doing anything—certain things happen to him, thoughts about father's death keep popping into his mind in certain situations, but they have no significance. This may be what Freud had in mind when he talked of how 'an act so often understands how to disguise itself as a passive experience' (1916, XV, p. 58).

of considering the economic factor' (1926, XX, p. 140): 'the question of what the material is out of which anxiety is made loses interest" (1933, XXII, p. 85). Moreover, what he now expresses in energetic terms can often be easily cashed in intentional terms, e.g., the 'technique of anticathexis ... in the phobias, whose interest is concentrated on removing the subject ... [from] the feared perception' (1926, XX, p. 158).

It is an essential characteristic of the neurotic's defenses that he must keep himself unconscious of the defenses he is using. The reason for this is that the neurotic's situation is always one of basic conflict: though he is defending against an id impulse because its expression would, so at least it seems to him, threaten danger, he also longs for the satisfaction of this impulse. If this conflict leads to his 'admission of helplessness in the face of it' (1926, XX, p. 166), he tries to avoid it instead of resolving it. He may not always keep anything that might remind him of the conflict out of consciousness, but he will at least keep himself from being conscious of the significance of the incompatible elements that he does remember. Thus, it is not only in repression, but also in other neurotic defenses, that conflict is 'fended off' through some modification of consciousness. This is why repression has paradigmatic importance for Freud and why he sometimes characterizes other defenses as 'surrogates of repression' (ibid., p. 119).

But in order to fend off a conflict by keeping incompatible elements, or their significance, out of consciousness, the neurotic must also keep himself from consciously knowing that this is what he is doing. Displacement of the object can enable 'Little Hans' to fend off consciousness of his conflict only if it is intentional but unconscious, something he does to deceive himself about his true feelings towards father but without being conscious of doing it. When Freud says that in an obsessional neurosis 'the actual wording of the aggressive impulse is altogether unknown to the ego . . . [but] the super-ego behaves . . . as though it knew the real wording' (ibid., p. 117), his point may be, not that we are to conceptualize the person in terms of homunculi, but that the neurotic has avoided the conflict by deceiving himself: his lack of awareness is motivated, he has made himself unconscious of an incompatible impulse which he knows, in one sense of that term, to be his. And he can do that only insofar as he can also keep himself unconscious of the technique he is intentionally using to deceive himself.

The connection between self-deception and psychoanalytic phenomena has been noted by some philosophers. Fingarette (1969) presents his account of the self-deceiver who tacitly adopts a 'policy of not spelling out', so as to keep himself from having to avow his 'engagement in the world', as, among other things, an explication of Freudian theory. But while a tacit policy of not explicitly spelling out one's situation may enable us to understand how self-deception works in the case of repression—e.g., how hysterics can bring it about that 'the perceptual content of exciting experiences . . . were forgotten and debarred from being reproduced in memory' (Freud, 1926, XX, p. 163)—there are other 'mechanisms of defense'. Hamlyn (1971) has stressed the variety of ways in which self-deception can come about, and provided an account of how what seems like 'sweet reasonableness' may 'involve a blocking of natural human feeling' and become a device the 'person uses to protect himself from his true nature', an account which he links to what Freud says about 'isolation' (1971, pp. 50–1). I am suggesting that a variety of normal cognitive processes can, as Freud put it, 'provide a pretext for neurotic procedures'; that is, different 'mechanisms of defense' can be construed as intentional but unconscious uses of different forms of thought and perception for the purpose of protecting oneself from the anxiety of an unbearable conflict by fending off consciousness of that conflict. In other words, neurotics attempt to cope with their anxieties by deceiving themselves about their real feelings towards others, and different neurotic defenses are different modes of normal cognition that have been distorted by this unconscious defensive aim.

To see this, consider another defense of a rather different sort, 'projection'. In connection with the Schreber case, Freud says that in paranoia 'the propostion "I (a man) love him" ' is contradicted by delusions of persecution which assert 'I do not love him—I hate him'. But 'this contradiction, which must have run thus in the unconscious' (*sic*.) could not serve as a defense if it were to become conscious in this form, and so is 'transformed by projection into . . . "*He hates* (persecutes) me, which will justify me in hating him" ' (1911, XII, p. 63). Paranoia is thus a defense against homosexuality which, through projection, substitutes an external danger for an internal one. But how can the delusions of persecution that befall the paranoiac be construed intentionalistically, as something he does or brings about? Freud says that while paranoiacs 'project outwards on to others what they do not wish to recognize in themselves . . . they do not project it into the blue, so to speak, where there is nothing of the sort already' (1922, XVIII, p. 226). Rather, they 'take up minute indications with which these other, unknown, people present them' (ibid.); the paranoiac's relations with men were 'dominated by suspiciousness; his keen intellect easily rationalized this attitude; and he knew how to bring it about that both friends and acqaintances deceived and exploited him' (ibid., p. 228). Far from 'debarring perceptual content' by consistently failing to spell things out, the paranoiac suspiciously searches the behavior of others for clues that can confirm what he (unconsciously) wants to see in them. In accordance with his (unconscious) defensive aims, he is constantly on the lookout for indications of hidden motives and intentions, and the unconscious bias which informs his perception allows him to find something in the behavior of others that could be interpreted in that way. (Would it have been hard for Schreber to find some 'confirmation' of his suspicion that his physician was trying to commit 'soul-murder' upon him?) This is how the paranoiac brings it about that 'the impelling unconscious feeling makes its appearance as though it were the consequence of an external perception' (1911, XII, p. 63). By intentionally, but unconsciously, interpreting the behavior of others in this systematic-ally biased way, the paranoiac can deceive himself both about the intentions of others and about his own feelings. The perception of other men's motives and intentions, when systematically distorted by the unconscious aim of finding in them a hostility that will fend off consciousness of the love one feels for them, is thus the core of the 'mechanism' of projection as a defense against homosexuality.

Of course, the neurotic is not conscious of using any technique and sees the unfortunate results he brings about as things that just happen to him. But the person himself is not the sole judge of what he is doing, any more than he is the sole judge of his own attitudes and feelings. Even if, e.g., Lorenz sincerely denies any hostility towards his father, the psychoanalyst may recognize that hostility from what he says and does—as well as what he doesn't, e.g., 'breaks' in his associations, his failure to draw obvious conclusions, etc.—in a way that does not differ, in principle, from the way in which we can often recognize another's conscious hostility, even if he does not tell us what his feelings in the matter are. And this may enable the psychoanalyst to interpret, e.g., Lorenz's nocturnal ritual as in part, an attempt to defy father, thus adducing Lorenz's unconscious hostility as a motive that helps to explain what he is up to. Since the Wundtian identification of the mental with that of which we are immediately conscious has now been discredited by numerous arguments, few would find it problematic that we can have good grounds for attributing attitudes to someone even if he sincerely denies having them.

What may still present difficulty is the fact that Lorenz can recognize his own feelings and intentions in a way others cannot. The difficulty is that if the analyst's interpretations help Lorenz to discover what his intentions were in performing his ritual, then it seems that he finds out about his own intentions in much the way in which one normally finds out about the intentions of others. But I do not normally 'find out' that, e.g., I intend to open the door. While others may find this out from various indications and may or may not be right in attributing this intention to me, if I say that I intend to open the door then, unless I am lying, what I say is normally not subject to correction. And this may make it hard to see how a person could ever be unconscious of his own intentions. But while it is, normally, for Lorenz himself to say whether or not he intends to open the door, this may not be true of the further intentions Lorenz may have in opening the door. If, e.g., Lorenz is opening the door in order to show father something that will please him while, at the same time, expressing his defiance of him, then he intends what he is doing to be taken by his father in certain ways; he is committed to patterns of conduct that extend over time and cannot, as it were, be 'seen' in a moment, he is committed to certain kinds of responses if certain situations were to arise, and to certain ways of accounting for what he is doing if he were challenged or were to reflect on the reasons for his conduct, etc., all in a context that makes these responses and appraisals reasonable or not. The point is that Lorenz's recognition of his own further intentions, when these are reasonably complex, requires judgment and inter-pretation, so that there is plenty of room for bias and self-deception. Consequently, others may even be in a better position than Lorenz to recognize the hostility which he himself does not want to see. Though Lorenz can recognize his own feelings in a way others cannot, this does not mean that he can never be mistaken about them, or that it makes no sense to suppose that he could ever find out, perhaps with the help of others, what his feelings and intentions really are.

If others know enough about Lorenz, about the patterns of his thoughts, feelings and behavior in various contexts, they may even have grounds for saying that he must, in some way, really know that he hates his father and that his sincere denials only show that he has deceived himself about his real feelings. After all, the concept of self-deception is not a theoretical construct first introduced by psychoanalysis, and it is hardly plausible to suppose that everyone, before and after St. Augustine, must have been talking nonsense when they appealed to it in interpreting human behavior. In confirming such interpretations one of the things we do, of course, expect is that, in the end, the person himself will come to recognize and admit that this is what he really felt or intended. But such avowal under ideal condition, i.e., if all resistances were overcome, etc., is part of what psychoanalysts mean by a 'correct interpretation'.

To see neurotic defenses as techniques of self-deception is to put them at the end of a continuum that begins with quite ordinary cases: from the 'point of view' involved in all interpretation of reasonably complex situations, through the bias ('prejudice') that leads to mistakes in interpretation, to the 'blinding', systematic bias of self-deception in which 'mistakes' are no longer really mistakes because there is a point to them in relation to the facts which the self-deceiver is (unconsciously) trying to 'fend off'. This fits in nicely with Freud's observation that 'between repression and what may be termed the normal method of fending off what is distressing or unbearable . . . there lie a whole series of more or less clearly pathological methods of behavior on the part of the ego' (1936, XXII, pp. 245–6). It may also be that the neurotic, whose 'primal repression' in early childhood is succeeded by the 'after pressure' of subsequent repressions that always follow the pattern of his childhood repressions (cf. 1937, XXIII, p. 227), goes through various degrees of self-deception before his lack of self-consciousness becomes invincible to anything but psycho-therapy.[4] As we go along this continuum, the issues involved in the confirmation of claims about unconscious intentions become more and more complex; but we do not suddenly lapse into incoherence in supposing that the neurotic intentionally, but unconsciously, uses techniques to fend off consciousness of his conflict.

If, as psychoanalysts claim, the patient in analysis 'repeats' his defenses in the transference (cf. IV, below), then the analyst may be able to spot the technique he unconsciously uses to keep himself deceived about his real feelings, much as we can sometimes spot the technique another person is using consciously, even if he does not tell us what it is. Given what Anna Freud calls 'the transparency of the repressive process . . . when the repressed material returns' (1937, p. 9), there can, in principle, be evidence for claiming that the neurotic is, e.g., intentionally isolating, even though he himself is not conscious of doing anything of the sort—he is merely concentrating on what is relevant. When psychoanalysts make such claims, we need to elucidate carefully what is being asserted and it may be difficult to assess the evidential status of their claims in particular cases. But there is no general incoherence in the attributing unconscious intentions to the neurotic (cf. Hamlyn, 1971b).

IV

I now want to show that this way of construing neurotic defenses can do justice to the clinical facts. Can it explain the derivation of adult symptoms from childhood experiences? According to Freud, 'the conflict at the root of his [Lorenz's] illness' was between 'his father's wishes and his own amatory predilections . . . and had arisen as far back as in his childhood' (1909, X, p. 200). Suppose

---

[4] This would be consistent with the conclusion, defended by some experimental psychologist on empirical grounds, that 'repression is only a very well-learned or overlearned response suppression' (C. W. Eriksen, 1966, p. 354).

that the beating father gave Lorenz for sexual misdemeanor, or some other incident or series of incidents that were seen by the child as having that general import, led to a hopeless conflict in Lorenz's attitude towards his father. Suppose also that, e.g., 'out of the fear of the violence of his own rage' (ibid., p. 206), he sought to fend off consciousness of that conflict by deceiving himself about his rage and that, whatever the reason for this may be (cf. V below), he did so primarily by isolating. The result of such 'primal repression' (in the generic sense) will be that a complex of childish attitudes and feelings, having been excluded from consciousness, may persist unaffected by subsequent learning and development (i.e., a 'fixation' is established). What makes defense potentially neurotic, according to Freud, is that in defending itself against the id, the ego 'has at the same time given it some independence and renounced some of its own sovereignty' (1926, XX, p. 153); this is what happens to one's feelings or desires when one attempts to cope with them by deceiving oneself about their real nature. Anything associatively connected with that conflict might bring it back and so will arouse signal anxiety and be defended against by more isolation (the 'after-pressure' of subsequent repressions). All sorts of 'secondary' defensive struggles may then ensue, as anything incompatible with the conscious love for father must somehow be 'rationalized' and rendered harmless.

While these defenses make is possible for Lorenz to function relatively free of anxiety, the psychological equilibrium which he thus achieves is unstable. For the infantile conflict about which Lorenz has been deceiving himself has persisted, without his being conscious of it, through the years, and so he 'behaves as though the old-danger situations still existed' (ibid., p. 147). Some people remain 'infantile' in the dangers they fear and, says Freud, 'it is precisely such people whom we call neurotics' (ibid., p. 148). Lorenz not only continues to be (unconsciously) afraid of what his father will do about his sexual impulses (castration fear), he also continues to keep himself unconscious of this, and of anything associatively connected with it, by means of his old techniques of self-deception, techniques which have now become habitual. As Freud puts it:

Q

the adult's ego, with its increased strength, continues to defend itself against dangers which no longer exist in reality; indeed, it finds itself compelled to seek out those situations in reality which can serve as an approximate substitute for the original danger, so as to be able to justify, in relation to them, its maintaining its habitual modes of reaction. Thus we can easily understand how the defensive mechanisms, by bringing about an ever more extensive alienation from the external world and a permanent weakening of the ego, pave the way for, and encourage, the outbreak of neurosis (1937, XXIII, p. 238).

That is, when, e.g., intentional but unconscious isolation, begun in childhood, succeeds in fending off consciousness of a conflict, the tendency to isolate will gain 'increased strength' with the years, it will be generalized to other situations and become more automatic, like any habit that is continually reenforced; a 'permanent weakening of the ego' will result as this tendency becomes less and less like a potentially intelligent technique and more and more like a blind 'mechanical' response activated by anything that arouses anxiety because of its connection with the conflict against which the person is defending. The price of coping with anxiety in this way will be an 'ever more extensive alienation' from reality in the social sense—alienation from other persons, whose character and aims get misconstrued in the attempt to defend against 'dangers which no longer exist', and alienation from oneself, from one's real attitudes and feelings. In this way, the potential neurotic's deepening immurement in his own self-deceptions can 'pave the way for, and encourage, the outbreak of neurosis'. A situation related to the conflict of which he has made himself unconscious—e.g., the need for deciding whether to marry Gisella, whom his father opposed, (the 'precipitating cause' of his illness, cf. 1909, X, p. 198)—can then bring on the 'return of the repressed' with the full-blown symptoms of neurosis.

The similarity between Lorenz's present predicament—to marry the girl he loves or to obey father by renouncing her—and the infantile conflict he has been keeping out of consciousness leads Lorenz to respond now as he did then; this is what Freud calls 'the influence of the compulsion to repeat' (1926, XX, p. 153). That is, he not only re-enacts his ancient love-hate conflict in relation to Gisella, he also atempts to fend off the conflict by means of his old techniques of self-deception. For example, though he is not conscious of rage against Gisella, he finds himself 'obliged' to remove a stone from the road because 'the idea struck him that her carriage . . . might come to grief against this stone' and then, a few minutes later, feels compelled to go back and replace the stone (1909, X, p. 190). The rage he is fending off makes him wish (unconsciously) that she would come to grief and this is why the stone seems like a real danger, against which he first tries to protect the woman he loves; it is then put back, where it might fulfill his unconscious wish to do her harm, with the 'rationalization' that the first action was silly (ibid., p. 192). But, characteristically, the elements have been isolated so that he is not conscious of his further intentions in moving the stone—by intentionally but unconsciously restricting what he sees as relevant, he has managed to keep himself unconscious of his rage against the woman he loves, though it explains what he is really up to. Moreover, Lorenz's ambivalent feelings toward Gisella are themselves rooted in his infantile love-hate conflict with father (ibid., p. 238 ff.).

The anxiety that comes when the conflict about Gisella begins to bring back the conflict about which he has been deceiving himself sets symptom formation going (cf. 1926, XX, p. 144). The symptoms alleviate the anxiety by fending off the 'dangerous' impulse. That is, though the impulse against which he is defending comes to expression in the symptom, it does so in a form that is 'safe' because the symptom also expresses the defending ego and through isolation, compartmentalization and the like, consciousness of the conflict is fended off. But Lorenz's attempts to continue his self-deceptions become more and more desperate as the repressed returns; what he takes things to be and how he responds to them comes to depend less and less on what they really are, and becomes increasingly a function of his (unconscious) defensive aims and what happened in the past. For example, since father's death fulfills the (unconscious) childhood wish to do violence to him, he is overcome with 'pathological mourning'—though he character-istically deceives himself into believing that his 'guilt' lies in having been asleep when he died (1909, X, p. 174 ff.)—and even attempts to 'prove' that, in some way, he is still alive (e.g., the nocturnal ritual performed 'at the hour when ghosts are abroad'). Surely an account along such lines does enable us to understand the relation between Lorenz's childhood experiences and his adult symptoms.

An intentionalistic account of defenses as techniques of self-deception also enables us to understand the 'dynamically unconscious' character of neurotic behavior. It is not merely that Lorenz is not conscious of his intent to harm Gisella, or defy the father who opposes his sexual urges, in going through his rituals. The routine things which we do intentionally, e.g., in driving a car, are not normally accompanied by any consciousness of our intentions, but we are not here talking about such 'preconscious' intentions. Freud was convinced, as a result of what he observed in the psycho-analysis of his patients, that a person can do something that is, in a sense, intentional even if he is unable to say, as he can when, e.g., steering to his right while completely absorbed in conversation, what he intended to do; he can do something intentionally even if something prevents him from recognizing his own intention in the usual ways, by reflection and the like. This led him to distinguish sharply between intentions that are dynamically unconscious (i.e., 'forced' into the unconscious) and merely preconscious ones ('the system Pcs (Cs)'). But this difference can be conceptualized in terms of unconscious intentions, without appealing to special 'mechanisms'. If defenses are techniques of self-deception, then Lorenz's rituals are structured, in part, by what he intentionally but unconsciously does to fend off consciousness of his conflict; the compulsion is itself designed to keep consciousness of the hostility it expresses at bay, to make it seem to himself as if he were not really hostile. His intentional but unconscious use of isolation thus keeps him from recognizing his own feelings and intentions. Since Lorenz cannot really account for what he is up to in terms of intentions of which he is, or can readily become, conscious—these can only provide 'rationalizations'—and since his self-deception consists in keeping himself from becoming conscious, by means of isolation, of the further intentions that could account for what he is doing, these behaviors of his become something that he himself can neither understand nor control: compulsions that come over

him rather than things he does. The usual ways of understanding
and controlling one's behavior through self-monitoring, by taking
thought, deciding that there is no reason, e.g., to open the door and
setting oneself against doing that, etc., are of no avail. Rational
considerations pertaining to Lorenz's actual situation are directed
at the wrong thing and can no more influence him, than assurances
that it was no 'crime' to take a nap during his father's long illness
can assuage the guilt he feels.[5]

But while Lorenz's behavior ceases to make sense when seen
only in relation to his actual situation, we can still understand it
in terms of his intentions when we widen the context to include his
infantile conflicts and the techniques which he (unconsciously) uses
to fend of these conflicts by deceiving himself about his true feelings
towards others. Given the ineffectiveness and inappropriateness of
these techniques for really solving his problems, we can certainly
say that he behaves irrationally; there is no good reason for what he
does. But only a potentially rational being is capable of such
irrationality. And no matter how self-defeating and pointless these
defensive struggles may be from an objective, external point of view,
they have 'sense'—there is internal consistency and, in a sense,
something calculated in the way they evade the hopeless conflict.
They represent, to use a quotation from *Faust* which Freud himself
cites in a similar context (1937, XXIII, p. 238), behavior in which
'*Vernunft wird Unsinn*' (reason becomes unreason).

Such an account of defense also enables us to make sense of what
happens in psychotherapy. Here the compulsion to repeat, which
is the neurotic's 'way of remembering', takes the form of a transference neurosis—'the transference is itself only a piece of
repetition' (1914, XII, pp. 150–1). Not only does the patient
reenact the conflict relating to a major figure of his childhood with
respect to the analyst, he also repeats his old techniques for fending
off consciousness of the conflict by self-deception: 'the patient
repeats these modes of reaction during the work of analysis as well
. . . he produces them before our eyes, as it were' (1937, XXIII,

---

[5] Indeed, even if such rational considerations were not misdirected, they
would be ineffective since 'insight' is not enough without 'working through'
(cf. below).

p. 238). The analyst must then try to bring to consciousness not only the instinctual impulses about which the patient has been deceiving himself ('content interpretations'), but also the maneuvers he has been unconsciously using to keep himself deceived ('defense interpretations'). Since it is 'hard for the ego' to face up to ideas or impulses which 'it has up till now made a rule of avoiding' (1926, XX, p. 159), the person 'resists' becoming conscious of them; and since self-deception depends on not being conscious of the techniques used for that purpose (cf. III above), he also resists becoming conscious of his defenses. Indeed, such precarious stability as has been achieved depends on these self-deceptions, so that 'the defensive mechanisms directed against former danger recur in the treatment as *resistances* against recovery . . . the ego treats recovery itself as a new danger' (1937, XXIII, p. 238). If these resistances can be overcome, the neurotic becomes conscious of the futility and inappropriateness of defending himself by self-deception and can then begin to cope with his situation in more realistic ways.

How is this accomplished? Interpretations make what was unconscious conscious by bringing the meaning of the patient's behavior to light—both what he unconsciously intended to fend off (content) and the way he is trying to fend it off (defense) are made explicit. These interpretations could not play the role they do in psychotherapy unless the analyst's interpretation of, e.g., Lorenz's ritual as due, in part, to unconscious hostility, were very much like an explanation in terms of conscious hostility—i.e., like an ordinary motive explanation that accounts for what a person did in terms of what he intended. The analysand's 'insight' simply cannot be an external 'third person' understanding of his behavior derived from psychoanalytic theory; it cannot be like the understanding a person might get of why he is unable to shift from one task to another when he learns that he suffers from a certain sort of brain damage and that people who suffer from this are never able to do that (cf. Goldstein and Scheerer, 1941). The reason for this is that the aim of interpretations is to get the neurotic to see

something like this: 'This thing, then—(this trick, this experience, this defense, this defeat)—happens to you repeatedly; it seems to happen especially to you. You seem to have something to do with its happening. Perhaps it doesn't just *happen*, possibly you actually do it. You have done it before. Perhaps you have some hidden purpose behind it, a purpose which was once valid but which is no longer valid (Menninger, 1958, pp. 136–7).

This shifting of responsibility from the outside to the core of the personality—helping the patient to be 'increasingly "behind" or at one with his own words and actions' (Kaiser, 1955, p. 211)—can only occur if the analyst's interpretations enable the neurotic to see that this is what he himself really intended in going through the ritual, though he was not conscious of it. Only if unconscious intentions are, in this way, like conscious intentions can the analyst's interpretations, by making conscious what was unconscious, allow repression to be replaced by 'rejection based on judgment (*condemnation*)' (1915, XIV, p. 146).

When a resistance has been made conscious we can, says Freud, 'bring forward logical arguments against it', but this is not enough because 'even after the ego has decided to relinquish its resistances' there must follow the 'strenuous effort . . . of "working through"' (1926, XX, p. 159). 'Insight' can no more be enough to change the neurotic's behavior than merely telling someone what is wrong with his serve in tennis can be enough to change his style; such re-learning also requires effort, practice, correction and the like. But while there is a point to comparing psychotherapy to other forms of learning, there are also crucial differences—perhaps this is why Freud compared therapy to 'a sort of *after-education* of the neurotic; it can correct mistakes for which his parents were responsible in educating him' and yet denied that the psychoanalyst is a 'teacher, model and ideal' (1940, XXIII, p. 175). Even apart from the fact that the neurotic is defensively motivated not to change, what he has to learn is not a relatively isolated bit of behavior but something that involves a reconstruction of his whole personality and so has to be worked through in many contexts and on many levels (cf. Kris, 1956). Closely related to this is the fact that the neurotic's self-deceptions have distorted his relations with significant figures of his childhood and that he has tended to perceive others who entered into the orbit of his neurotic conflict as specters of these childhood figures. Unable to enter into open and reciprocal personal relations with significant others, he has been prevented by defensive self-deceptions from understanding their intentions towards him and from perceiving them as the persons they really are. (Cf. Hamlyn, this volume, on the connection between personal relations and our understanding of others.) This is what the neurotic now has to 'learn' as he works—through his insights with the therapist.

The transference, which psychoanalysts regard as the core of their therapeutic technique (cf. Sandler, *et al.*, 1970, p. 667), provides a unique opportunity for this. Strachey speaks of 'the neurotic vicious circle', i.e., the way the neurotic tends to turn new persons he encounters into 'phantasy objects' that are replicas of the 'archaic objects' of his past, so that he relates to them as he did in his childhood, with the result that his expectations about them get 'confirmed'. Thus 'the pathological obstacle to the neurotic individual's further growth is in the nature of a vicious circle' (1969, p. 280), a circle that is broken through 'mutative interpretations' of the transference relation. What makes these interpretations 'mutative' is that through them 'the patient's ego will become aware of the contrast between the aggressive character of his feelings and the real nature of the analyst, who does not behave like the patient's "good" or "bad" archaic objects' (ibid., p. 283). Doesn't this mean that the analyst's handling of the transference enables the neurotic to break out of a pattern of defensive self-deceptions in his relations with other persons? In order to explain what transpires in psychotherapy analysts appeal, not to the medical model, but to the notion that 'it is the analyst's task to resolve the patient's propensity toward archaic relationships' (Kaiser, 1955, pp. 206–7), or to the way in which the new 'object-relation' that develops between patient and analyst in the transference becomes the source of 'healthier object relations' (Loewald, 1960).

Our understanding of the efficacy of psychotherapy thus depends on intentionalistic concepts: 'resistance', 'interpretation', 'insight', 'working-through' to new 'personal relations'. An intentionalistic account of how defense against conflict leads to neurosis, along the lines sketched above, is able to provide a framework in which the therapeutic action of psychoanalysis is intelligible. But it is hard to see how an account in terms of concepts of an entirely different type (e.g., 'mechanism' and 'cathexes') could do that.

V

But why should Lorenz fend off his conflict by isolating rather than, e.g., repressing? If defenses can be construed as techniques of normal cognition which have been distorted by the unconscious aim of fending off consciousness of an anxiety provoking impulse, then we should expect the 'choice' of defense to be related to ways of thinking and perceiving that may be characteristic of different people. Psychologists have started investigating the 'typical strategies of perceiving, remembering and thinking' that people use (cf. Klein, 1958), and there is now considerable empirical evidence showing that there are 'stable individual preferences in mode of perceptual organization and conceptual categorization' (Kagan, *et al.*, 1963, p. 74). That is, normal people differ in their 'cognitive styles'; for example, some are 'field dependent' and tend to organize their experience in relatively undifferentiated, global and diffuse ways, while others are 'field independent' and their experience tends to be sharply differentiated, focused and structured (Witkin, *et al.*, 1962). These differences are already apparent in children at various developmental stages, and while there is a general increase in analytic perception and cognitive differentiation with development, the tendency towards greater or lesser differentiation remains stable as the child develops. On the interpretation of defense which I have suggested, the choice of defense should be related to such differences in cognitive styles.

A step in this direction has already been taken by David Shapiro in *Neurotic Styles* (1965). Shapiro starts from the recognition that the 'choice of neurosis' cannot be explained solely in terms of a theory of libidinal development. For even if the 'content' of a symptom be determined by the fixation of an instinct at some developmental stage, the 'form' of the symptom will depend on the defense mechanism which the ego deploys against the instinct. In order to account for the form which symptoms take (e.g., why

Lorenz's fixation at the oedipal stage leads to obsessive-compulsive symptoms while, in another case, it might lead to a different syndrome) Shapiro suggests that 'style of thinking may be considered a matrix from which the various traits, symptoms, and defense mechanisms crystallize' (1965, p. 2). On Shapiro's view, the obsessive-compulsive 'performs his rituals not only because of the balance of instinctual and counterinstinctual forces, but also because he is a compulsive person, that is, because he is a person with certain relatively stable ways of thinking and cognition' (ibid., p. 17). And the book presents a detailed clinical description of four 'forms of functioning . . . characteristic of the various sorts of pathology' (ibid., p. 3)—the obsessive-compulsive, paranoid, hysterical and impulsive 'styles'.

Shapiro characterizes the cognitions of hysterical people as 'impressionistic', their capacity for 'sharply focused attention and concentration' is limited, so that what they see and remember lacks definition and detail and they live more in a world of 'romance and fantasy' than in a world of solid facts. Since the hysteric's conception of himself is equally impressionistic, he lacks a 'sense of personal substance and definiteness' and his behavior often strikes others as histrionic; while he is not playing a part, he responds largely on the basis of his vague and fluctuating impressions of the situation confronting him, so that neither his emotional outbursts nor his other behaviors are 'anchored in a real and deep interest, a long history, or an abiding purpose' (ibid., p. 121). That is, the hysteric's volatile emotional life parallels his impressionistic cognitions; the hysterical style grows out of a 'relative absence of complex cognitive integration' (ibid., p. 130) which allows half-formed whims and transient impressions to dominate, for the moment, his cognitions, affects or behavior.

Obsessive-compulsive people, on the other hand, characteristically concentrate rigidly and narrowly on 'technical details'; while this leads to sharply detailed perception and memory of what is in focus, 'the obsessive-compulsive's intellectual rigidity . . . [has] a quality of "active inattention" to any external influence or any new idea' (ibid., p. 30). This rigid mode of cognition is paralleled by rigid self-control; such people like to be absorbed in technical, relatively routine tasks, where what they are supposed to do fits a role, they become anxious when they encounter situations that are novel and call for choice. Since this style generates responses that depend, not so much on what the person himself really thinks, wants or feels, as on what 'fits', what cannot be managed in this way is avoided, with the result that 'much of life aside from work, shrinks and is severely restricted in this style of functioning' (ibid., p. 43). The style encourages 'ritualistic behavior', where what should be done is externally defined, and a ritualistic interest in 'indicators or technical signs' rather than substantial reality (ibid., p. 50).

If the hysteric's lack of cognitive integration makes it seem as if he were 'playing for fun' rather than 'for keeps' (ibid., p. 121), the obsessive-compulsive seems to be trying to control everything through rigid and excessive integrations that will make it 'fit' a preconceived pattern. As for the paranoid and impulsive styles, Shapiro describes them as 'more psychologically primitive' variants of the other two style (cf. ibid., pp. 107, 136, 142, 150). All the styles are 'neurotic' because they lead to 'the exclusion from consciousness of certain classes of subjective experience and mental content' (ibid., p. 196). The style is the 'aspect of neurotic functioning' that explains the form of symptoms, different defenses being manifestations of 'the operation of that style under special conditions of tension' (ibid., p. 194).

But do neurotics develop special cognitive styles, that differ in their nature from the styles developed by normal people, or is Shapiro describing what happens when normal styles of cognition, which may be used intelligently for adaptation, are used defensively for self-deception? The relation between normal adaptation and neurotic defense has become an increasingly vexing problem for psychoanalytic theory as a result of the new emphasis on ego-psychology that grew out of Freud's writing in the 1920s. While Freud's interest was focused on instincts and ego activities were seen as conscious responses which fall into the domain of academic (Wundtian) psychology rather than psychoanalysis, it was easy for him to think of defenses as quasi-biological 'counter-forces' directed against instinctual forces. But when the structural point of view led Freud to focus on the (unconscious) activities of the defending ego, he began to stress, as we have seen, similarities between defense against internal (instinctual) and external dangers. Attention shifted from speculation about the workings of mysterious intrapsychic mechanisms to consideration of what the neurotic is afraid of, and what he does to cope with the danger he fears, whether or not he is conscious of doing that.

Anna Freud continued this line of thought, pointing out not only that all defense mechanisms 'have their counterpart in the ego's attempts to deal with the external danger' and develop hand in hand with techniques for such coping as the child's ego 'adapts its weapons to the particular need' (1937, p. 174), but also that the very same mechanisms (e.g., introjection and projection) that are operative in neurotic symptoms play an essential role in normal ego and super-ego development (ibid., pp. 188ff; 123ff). But then, as Anna Freud herself came to say, it is misleading to go on 'differentiating between defense and adaptation and labelling the ego-mechanisms employed as either pathological or normal' (1965, p. 177). For everything will depend, not on *what* mechanisms are employed, but on *how* they are employed. Psychoanalysts began to suggest 'that we view the neurotic defense mechanisms as pathologically exaggerted or distorted regulation and adaptation mechanisms, which in themselves belong to normal development' (Lampl-de Groot, 1957, p. 117). And when the American Psychoanalytic Association recently convened a panel on 'Defense Organization of the Ego', there was much emphasis on the notion that

what determines whether a defense is normal or abnormal is its functional relevance; is it predominantly in the service of conflict or is it developmentally phase adequate, reality appropriate, and predominantly in the service of healthy adaptation? (Pumpian-Mindlin, 1967, p. 160).

Though some analysts still think of 'defense mechanisms as constructs . . . theoretical abstractions describing a way of working of the mind' (Wallerstein, 1967, pp. 135–6), the development of ego-psychology has led many others to realize that 'we conceive the characteristics of unconscious mechanisms to some extent in the image of these conscious defensive reactions' (Loewenstein, 1967, p. 804), and that the difference between pathological and normal defense lies in the 'inappropriateness of these defences in regard to the reality situation' (ibid., p. 798).

But in that case, why not construe neurotic defenses as attempts to cope with conflict that differ from normal problem solving, not because they are the result of non-cognitive mechanisms, but because the person is deceiving himself about the real nature of his conflict or problem? If neurotic defense differs from intelligent adaptation, not in its origins or aims but only in its outcome—'the processes that resulted in a neurosis were *adaptational* . . . although they did not end up being *adaptive*' (Loewenstein, 1967, p. 800)—then isn't it misleading to go on talking about defenses as 'mechanisms'? Shouldn't they be regarded as cognitively structured techniques (like Piaget's schemas) that fail to be adaptive when they are used to fend off consciousness of a conflict? Waelder reports that when something like this issue was raised, 'Anna Freud maintained that "mechanism" was appropriate because the defenses are automatic and stereotyped' (Pumpian-Mindlin, 1967, p. 152). But this may mean that some behavioral pattern is triggered independent of the person's thoughts and intentions, as in Freud's speculations about the relation between repression and the physiology of the reflex arc; or it may mean that the person does not choose to respond in the way he does, that his behavior does not arise from, and cannot be directly influenced by, rational considerations and that his responses do not vary appropriately in relation to the requirements of his real situation.

The interpretation of defense which I have suggested would certainly account for the fact that the neurotic's behavior is 'automatic and stereotyped' in the second sense. The appeal to defense becomes, in effect, a motivational explanation which seeks to account for the neurotic's cognitive failures—his inability to understand and control his own behavior (its 'dynamically unconscious' character), his inability to see his situation for what it is and to deal with it in 'reality appropriate' ways, his tendency to 'repeat' developmentally earlier ('phase inadequate') techniques of coping —in terms of his unconscious intention to 'fend off' a conflict, rooted in childhood, when consciousness of that conflict would overwhelm him with anxiety.

Seen in this way, the story about the etiology of neurosis would be, not about the vicissitudes of instincts, but about the vicissitudes which Piagetian cognitive development may suffer under the impact of anxieties characteristic of different developmental stages. For in order to perceive things that make him anxious (e.g., the difference between the sexes), the child must already have acquired the capacity to perceive and categorize things in certain ways, and in order to 'deny' reality in fantasy, or by play-acting a 'reversal' of the real situation, he must already have some ability to imagine and to act. (Cf. A. Freud, 1937, Chs. 6 and 7 for an account of these infantile defenses.) And the move from such primitive defenses to more sophisticated ones, like 'sublimation', 'rationalization' or 'altruistic surrender',[6] requires not only more and more complex cognitive capacities, but also more and more complex interpersonal relations which make it necessary to take the expectations and pressures of others into consideration and to justify one's conduct and aims, not only to them but also to oneself. The point is that the conception of defense in response to anxiety, at which Freud finally arrived, logically presupposes cognitive structures. How could there even be signal anxiety without some capacity to remember and anticipate? How could there be repression before there is perceptual discrimination and memory? How could there be projection or introjection without the capacity to distinguish between self and world? How could there be sublimation before there is some understanding of social values? Or rationalization without a fairly sophisticated capacity for justificatory reasoning? And if different defenses must make use of cognitive structures that have already developed, then it becomes plausible to reverse Freud's earlier view (1908) that the styles of cognition and response that constitute a person's character arise from non-cognitive defense mechanisms directed against instincts, and to say instead that the

[6] Anna Freud included this, as well as 'identification with the aggressor' among the ego's mechanisms of defense (cf. 1937, Chs. 9 and 10). A more recent classification of defenses (Valerstein and Bibring, 1961) has 45 entries, including, e.g., 'ascetisism', 'compliance' and 'identification with the loved object'; Laughlin's (1970) textbook lists 22 'major defenses' (including 'compensation' and 'restitution') and 26 'minor defenses' (including 'atonement' and 'retrospective devaluation').

choice of defense depends on the cognitive structures and styles which the child has already developed.[7]

It is no secret, even among psychoanalysts, that Freud 'has said a good many contradictory things . . . [and] can be quoted in support of many different ideas' (Loewald, 1960, p. 32). While I do not imagine that my analysis of defense can fit everything Freud ever said on the subject, I do think it presents a plausible reading of the direction of his thought. Freud began his investigations with an intellectual background that inclined him to suppose that the scientific understanding of persons requires that they be conceptualized as complex biological structures whose behavior is brought about by various physio-chemical mechanisms. But Freud's clinical practice and the germinal discoveries he made in that practice— particularly that symptoms, as well as some other phenomena, which were previously regarded as having causes but no sense, do have sense because they are brought about intentionally but unconsciously by the agent himself—required a very different conceptualization of persons as thinking, social beings who act intentionally in a matrix of personal relations with others. Freud began to resolve this tension in the 1920s, after he came to see that the activities of the ego may be unconscious so that they, and not just the repressed instincts on which he had previously concentrated, fall into the domain of psychoanalysis. For he then proceeded to treat the so-called 'mechanisms of defense' as techniques which the neurotic unconsciously uses to fend off consciousness of an anxiety provoking conflict that is rooted in instinctual urges with which he could not cope in childhood; and he held that these techniques are to be understood by analogy, not to physiological processes, but to normal purposive and intentional behavior. Perhaps this is also part of the

---

[7] All sorts of further questions arise here about the origin of cognitive styles and the relation of these styles, which serve to organize the way, or manner, in which one construes situations, to dramaturgical styles of performance (cf. Harré, this volume) that control the presentation of the self to others. Can different 'developmental lines' (cf. A. Freud, 1963) involve different cognitive and dramaturgical styles so that the same person may develop different defenses as well as 'personas' in different arears of endeavor and interpersonal relationship? etc. But these questions are beyond the scope of this paper.

reason why Freud came to think that 'the theory of the instincts is so to say our mythology' (1933, XXII, p. 95).

I have tried to show that the nature of defense, the dynamically unconscious character of neurotic behavior, the etiology of neurosis and the therapeutic action of psychoanalysis, all become intelligible in the framework of intentionalistic concepts that informs our understanding of persons. Such a de-mythologized, but properly anthropomorphic, reading of Freud is in line with current psychoanalytic ego-psychology, as well as with the general approach to the understanding of persons exemplified by most of the essays in this volume.

REFERENCES

Alexander, P., 'Rational Behavior and Psychoanalytic Explanation', *Mind*, lxxi, 1962.

Amacher, P., 'Freud's Neurological Education and its Influence on Psychoanalytic Theory', *Psychological Issues*, Vol. IV, No. 4, International Universities Press, Inc., New York, 1965.

Brenner, C. 'The Nature and Development of the Concept of Repression in Freud's Writings', in *The Psychoanalytic Study of the Child*, Vol. XII, International Universities Press, Inc., 1957.

Dorer, M., *Historische Grundlagen Der Psychoanalyse*, Felix Meiner, Leipzig, 1932.

Eriksen, C. W., 'Cognitive Responses to Internally Cued Anxiety', in Charles D. Spielberger (editor), *Anxiety and Behavior*, Academic Press, New York, and London, 1966.

Fingarette, H., *Self Deception*, Humanities Press, New York, 1969.

Freud, A., *The Ego and the Mechanisms of Defense*, International Universities Press, Inc., New York, 1937 (1954).

—— 'The Concept of Developmental Lines', in *The Psychoanalytic Study of the Child*, Vol. XVIII, International Universities Press, Inc., New York, 1963.

—— *Normality and Pathology in Childhood*, International Universities Press, Inc., New York, 1965.

Freud, S., *The Origins of Psycho-Analysis: Sigmund Freud's Letters*, 1887–1902, Basic Books, Inc., New York, 1954.

—— *Gesammelte Werke* (1892–9), Vol. I, Imago Publishing Co., Ltd., London, 1952.

—— 'Some Points for a Comparative Study of Organic and Hysterical Motor Paralyses' (1893), *The Standard Edition of the Complete Psychological Works of Sigmund Freud*, Vol. I, The Hogarth Press, London, 1953.

—— (and Breuer), *Studies on Hysteria*, (1893–5), S. E. Vol. II.

—— 'The Neuro-Psychoses of Defence' (1894), S. E. Vol. III.

—— *Project for a Scientific Psychology* (1895), in Freud, 1887–92).

—— 'Further Remarks on the Neuro-Psychoses of Defence' (1896), S.E. Vol. III.

—— *The Interpretation of Dreams* (1900), S.E. Vol. V.

—— *Jokes and Their Relation to the Unconscious* (1905), S.E. Vol. VIII.

—— 'My Views on the Part Played by Sexuality in the Aetiology of the Neuroses' (1906), S.E. Vol. VII.

—— 'Character and Anal Eroticism' (1908), S.E. Vol. IX.

—— 'Notes Upon A Case of Obsessional Neurosis' (1909), S.E. Vol. X.

—— 'Analysis of a Phobia in a Five-year-old Boy' (1909b), S. E. Vol. X.

—— 'Psycho-Analytic Notes on an Autobiographical Account of a Case of Paranoia (Dementia Paranoides)' (1911), S.E. Vol. XII.

—— 'Remembering, Repeating and Working-Through' (1914), S.E. Vol. XII.

—— 'Repression' (1915), S.E. Vol. XIV.

—— 'Instincts and Their Vicissitudes' (1915b), S.E. Vol. XIV.

—— 'The Unconscious' (1915c), S.E. Vol. XIV.

—— *Introductory Lectures On Psycho-Analysis* (1916–17), S.E. Vols. XV and XVI.

—— 'Some Neurotic Mechanisms in Jealousy, Paranoia and Homosexuality' (1922), S.E. Vol. XVIII.

—— *The Ego and the Id* (1923), S.E. Vol. XIX.

—— 'Psychoanalysis' (Encyclopedia Article), (1923b), S.E. Vol. XVIII.

—— *Inhibtions, Symptoms and Anxiety* (1926), S.E. Vol. XX.

—— *New Introductory Lectures on Psycho-Analysis* (1933), S.E. Vol. XXII.

—— 'A Disturbance of Memory on the Acropolis' (1936), S.E. Vol. XXII.

—— 'Analysis Terminable and Interminable' (1937), S.E. Vol. XXIII.

—— *An Outline of Psycho-Aanalysis* (1940), S.E. Vol. XXIII.

Goldstein, K. and Scheerer, M., 'Abstract and Concrete Behavior; An

R

Experimental Study with Special Tests', *Psychological Monographs*, LIII, No. 2, 1941.

Hamlyn, D. W., 'Self-Deception', *Proceedings of the Aristotelian Society*, Sup. Vol. XLV, 1971.

—— 'Unconscious Intentions', *Philosophy*, XLVI, 1971b.

Hartman, Kris and Loewenstein, 'Comments on the Formation of Psychic Structure', *The Psychoanalytic Study of the Child*, Vol. II, International Universities Press, Inc., New York, 1946.

Kagan, J., Moss, H. A. and Sigel, I. E., 'Psychological Significance of Styles of Conceptualization', in J. C. Wright and J. Kagan (editors), *Basic Cognitive Processes in Children, Monagraphs of the Society for Research in Child Development*, Vol. 28, No. 2, 1963.

Kaiser, H., 'The Problem of Responsibility in Psychotherapy', *Psychiatry*, Vol. 18, 1955.

Klein, George S., 'Cognitive Control and Motivation' in Gardner Lindzey (editor), *Assessment of Human Motives*, Grove Press Inc., New York, 1958.

Kris, E., 'The Recovery of Childhood Memories in Psychoanalysis' in *The Psychanalytic Study of the Child*, Vol. XI, International Universities Press, Inc., New York, 1956.

Lampl-de Groot, J., 'On Defense and Development: Normal and Pathological' in *The Psychoanalytic Study of the Child*, Vol. XII, International Universities Press, Inc., New York, 1957.

Laughlin, H. P., *The Ego and Its Defenses*, Appleton-Century-Crofts, New York, 1970.

Loewald, H. W., 'On the Therapeutic Action of Psycho-Analysis', *International Journal of Psychoanalysis*, 41, 1960.

Lowenstein, R., 'Defensive Organization and Autonomous Ego Functions', *Journal of the American Psychoanalytic Association*, Vol. 15, 1967.

MacIntyre, A. C., *The Unconscious: A Conceptual Analysis*, Humanities Press, New York, 1958.

Madison, P., *Freud's Concept of Repression and Defense, Its Theoretical and Observational Language*, University of Minnesota Press, Minneapolis, 1961.

Menninger, K., *Theory of Psychoanalytic Technique*, Basic Books, Inc., New York, 1958.

Mischel, T., 'Wundt and the Conceptual Foundations of Psychology', *Philosophy and Phenomenological Research*, Vol. XXXI, 1970.

Nagel, E., 'Methodological Issues in Psychoanalytic Theory' in Sidney

Hook (editor), *Psychoanalysis: Scientific Method and Philosophy*, Grove Press, Inc., New York, 1959.

Nunberg, H. and Federn, E. (editors), *Minutes of the Vienna Psychoanalytic Society, Vol. I, 1906–1908*, International Universities Press, Inc., New York, 1962.

Peters, R. S., *The Concept of Motivation*, Humanities Press, New York, 1958.

Pumpian-Mindlin, E., 'Panel Report B: Defense Organization of the Ego and Psychoanalytic Technique', *Journal of the American Psychoanalytic Association*, Vol. 15, 1967.

Rangell, L., 'On the Psychoanalytic Theory of Anxiety: A Statement of a Unitary Theory', *Journal of the American Psychoanalytic Association*, Vol. 3, 1955.

Sandler, J., Dare, C. and Holder, A., 'Basic Psychoanalytic Concepts: III, Transference', *British Journal of Psychiatry*, Vol. 116, 1970.

Shapiro, D., *Neurotic Styles*, Basic Books, Inc., New York and London, 1965.

Shope, R. K., 'The Psychoanalytic Theories of Wish-Fulfillment and Meaning', *Inquiry*, Vol. 10, 1967.

Strachey, J., 'The Nature of the Therapeutic Action of Psychoanalysis', *International Journal of Psycho-Analysis*, Vol. 50, No. 275, 1969 (Reprinted from *Int. J. Psychoanalysis*, Vol. 15, 1934).

Szasz, T. S., *The Myth of Mental Illness*, Martin Secker and Warburg, Ltd., London, 1962.

Ullmann, L. P. and Krasner, L., *A Psychological Approach to Abnormal Behavior*, Prentice-Hall, Inc., 1969.

Valerstein, A. F. and Bibring, E., 'Glossary of Defenses' in *The Psychoanalytic Study of the Child*, Vol. XVI, International Universities Press, Inc., New York, 1961.

Wallerstein, R. S., 'Panel Report A: Development and Metapsychology of the Defense Organization of the Ego', *Journal of the American Psychoanalytic Association*, Vol. 15, 1967.

Witkin, Dyk, Faterson, Goodenough and Karp, *Psychological Differentiation; Studies of Development*, John Wiley and Sons, Inc., New York, 1962.

Index